WASHINGTON BABYLON

Alexander Cockburn
&
Ken Silverstein

VERSO

LONDON • NEW YORK

First published by Verso 1996
© Alexander Cockburn and Ken Silverstein 1996
All rights reserved

The rights of Alexander Cockburn and Ken Silverstein to be identified
as the authors of this work have been asserted by them in accordance
with the copyright, Design and Patents Act 1988

Verso
UK: 6 Meard Street, London W1V 3HR
USA: 180 Varick Street, New York, NY 10014-4606

Verso is the imprint of New Left Books

ISBN 1–86091-427-5
ISBN 1–85984–092–2

British Library Cataloguing in Publication Data
A catalogue record for this book is available from the British Library

Library of Congress Cataloging-in-Publication Data
A catalog record for this book is available from the Library of Congress

Manufactured in the USA by The Courier Companies

Book design by Deborah Thomas

To Ben Sonnenberg

CONTENTS

INTRODUCTION

One of the rituals of public life in America is the anxious pronouncement, every few years, that a virus is sapping the nation. In the mid-1970s it was called "a crisis in democracy". Nelson Rockefeller paid scores of scholars to write papers on the topic.

What it boiled down to was something fairly simple: the elites were badly frightened by the 1960s' upsurge and were asking basic questions such as, Is democracy really the way to go? As one troubled CEO in a meeting of tycoons put it, "One man, one vote has undermined the power of business in all capitalist countries since World War II."

In January of 1996, it was *The Washington Post* that spotted trouble. The newspaper fired off a six-part series, concocted with the help of Harvard profs, decked out with doleful front-page headlines such as "In America, Loss of Confidence Seeps Into All Institutions" and adorned by graphs about "public trust" with the trend lines all pointing down. Cut through the underbrush of graphs and pizza-slice charts in the *Post's* series and again we find something simple: it's as if P.T. Barnum set forth across the country to see if one was still being born every minute, got to the edge of the Midwest, looked around and then muttered to himself mournfully, "No suckers!"

Of course, the *Post's* series didn't put it that way. The word is that people don't trust government because we don't trust each other. It's all our fault. "The reason our politics is behaving badly", the *Post* quoted Eric Uslaner of the University of Maryland as saying, "is because the whole country is behaving badly." (Dr. Uslaner is reverently billed as "one of the first to identify the relationship between declining trust in human nature and attitudes towards politics and government".)

The *Post* launched its entire "waning trust" thesis on a couple of vignettes. In the opening paragraph of its first article in the series, Janice Drake, mother of three in Detroit, doesn't trust the neighborhood teenager who doesn't pull his pants up properly. In paragraph three, 18-year-old Lori Miller of Madison, Wisconsin, says she never knows who the next Jeffrey Dahmer might turn out to be.

Drawing on this data base, paragraph four says we've become "a nation of suspicious strangers", and this explains why we've lost confidence in the federal government.

So if Janice Drake had told the *Post* reporters that she puts in three hours a week running errands for old folks and young Lori said she relied on her friends for emotional back-up, we wouldn't have had a crisis.

The *Post* thinks it's good to trust the government, as in the golden 1950s which, you may recall, was a time when government told trusting soldiers it was safe to march into atomic test sites, and when government-backed doctors offered radioactive oatmeal to retarded kids without their parents' knowledge.

The one thing the *Post* and all the other crisis-identifiers can't face is that for an independent citizenry the correct, and indeed democratic, approach is not to trust government—not in ancient Greece, not in America today.

Aside from that, across the last thirty years, government has willfully forfeited such scant reservoirs of trust as might have remained. On top of which, for all the wrong reasons, politicians ranging from Jimmy Carter to Ronald Reagan spent the second half of the 1970s and the whole of the 1980s campaigning against government. By the time Clinton got to his State of the Union address in 1996, he faithfully echoed Reagan in declaring, "The era of big government is over." Of course, when it comes to corporate welfare or policing powers, Clinton, like Reagan, adores big government and only derides its role in helping the poor.

Washington Babylon shows why the people are right and the profs, the pundits and pollsters at places like *The Washington Post* are wrong. Americans don't trust government, politicians and the press because they see them, rightfully, as corrupt. The story of *Washington Babylon* is of how a moment of optimism in American political life, in the immediate aftermath of Watergate and the exposure of that scandal, was betrayed and destroyed. What's remarkable, indeed, is how the Nixon era, when contrasted with the current state of affairs, seems like an age of enlightenment and promise. Most people still looked upon government as a positive good, capable of redressing economic and social injustices. To that end, President Nixon passed a wide variety of environmental laws, created the Occupational Safety and Health Administration, and even felt obliged to rebuke corporations publicly for profiteering. The postwar social compact between labor and capital, which guaranteed workers at least a slow rise in the standard of living, was still intact, only coming slowly apart during the Carter years and then very rapidly with the Reagan administration.

Washington Babylon focuses on the way in which both major political parties have been bought up by big money from corporations and wealthy Americans, and how this has affected the rest of the country. More than 100 corporate political action committees contribute to both "liberal Democrat" Richard Gephardt and "right-wing Republican" Newt Gingrich. Never have Tweedledee and Tweedledum been so indistinguishable.

There are, of course, some honorable men and women in Congress whose votes are not for sale, but these are more and more the exception. Knowing that the espousal of even remotely populist views will make it impossible to raise the huge sums of money now needed to run for elected office, few Democrats dare step outside the narrow boundaries of accepted opinion. There are only 46 members of the Democrats' "Progressive Caucus" and more than a few of those don't deserve the name. Similarly, there are diligent journalists working in and outside of Washington. But these are increasingly rare, and their integrity relates directly to the distance they keep from the world of power and money they must watch.

Some pundits have described the big group of Republicans elected in 1994 as representing Main Street versus Wall Street. Congressman Jon Christensen of Nebraska is fairly representative of these crusaders for the average American. He campaigned on a platform that attacked "special interests" but soon after winning office was holding fund-raisers on the Potomac aboard a Mutual of Omaha yacht.

As the differences between the parties narrow to the point of invisibility, the "either/or" choices Americans are given in a fixed political system are meaningless or precisely the reverse of what people suppose them to be. There's no question that if George Bush had defeated Bill Clinton in 1992, Newt Gingrich would not today be Speaker of the House, and the environment and social welfare programs would be in far better shape.

Nineteen ninety-six is a big year for Lesser-of-Two-Evilism. In February, Dennis Rivera, head of a hospital workers' union in New York City, said the most important labor project of a half-century is the re-election of Bill Clinton in November. He and other labor leaders, joined by other core groups of the old liberal coalition, will scramble to get out the vote for a man whom political columnist Kevin Phillips described a couple of years ago as the most anti-labor president of the 20th century.

Here's a little parable about Lesser-of-Two-Evilism from the 1996 special election in Oregon to replace Senator Bob Packwood. At one point in the race between Democrat Ron Wyden and Republican Gordon Smith, there was a green candidate called Lou Gold. As the race came down to the wire, the green establishment in Oregon told Gold that every vote counted and that if he stayed in, his third party candidacy could throw the race to the man of darkness, Smith. So Gold stood down.

The Oregon green establishment took out ads saying that it was a choice between Despoilers and Protectors, that a vote for Wyden was a vote for the temple of nature. Wyden rewarded these expressions of support with stentorian speeches to the effect that the Clinton logging plan—under whose auspices old-growth is falling and the spotted owl going to its long home—wasn't cutting enough.

In the end, Wyden won the race by 1.5 percent. The green vote put him over the top. Even before taking office he began saying that since he represents all the people of Oregon, including the chainsaw faction that voted for Smith, he wants to lay Oregon waste in the manner that Smith had proposed.

Nearly three decades ago, Hal Draper wrote an article in *Independent Socialist* called "Who's Going to be the Lesser Evil in 1968?" Draper made a comparison between Pat Brown, the liberal governor of California, and his successor, Ronald Reagan. Draper noted that it was Brown who had sold out the water program to the big land-holding companies and fought for the *bracero* program in a way no Republican governor would have dared. It was Brown who'd unleashed an army of cops against the students in 1964, had named John McCone's commission to whitewash police conduct in the Watts rebellion in Los Angeles, and had supported the right-wing's anti-riot law. "If half of this had been done by Reagan, the lib-labs would be yelling 'Fascism' all over the place", Draper wrote.

He concluded: "We increasingly are getting ... Lesser Evils who, as executors of the system, find themselves acting at every important juncture exactly like the Greater Evils, and sometimes worse. They are the products of the increasing convergence of liberalism and conservatism under conditions of bureaucratic capitalism. There never was an era when the Policy of the Lesser Evil made less sense than now. That's the thing to remember for 1968, as a starter."

And for 1996.

A few final notes. We must thank a number of people and organizations who helped us prepare this book. We're deeply indebted to Jeffrey St. Clair of Oregon City, editor of *Wild Forest Review* and contributor to our newsletter, *CounterPunch*, for his work on the chapter on the environment and for his help overall.

Much of the information we gathered on the influence of money in the political system came from two outstanding Washington-based watchdog groups, the Center for Public Integrity and the Center for Responsive Politics. We're also grateful to Jake Lewis of Ralph Nader's Center for the Study of Responsive Law, who long worked in Congress and who spent much time helping us detail the changes that have swept through the capital during the past two decades.

From Point Arena, California, Carolyn Cooke helped greatly in buffing up the chapters. In New York, JoAnn Wypijewski, as so often before, was the reader of last resort. Deborah Rust was heroic in helping us across the finishing line with production. Ken Silverstein is especially grateful to Clara Rivera for her support and generous spirit. Our final thanks to Deborah Thomas, who designed and did the production on *Washington Babylon,* and organized the photographs that adorn it.

BABEL'S TONGUES

Katharine Graham: In Watergate's afterglow she counseled caution, urged probes of geology, beckoned press back to lapdog role. Escorted by one of America's richest men, Warren Buffett, Omaha's answer to Jay Gatsby, Graham drifted rightwards. The *Post* grew steadily duller under the hand of editor Len Downey. (Les Stone/Impact Visuals)

COURTIERS TO POWER:
THE PRESS AND INTELLECTUALS
STEER RIGHT

In the late fall of 1974 Katharine Graham, boss of the Washington Post Company, rose to address the annual meeting of the Magazine Publishers' Association. It was a year of supreme triumph for the *Post*. After the long siege of Watergate Richard Nixon had tumbled on August 7. The *Post*'s reporters, Bob Woodward and Carl Bernstein, were credited with bringing him down. After two years of abuse by the Nixon administration the *Post* was vindicated. Journalists across the country were casting themselves as "investigative reporters", eager to do battle with vested power, the high and the mighty.

Mrs. Graham chose this exhilarated moment to strike a note of prudence. "The press these days", she sternly told the audience, "should . . . be rather careful about its role. We may have acquired some tendencies about over-involvement that we had better overcome. We had better not yield to the temptation to go on refighting the next war and see conspiracy and cover-up where they do not exist."

The chairman of the Washington Post Co. was not alone among her fellow proprietors in the publishing industry in feeling that the time had come to cry halt. Watergate had encouraged the press corps to advance recklessly across traditional boundaries and probe hitherto sacrosanct aspects of the social, political and, above all, corporate landscape. Vested power, in whose ranks stands Katharine Graham, always fears moments of populist opportunity. The story of the New Deal—as the late Walter Karp showed in a brilliant book, *Indispensable Enemies*—is in large part that of Franklin Roosevelt desperately trying to contain the popular anger threatening to overwhelm the corrupt financial institutions that presided over the onset of the Great Depression. He finally distracted this anger and the militant Democratic majority of 1937 from constructive reform with his self-consciously preposterous court-packing scheme.

Thus also was it in late 1974. The people had seen institutions corrupted, politicians plying corporate leaders for the beneficence of a bribe. They were eager for change. It was the profound, urgent task of vested power to contain that urge and to deflect it.

Graham called for a return to basics. Journalists, she said, should stop trying to be sleuths, and instead master "the ability to comprehend a number of extremely arcane fields, ranging from macroeconomics to geology to antitrust. It is no mean trick to become conversant in a specialty which experts spend their whole lives mastering—especially if practitioners devote much energy to keeping their field obscure."

The press had always been terrified of accusations that it was unreasonably hounding Nixon. Even before Nixon finished himself off with the June 23 tape, *Time* had suggested that the media was overstepping its bounds, asking in a mid-summer 1974 cover story, "Has the press gone too far?" Then the "smoking gun" tape surfaced and Nixon retired to San Clemente forthwith.

Graham's demand that journalists behave with more deference towards the powerful was widely noted. It helped set the tone for the post-Watergate period. As one of her employees put it, "The feeling behind the talk was, 'We did this [Watergate], we removed the glue, so now what?' It called for a new definition of 'responsibility'."

The early Seventies found a substantial section of America's corporate, political and academic elites profoundly alarmed by the seeming collapse of normal controlling mechanisms and values. Vietnam externally, and Watergate internally, symbolized the crisis.

To business the press was the enemy, indecently reveling in corporate malfeasance during the Watergate affair, poisoned by the radicalism of the 1960s.

In 1974 and 1975, the Conference Board arranged a series of meetings of top corporate officials who brooded jointly about the

Dinesh D'Souza: Welfare ward of right-wing foundations; gives the white man his greatest pleasure, paying a brown man to attack black ones; once squired Laura Ingraham, the right's vampette scrivener. (Len Be Pas)

future for business. The assembled CEOs believed that it was crucial to win over the press. Among the complaints: "Even though the press is a business, it doesn't reflect business values"; "Unless the press stops tearing down our system and begins to tell the public how it works, business leaders will not be permitted any future participation in the formation of social goals" and, from the wife of one CEO, "It makes me sick to watch the evening news night after night and see my husband and the efforts of his industry maligned."

The idiom of the day was that of the press insurgent: Woodward & Bernstein overthrowing Nixon; Seymour Hersh evicting James Angleton from the CIA; Nader's investigators pillorying US business.

Less than a decade later, Woodward was writing a book about

Martin Peretz: Has owned *The New Republic* since mid-1970s; lapped by wife Anne's vast Singer Sewing Machine fortune; told Blair Clark in 1968, "I have been in love only three times in my life. I was in love with my college room-mate. I am in love with the state of Israel and I love Gene McCarthy." The McCarthy thing is over, the whereabouts of the room-mate unknown, but third love still burns brightly. In 1982 Marty tossed flowers at Israeli pilots returning from bombing runs on Lebanese refugee camps; later, as Reagan groupie, published editorials favoring the contras. Scatters favors on acolytes, thus ensuring their loyalty; entertained on white fur sofa in nest atop the Sherry Netherland. Uses magazine to heap abuse on foes, then refuses to print their rebuttals. Racist outbursts about Arabs and blacks greeted with tolerance by Babylon's elites. After glory years as Reaganauts' in-house neo-lib magazine, *TNR*, now edited by gay rightist Andrew Sullivan, swivels between what Frank Mankiewicz called "a Jewish version of *Commentary*" and *GQ.* (Vivian Ronay/Photoreporters)

John Belushi, and the journalists most honored by their peers included William Safire, Nixon's former speech writer, and George Will,
who hosted the welcoming party for Ronald Reagan when he came
to Washington for his first term. In 1984, Dinesh D'Souza was writing
(with the pomposity that only a young man with right-wing foundation dollars in his pocket can muster) in the Heritage Foundation's
Policy Review that under the leadership of A.M. Rosenthal, *The New
York Times*—which along with the *Post* had long been seen by conservatives as a tool of the Kremlin—was "reaffirming its greatness by
retreating from the radicalism of the last two decades and once again
taking up responsible journalism. It is the first liberal institution to
identify the excesses of liberalism, mainly its flirtation with Com-
munism, and to seek to correct them."

Today, the final vestiges of critical thought in the press have been
all but extinguished, and mainstream journalists are as much a part
of the ruling class as the political and business elite.

During Bill Clinton's first six months in office, he and his wife
Hillary hosted a series of private dinner parties—"as a way to meet
some of his new neighbors", explained Roxanne Roberts of *The
Washington Post* when writing about these "private soirees for the
elite". On her account, the Clintons' guests drank fine wines and
feasted on pan-seared lamb. On one occasion, the women joined
Hillary Clinton for a private screening of the film *Sleepless in Seattle*
while male guests chatted with the president and watched a basket-
ball game.

Heavily represented among the invitees—which included political
leaders, business officials and personal friends—were leading members of the Washington press corps: notorious Clinton brown-noser
Sidney Blumenthal of *The New Yorker*, Rita Braver and Susan Spencer
of CBS ("You have to be jaded not to admit that being at the White
House is a pretty interesting experience"), Katharine Graham and
three others from the *Post*, Dan Goodgame of *Time*, Evan Thomas of
Newsweek, Jack Nelson of the *Los Angeles Times*, Charles Peters of the
Washington Monthly and R.W. Apple of *The New York Times*.

The latter, a swag-bellied gormandizer of international repute, was
particularly moved by his evening at the White House. Apple shared
Clinton's table for a dinner on June 3, 1993, the night that the president, with incomparable servility to right-wing bluster, withdrew Lani

Guinier's nomination as his assistant attorney general. Two days later, Apple paid for his dinner with a front-page story about Clinton's "brutal, heartbreaking" decision to abandon Guinier, about the pain etched on his face as he arrived at the dinner when many guests were already "halfway through their beef Wellington and some . . . on their second glass of Jordan cabernet sauvignon".

Behind the media's violent swing was an expensive, carefully planned corporate campaign to recapture the culture. Panic among the elites in the mid-1970s was very high. This was the period when Samuel Huntington of Harvard University and Nelson Rockefeller's Trilateral Commission wrote of the need to curb the "excess of democracy" in the US, Japan and Western Europe. Comments at the Conference Board meetings indicate that CEOs believed a popular uprising could be imminent: "Can we still afford one man, one vote? We are trembling on the brink"; "We are terribly scared within this room. We are in serious trouble"; "One man, one vote has undermined the power of business in all capitalist countries since World War II."

Corporate executives also felt pressured by labor unions, then still relatively powerful, and by the rising expectations of the citizenry. "We have been hoist with our own petard," complained one business leader at the Conference Board meetings. "We have raised expectations that we can't deliver on."

Profit margins were down; corporate debt was up. The rules of the game needed to change in favor of business. *Business Week* put the matter squarely in a mid-1970s issue: "It will be a hard pill for many Americans to swallow—the idea of doing with less so that business can have more. . . . Nothing that this nation, or any other nation, has done in modern economic history compares in difficulty with the selling job that must now be done to make people accept the new reality."

The first target of the conservative counterculture was not the press, but intellectuals. In 1970, Patrick Buchanan, then a Nixon speech writer, complained in a memorandum to the president that conservatives desperately needed to set up a think-tank to counter the malign influence of the Brookings Institution, which then reigned supreme in Washington and was considered (wrongly) to be an extremely liberal outfit.

Charles Peters: Former Peace Corps bureaucrat who started *The Washington Monthly* in 1969 on money from Jay Rockefeller, plus a department store heir and toy magnate. Like *The New Republic*, the *Monthly* has given enormous pleasure to Babylon's elites with its safe essays in neo-liberal iconoclasm. Jack Shafer, then of Washington's *City Paper*, once persuasively argued that the worship of Peters by his disciples amounts to a Peters Cult, with its own initiatory rites and sacred mysteries. This stable of acolytes—James Fallows, Michael Kinsley, Nicholas Lemann, Mickey Kaus, Gregg Easterbrook, Jonathan Alter, Timothy Noah, Jason DeParle—all carry the Peters mark, a bright boy-ism represented in its most undiluted and irksome form in Kinsley. Main characteristics of breed are extreme political orthodoxy, sedulous careerism, smugness.
(The Washington Monthly)

Robert Bartley: Editor of *Wall Street Journal's* editorial pages; a manic ideologue whose enthusiasms are decorously buttoned behind an Iowan's well-scrubbed Christian mien. Bartley's most notable passion in life has been supply-side economics, whose chief propagandist—Jude Wanniski—once worked for him. Other Bartleyesque passions down the years have included yellow rain, the Bulgarian connection in the Pope assassination plot, the Soviet threat in the South Pacific, the Star Wars system and gold. At the thought of returning America to the gold standard Bartley's eyes gleam and his breath comes faster. His pages are an important staging post in the transmission of right-wing obsessions into the larger culture. Charles Murray, James Q. Wilson and others regularly graze in the *Journal's* pasture. Bartley's underling John Fund co-wrote Rush Limbaugh's "book", and indeed the great Dirigible of Drivel is the fat man inside the trim Bartley who screamed all those years to be let out. In the neo-liberal swamp that constitutes most editorializing in America, Bartley stands out as a man who has held steadfastly to the tenets and fantasies of supply-siders and who has realized that successful propagandizing stems from saying the same thing at the top of one's voice for a very long time. (AP)

In the war of ideas, the right had grown a little slack. The fierce post-World War II corporate campaign against labor had achieved its objective and faded. The American Enterprise Institute (AEI) was founded in 1943, but three decades later lacked prestige, and was home to but a dozen full-time "scholars". The Heritage Foundation, born in 1973, was regarded as an institution of the lunatic fringe.

In the Watergate emergency this tranquil panorama underwent a seismic shift. In 1973, as the reputation of big business plummeted, corporate leaders formed the Business Roundtable. They reactivated the moribund US Chamber of Commerce and made it a potent lobbying force. Intensive recruitment of "opinion makers" went into high gear. Led by the John M. Olin Foundation—chaired by former Treasury Secretary William Simon—corporations and wealthy individuals were soon funneling tens of millions of dollars annually to right-wing thinkers. Recipients of Olin's cash over recent years include the late Allan Bloom, author of *The Closing of the American Mind*; the neo-conservative Irving Kristol, who took in $376,000 for general support in 1988 alone; and David Brock, for support of his book, *The Real Anita Hill: The Untold Story*. Joseph Coors put up the initial $250,000 in seed money to start Heritage in 1973. Since then, he has funded Paul Weyrich's Free Congress Foundation, the reclusive Council for National Policy (the far right's answer to the Council on Foreign Relations), the Hoover Institution, the American Defense Institute and Accuracy in Media.

Another major funder of the conservative counterattack was Richard Mellon Scaife. By 1981 *Columbia Journalism Review* was reporting that through his various foundations, Scaife had during the previous eight years given $1 million or more to a score of right-wing institutions, making him someone who "could claim to have done more than any other individual [in recent times] to influence the way in which Americans think about their country and the world".

Among the groups receiving substantial funding from Scaife were Georgetown University's Center for Strategic and International Studies, the Committee on the Present Danger, James Watt's Mountain States Legal Foundation and *The American Spectator* magazine. (When asked about his support for such outfits by the *Review*'s Karen Rothmyer, Scaife gallantly replied, "You fucking Communist cunt, get out of here.")

In the decade after Watergate, corporate money helped found several dozen conservative think-tanks. Aside from those already cited, they include the Cato Institute, the Manhattan Institute, and the Ethics and Public Policy Center. Meanwhile, the American Enterprise Institute's budget grew from $4 million in the mid-Seventies to $12.5 million in the mid-Nineties. By 1985, 12 years after it was founded, Heritage's annual budget had reached $11.6 million; nine years later that figure had grown to $25.5 million. Both of these outfits provided the Reagan administration with dozens of staffers.

The right's think-tanks know how to ventilate their views. The Heritage Foundation publishes hundreds of books, monographs and studies annually, with complimentary copies mailed to journalists across the country. Heritage's 1995-1996 *Guide to Public Policy Experts* lists some 1,800 policy wonks and 250 policy groups which "share our commitment to public policies based on free enterprise, limited government, individual freedom, traditional American values, and a strong national defense". The cross-referenced guide provides deadline-weary journalists with cooperative specialists in dozens of areas, ranging from "intelligence and counter-terrorism" to "wildlife management" and "bilingual education".

Think-tank scholars make money on the side by renting themselves out to public relations firms and lobbyists looking for "independent" supporters of their clients' viewpoints. One PR industry rep describes his technique in the following way: "I call up an 'expert', feign interest in his or her work, confirm that it's consistent with the industry viewpoint and then seek to strike a deal", normally for either a study or an appearance at a press event. "We don't say that we want an industry mouthpiece, but that's what it amounts to—and they know it. There are many people in this town who are willing to prostitute themselves and their work." This person recalls asking the conservative economist Murray Weidenbaum, former head of Reagan's Council of Economic Advisers, to appear at a media briefing on behalf of an industry group. Weidenbaum said he was very busy, but would try to squeeze in half a day if the PR firm would pony up $15,000—about three times the normal rate paid to industry flacks.

It's now all but impossible to keep track of the proliferating number of think-tanks and pressure groups, many of them benignly named fronts for corporate chicanery. Consumer Alert, formerly headed by John Sununu and funded by such companies as Chevron, Eli Lilly and Philip Morris, has fought mandatory air bags on the grounds that their expense is a burden to the consumers the group claims to represent; Citizens for the Sensible Control of Acid Rain is financed by major electric utilities and coal companies and battles tougher rules on air pollution; the Princeton Dental Resource Center, which once produced a study concluding that eating chocolate could be good for the teeth, is funded almost entirely by M&M/Mars.

ASIDE: ROBERT LEIKEN AND THE GOLDEN ROLODEX

It's called the "Golden Rolodex" and it refers to what the *National Journal* once called the "informal but intricate network . . . of former government officials, academic specialists, think-tank associates and a few journalists who advise decision-makers and . . . help frame the public debate". The privileged group of "experts" who make it to the Rolodex are always first to be called to appear on TV talk shows, to write op-ed pieces for major newspapers, to testify before Congress, to serve on government commissions.

The spectrum of opinion among Rolodexers is narrow. In 1989 Fairness and Accuracy in Reporting surveyed guest lists for *Nightline*. Tied for first place with 14 appearances were Henry Kissinger ("It was something akin to playing tennis with Boris Becker every day for a year and then going back to the club and playing everyone else", the program's host, Ted Koppel, once said of his days covering Kissinger at the State Department) and Al Haig, followed by Elliott Abrams and Jerry Falwell (12 appearances each), Alejandro Bendana, a spokesman for Nicaragua's Sandinista government invariably called upon to be abused by Koppel and invited guests (11), and Lawrence Eagleburger, one-time president of Kissinger Associates, and Jesse Jackson (10 each).

Of 19 US guests who appeared more than five times, 13 were conservatives, all were men and 17 were white.

For a brief period during the 1980s, Robert Leiken was awarded a card on the Golden Rolodex. His case offers a useful lesson in how one gets ahead in Washington.

Back in the Sixties, Leiken was a student of French literature at MIT. In the early Seventies he had a sudden conversion to Maoism and moved to Mexico to organize the peasantry. Associates were soon receiving letters from Leiken, who claimed to be living with a group of Maoist guerrillas in the highlands (though one old friend claims that he never left Mexico City).

After disappearing for a few years, Leiken emerged in the early Eighties at the liberal-ish Carnegie Institution. He published a book on Soviet influence in Central America. Reagan's war on Nicaragua was heating up, and Leiken, no fool at this game, began to auction himself as that most irresistible of PR commodities, a leftist who'd grown disillusioned with the Sandinistas.

On January 19, 1985, Walter Raymond, a long-time CIA employee who then headed the Office of Public Diplomacy, sent a memo to National Security Adviser Robert McFarlane. Leiken had approached him "at a face-to-face dinner and suggested that he would like to help":

"[Leiken] believes we have a fairly good chance of winning the Contra fight on the Hill if we play our cards right.... His proposed package includes several elements which I will tick off for you below:

• Build a positive image of the [Contras]. To do this we should send down one or more key journalists to start developing major positive stories.

• We must clean up the image of the [Contras], particularly removing known violators of human rights ... we need a cleaned up package."

Hence was born the "Gang of Four", a quartet of Democratic Party regulars in Washington. In addition to Leiken they were Penn Kemble, Bernard Aronson and Bruce Cameron, who helped line up congressional support for Ronald Reagan's war on the Sandinista government.

Leiken was the Gang's star. The former Maoist was suddenly a media darling, berating the Sandinistas in testimony before Congress, and in articles for *The New Republic* and *The New York Review of Books*. *Time* magazine commissioned an admiring profile. In a 1986 address to the nation, Reagan cited Leiken's hostility to the Sandinistas as proof that even bleeding hearts had given up on them.

Leiken soon moved on to Harvard's Center for International Affairs. His work there was financed with a $75,000 grant from the Olin Foundation.

After the wars in Central America wound down, Leiken's value as an officially sanctioned intellectual fell. He went on to Oxford to do a Ph.D., then returned to Washington in 1994 to become executive director of the US Information Agency's (USIA) advisory panel on TV and Radio Marti, the gov-

Gang of Four member Bernard Aronson.
(Shia photo/Impact Visuals)

ernment-funded propaganda vehicles controlled by the anti-Castro zealots at Miami's Cuban American National Foundation. Predictably, the panel he headed recommended the continued operation of both Radio and TV Marti. (This display of US arrogance is particularly stupid, since the Cuban government jams TV Marti and thus it is virtually unseen on the island.)

Joining the Reagan administration's anti-Sandinista crusade proved even more rewarding to Leiken's "Gang of Four" colleagues: Penn Kemble, a prominent Democratic cold warrior, now has a top position at the USIA (he helped Leiken get the Marti panel position); Bernard Aronson became assistant secretary of state for inter-American affairs for George Bush; and Bruce Cameron now runs a Beltway lobbying outfit.

★

The classic think-tank for the Nineties is Citizens for a Sound Economy (CSE), with the "citizens" in question being companies like Amoco, Bell Atlantic, Citibank, General Electric and General Motors. During recent years, the CSE, headed by C. Boyden Gray, who acted as counsel to the president under George Bush, has opposed health care reform and a rise in the minimum wage, while championing corporate tax cuts, deregulation and a balanced budget.

In 1995, CSE's budget hit $10 million and its "research"—funded entirely by corporations, conservative foundations and wealthy businessmen—is tailored to ensure results favorable to its patrons. Hence, a recent CSE study found that the American people were furious with the Food and Drug Administration. The CSE discovered this by asking respondents if they agreed with rigged statements such as, "The additional years it takes for the FDA to approve products costs lives by forcing people, including those with incurable diseases, to go without potentially beneficial drugs." Sixty-eight per cent agreed.

Armed with this information, Gray went before a House subcommittee in early 1995 and demanded "reform" (that is, gutting) of the FDA.

Gray told members of Congress that as a result of FDA dawdling, tens of thousands of Americans die annually. One particularly absurd case was that of the miracle drug nitrazepam. Deprived by FDA bureaucrats of the right to take this drug, some 4,000 people had perished. Or so Gray claimed.

Questioned by committee members, CSE's head conceded that he wasn't sure what nitrazepam was used for. Rep. Richard Durbin informed him: insomnia.

Though the enrichment of think-tanks on the right has been paramount since the early Seventies, corporations have not neglected the vital task of financing Democratic Party policymakers. These liberal think-tanks, like their conservative counterparts, enjoy through their tax-exempt status the welfare they constantly denounce. They devote themselves mainly to keeping liberalism safely within the bounds of corporate tolerance.

Try to enter forbidden terrain and a volley of barking goes up from these liberal watchdogs. In 1992 Jerry Brown, running against Bill Clinton for the Democratic nomination, started talking about a flat tax. After some input from radical economists he even started talking about a progressive flat tax. But liberal Washington had already marked Clinton as its man, despite his lackluster performance in a right-to-work state run by the Stephens banking family, the Rose Law Firm, Tyson, Wal-Mart and the timber companies.

So liberal think-tanks in Washington, led by Citizens for Tax Justice, raced to belabor Brown and laud the "progressivity" of the existing system. The fact that one of the leaders of Citizens for Tax Justice—David Wilhelm—was now working for Clinton's campaign emphasized the commitment of Babylon's liberal sector to the New Democrat from Little Rock.

Throughout 1992 liberal nostrils snuffled eagerly at the entrancing aromas of impending power. It had been a long time—12 years of exile—since Carter crept back to Plains in January 1981. In the primary season of 1992 liberal Babylon quivered with tremendous presentiments.

"It's our turn," Jackie Blumenthal, Sidney's wife, cried impatiently

Al From: President of the Democratic Leadership Council and chairman of its half-thought-tank, the Progressive Policy Institute, corporate promotional vehicles promulgating Clintonism and other "New Democratic" ideas. PPI's function is to hand out press releases every few weeks stressing that Clinton must steer clear of left contamination from labor unions, the Economic Policy Institute and other sanctuaries of the plague bacillus of old liberal ideas. (Democratic Leadership Council)

when a friend questioned Clinton's integrity and competence.

Nowhere was the excitement keener than in the Democratic Leadership Council (DLC) and its modest half-thought-tank, the Progressive Policy Institute (PPI). Back in late 1992, at a dinner held to honor Clinton, the Council took in $2.6 million. Among sponsors of the $15,000-a-plate affair were the American Bankers Association, the Tobacco Institute, Merrill Lynch, Coca-Cola and Occidental Petroleum. The Council was designed by Clinton, Charles Robb and other southern politicians to extract money and political endorsement from these corporate bigwigs, while simultaneously selling to the ever-receptive pundits of the Fourth Estate the notion that here at last was an outfit prepared to do battle with the hated "special

interests", otherwise known as the base of the Democratic Party—
working people in unions, blacks, Hispanics, greens and so on.

PPI's budget is provided largely by a board of trustees, whose 21
members play a significant role in forming policy. The board includes
five investment bankers, three real estate barons, a Louisiana socialite,
a leading contributor to the Republican Party and officials from
Coca-Cola, Gilman Paper Co. and the Mars candy empire.

An important issue for the PPI in 1993 was the battle for NAFTA,
which it promoted in a series of position papers and in a corporate-
financed lobbying campaign. To the delight of the Institute's vice
chairman, Al From, the debate on the trade pact provoked a split
between the Clinton administration and organized labor, the PPI's
bête noire. Another priority of the Institute was "two-years-and-out"
welfare reform, an interest finally consummated in the welfare votes
of the fall of 1995.

The link between the Democratic Leadership Council's finances
and its ideology was vividly displayed in a fundraising campaign it
conducted in 1994. On March 7 of that year, development director
Winston McGregor sent PPI trustees a memo with the names of several hundred potential contributors. Many of the prospects were
culled from an earlier memo, dated February 28, which catalogues
all $5,000-plus donors to the Democratic Party. A note attached to
the latter document says the PPI "should explore almost all of the
individuals on these lists with the exception of those from the labor
community".

The PPI's targets are a resplendent mix of Fortune 500 firms and
wealthy individuals. They include prominent Republicans such as bil-
lionaire Walter Annenberg, Richard Nixon's ambassador to Britain,
who made it to the "A list" of top prospects. In some cases, the memo
selects "the individual who [would] be most successful in soliciting
the contribution":

• Bill Clinton was suggested to put the bite on Don Tyson, head
of Little Rock-based Tyson Foods, and on mega-investor Warren
Buffett, whose net worth is valued at $8.3 billion.

• VP Al Gore, the administration's point-man on the information
superhighway, was to extract money from John Cooke of the Disney
Channel. Cooke's firm has much at stake in federal policy on
telecommunications laws and regulations.

Barbara Walters: Fading empress of the "indiscreet" interview; here seen with Senator John Warner, Bob Zelnick and Donna Shalala, Secretary of Health and Human Services. (Vivian Ronay/Photoreporters)

• Senator John Breaux—who once announced that his vote could not be bought but "it can be rented"—was to coax funds from John Kluge of Metromedia, a company which Breaux oversees from the communications subcommittee of the Senate Commerce Committee. The Louisiana senator, a vigilant ally of agricultural interests, was also to solicit Grover Connell, the country's largest independent sugar and rice trader.

• Senator Sam Nunn was to solicit Ronald Allen, CEO of Atlanta-based Delta Airlines. In September 1994, Nunn lobbied the Transportation Department on Delta's behalf in negotiations with Germany on a new bilateral aviation accord.

The PPI's policy choices were particularly interesting in light of its funding base and donor targets. Take the issue of campaign finance reform, which vice-chair From once opposed in the Institute's soporific publication, *The New Democrat.* "For all the superficial appeal of replacing special interest money with public funding . . . I shudder at the thought that some day some government bureaucrat could decide which campaigns to fund", From wrote tactfully. "The best solution is lots of sunshine. Give voters the information they need to exercise their ultimate power."

Peering over From's shoulder was PPI board member Richard

Fisher, who spent $4.5 million of his own money to buy victory in Texas's Democratic senate primary in 1994. The Institute's major funders are the same corporations and individuals who, under the current system, purchase political influence with their campaign contributions.

The New Democrat also feels strongly about China, blasting Peking's "bully boys" for their "abysmal" human rights record while simultaneously demanding that Clinton renew that country's most-favored-nation trade status. Many DLC corporate contributors have important commercial relations with Peking, including at least three firms which hold seats on the Council's board: Xerox controls 45 per cent of China's desktop copier market, Pepsico recently announced new investments in China of $350 million and Merck's chairman, Roy Vagelos, last year visited Peking to explore business possibilities.

With regard to the budget, a *New Democrat* editorial in 1994 proposed reducing federal spending by $225 billion over the next five years. Not one of the recommended cuts would affect the military budget, a posture pleasing to such DLC donors as Martin Marietta, General Dynamics, Boeing and McDonnell Douglas.

ASIDE: MURRAY, THE THINKER

Charles Murray is a Thinker of the Right, a breed which leads an affluent and pleasant life. Natural habitat ranges from the Hoover Institute at Stanford to Washington's American Enterprise Institute, with herd members frequently spotted churning up topsoil on the editorial page of *The Wall Street Journal*. Prominent Thinkers of the Right include Murray, James Q. Wilson, Thomas Sowell and Milton Friedman. A notch below are Pamphleteers of the Right such as the Kristols, father and son, and William Bennett.

If Wilson's quarter-century mission has been to argue that crime is best dealt with by imprisonment (thus leading to one of the highest incarceration rates in the world), Murray's role is to attack subsidies to the poor, particularly welfare.

In the early Eighties, Murray was based at the Manhattan Institute for Policy Research, a think-tank founded by ex-CIA director William Casey. The Institute's president, William Hammett, was impressed by a Heritage

Charles Murray: Sold old Nazi and even older American racist dogma as bold new thought. Bogus statistics, cretinous ideas, treated with extreme seriousness in Babylon.
(The Free Press/1994)

Foundation booklet written by Murray and hired him as a senior research fellow. Murray's research during this period was funded by the Olin and Sarah Scaife Foundations.

It was at the Manhattan Institute that Murray wrote his 1984 book, *Losing Ground*, in which he argued that social programs were worthless and should be eliminated. The Institute financed a big publicity campaign for the book, mailing nearly a thousand free copies to journalists and academics. It also signed up a public relations firm to set up TV and radio interviews, a nationwide speaking tour and a two-day seminar in New York at which prominent writers and thinkers gathered to hear Murray pontificate.

In 1995 Murray moved to new ground, seeking to show the innate inferiority of blacks in *The Bell Curve,* the book he co-wrote with the late Richard Herrnstein. Murray's research for the book was sponsored by the American Enterprise Institute.

Open up *The Bell Curve* and glance at the introduction, where the authors list their intellectual ancestors. There on the opening page is Darwin's half-cousin Francis Galton, cited in blandly respectful terms. Galton's scientific procedures are well exhibited by an observation in his essay "Hereditary Improvement", that after the famine "the Irish type of face seemed to have become more prognathous, that is, more like the negro in the protrusion of the lower jaw; the interpretation of which was that the men who survived the starvation and other deadly accidents of that horrible time were more generally of a low or coarse organization."

In opposition to England's 19th-century public health movement, Galton denounced such efforts as wasted on the genetic *submenschen,* while announcing sadly that he had not "yet succeeded to my satisfaction to make an approximate estimate of the worth of a child according to the class he is destined to occupy as an adult". Most children should get nothing, for "the average citizen is too base for the everyday work of modern civilization" and should maintain celibacy, since their procreation of children "inferior in moral, intellectual and physical qualities" renders them fit to be considered "enemies to the State, and to have forfeited all claims to kindness".

Next up for kindly citation in *The Bell Curve's* introduction is Galton's assistant Karl Pearson, who measured the heads of Jewish children to prove their innate inferiority ("the defect of brachycephaly in our alien Jewish boys seems noteworthy"). Pearson arrived at such conclusions with the help of the "correlation coefficient" for which Herrnstein and Murray honor him.

Receiving most honorable mention by Herrnstein and Murray are important begetters of the pseudo-science of IQ testing, Henry Goddard and Lewis Terman. Goddard is defended from the charge that he used his modification of Binet's tests at Ellis Island to show that Jews were "feeble-minded".

Goddard's work at Ellis Island paved the way for the 1924 Immigration Restriction Act. Hitler and his fellow Nazis took the Act—and the pseudo-sciences behind it—as a model for their own efforts in applied eugenics. Herrnstein and Murray remark that the 1924 Act "tipped the flow of immigrants toward the western and northern Europeans". This is a typical disingenuous euphemism: between 1900 and 1924 the average annual arrival of immigrants from countries proscribed by the Act was 434,810, a total which dropped to an annual average of 24,430 after the Act passed. Many of those excluded as "dysgenic" were murdered by the Nazis, who applied with gusto the theories developed by their American tutors.

Herrnstein and Murray, lauded even by their press critics as scrupulous and fearless in their scholarship, trace their own intellectual heritage back to those instructors of the Nazis.

These spasms of racist IQ theory and persecution of the poor and minorities also coincide with economic and social upheaval. The Supreme Court's 1954 decision in Brown v. Board of Education provoked a wave of race inferiority work designed to demonstrate that there was no point in trying to educate the negro. The IQ racists of later years have wanted to justify the accelerating splits in American income between an elite and the broad and undeserving mass.

★

The DLC champions the middle class and berates "special interests", but its raison d'etre and the key to its financial success is keen solicitude for the ideological needs and spiritual fears of business. As Ellen Miller of the Center for Responsive Politics puts it, "The type of donors that give money [to the DLC] are expect-

Sidney Blumenthal: Part of boomer cohort chafing for a Democrat's return to the White House after the Reagan-Bush darkness. Blumenthal pastured at *The New Republic,* ended up at Tina Brown's *New Yorker,* where his Clintonophiliac ecstasies proved too much for the which-way-the-wind-blows snuffling Brown. Blumenthal went into eclipse, but with Clinton renascent Sid's star will also rise. Cultivates appearance of measured sagacity, like the man in Rebecca West's novel *The Thinking Reed* who, "even when he was peering down a woman's breasts managed to look as though he was thinking about India".
(Vivian Ronay/Photoreporters)

ing something in return, in this case favorable policies from an influential institution. And they [the DLC] are able to get money from these corporations because of the positions they take."

Reporters have always nuzzled close to power. The classic example is *The New York Times*'s James Reston, a man deeply involved in the struggles over the political contours of the postwar world. Along with Walter Lippmann he helped Senator Arthur Vandenberg write his famous speech of January 10, 1945, recanting isolationism and then, like Lippmann, gave it an ecstatic review without mentioning his own role. He had, however, made a coy gesture to his insider knowledge when, in a dispatch filed the day before the speech, he wrote, "These proposals are said to have been drafted not in a partisan sense but with the purpose of making clear that the Senate is prepared to favor putting American force behind American principles in the interests of a lasting peace."

Hugh Sidey, now at *Time*, was a fawning admirer of JFK. In *President Kennedy, Portrait of Power*, Richard Reeves revealed that Sidey, upon learning that the Evelyn Wood Institute estimated that JFK read 700 to 800 words per minute, called the president for confirmation. Kennedy said that the Institute's estimate was probably too low.

Sidey suggested 1,200 words, to which JFK replied, "OK." Sidey soon had a piece for *Life*—"He Eats Up News, Books at 1,200 Words a Minute." In 1994, Sidey told *The Washington Post*, "I haven't any idea how fast he read. The figure was kind of hoked up."

Today such collaborations are far more widespread, encompassing not just a handful of State Department reporters but many in the Washington press corps. When not sipping wine with the president, the *Times*'s R.W. Apple consorts with such friends as the quintessential lawyer-lobbyists Robert Strauss and Lloyd Cutler. He once told *The Washington Post*'s Howard Kurtz frankly enough that he's an "establishment" type of guy, and that "if Lawrence Eagleburger and Zbigniew Brzezinski and one or two others were to say to me, 'that's a lot of crap', I would tend to be hesitant to put it forward."

Reflecting their increased respectability and compliance, media figures now make up roughly 10 per cent of the membership of the Council on Foreign Relations. Once a tranquil watering-hole for

Michael Kinsley and William Bennett: Kinsley came to prominence as a novitiate in the Peters Cult. Held up neo-liberal end of *Crossfire* before entering holy orders at the Cathedral of St. Microsoft in Seattle. Thought to have been only virgin ever to have appeared on *Crossfire*. Bennett, author of uplifting homilies of appalling triteness, *The Book of Virtues*, venerated on right as thinker and other half of Limbaugh's brain. (Vivian Ronay/Photoreporters)

senior mass murderers, State Department veterans and a sprinkling of corporate and journalistic self-seekers, the Council is now headed by Leslie Gelb, whose serpentine career has shuttled him between Pentagon, State and *The New York Times*. CFR's snooze-producing *Foreign Affairs* is run by James Hoge, another ex-journalist. Hoge's media colleagues at the Council include Robert Bartley (*The Wall Street Journal*), Karen Elliott House (*Wall Street Journal*) and her husband, Peter Kann (CEO, *Wall Street Journal*), Roone Arledge (ABC News), Tom Brokaw, David Brinkley, John Chancellor, A.M. Rosenthal (*The New York Times*), Katharine Graham (*The Washington Post*), Robert Silvers (*The New York Review of Books*), Katrina vanden Heuvel (*The Nation*), R. Emmett Tyrell (*American Spectator*) and coffles of pundits great and small.

Truly "responsible" reporters also gain that most cherished of all Washington commodities: "access". Some reporters of the Federal Reserve win coveted invitations to the annual Fourth of July bash held on the Fed's roof, and to the Fed's annual economics conference in Jackson Hole, Wyoming, where reporters and their spouses wander toward seminars through an athletic haze of hiking, tennis and white-water rafting.

Another popular affair is the year-end Renaissance Weekend in Hilton Head, South Carolina. The 1993 event was attended by Bill Clinton, Supreme Court Justice Harry Blackmun, three US senators and hundreds of other powerful Beltway players. *Newsweek*'s Howard Fineman was among the journalists invited to attend on the condition that they not write about it. During the weekend, which cost roughly $1,500 per couple, Fineman attended such seminars as "Building an Inner Life", played touch football with the president and urged Clinton to send daughter Chelsea to Washington's Sidwell Friends Academy (annual tuition, $11,000), which Fineman's own daughter attends.

Not long afterwards, Fineman appeared on "Washington World This Week" to pontificate about the political culture of Little Rock, capital of Clinton's home state of Arkansas. The problem with Little Rock, Fineman said with scant self-reflection, was that politics is controlled by a small group of insiders: "They have the money. They've got the power. They're on a first-name basis with each other ... and

Thomas Friedman and Senator Pat Moynihan, a noted appreciator of inspiring liquids. Friedman himself is maturing in the cask of self-importance as a *New York Times* registered pundit. (Vivian Ronay/Photoreporters)

Leon Wieseltier: "Yet let me flap this bug with gilded wings/This painted child of dirt that stinks and stings . . ." The Tartuffe of Babylon, stabled at *The New Republic* where he has led the life of a second-tier literary dilettante, snorting cocaine and paltering with the interns, whose duties include walking his dog. Fainéant, full of pathetic self-conceit, Wieseltier evokes London's Grub Street of the 1890s, whose bohemian poseurs were so well recorded by Max Beerbohm (though Wieseltier would not have the courage to make a pact with the devil, as did Enoch Soames). Cover story for a life of marked though no doubt merciful lack of productivity is that he is at work on "a book about sighing".
(Vivian Ronay/Photoreporters)

Howard Fineman: *Newsweek*'s **national correspondent; pretends to deride Beltway's "insider" culture while enjoying all its vices and perks—married to a DC lobbyist and played touch football with Clinton at a Renaissance Weekend affair.** (Carl Cox Photography)

the line between public money and private business is very fuzzy."

The Gridiron Club, a society of successful journalists, holds an annual spring dinner which the capital's leading political figures attend. In *The Power Game, The New York Times*'s Hedrick Smith cheerfully relates such highlights from dinners past as the delightful jitterbug by Jimmy and Rosalyn Carter in 1978 and Ronald Reagan's softshoe routine a few years later. "But for a sheer turnaround—and a political facelift—no Gridiron guest in recent years has outdone Nancy Reagan," Smith remarks. Mrs. Reagan's immoderate spending had created a cold and unsympathetic image which the First Lady managed to reshape with one hearty song-and-dance routine at the

Club: "Secondhand clothes, I'm wearing secondhand clothes . . . Even my new trench coat with fur collar, Ronnie bought for ten cents on the dollar."

This performance earned Mrs. Reagan a standing ovation from the audience. "Only the inner core of the Washington community had seen this side of Mrs. Reagan," Smith observes. "But that community included most of the important journalists and politicians, and among this crucial audience Mrs. Reagan's image had been remade in a few short minutes. Inside the Beltway, people talked with amusement and warmth about her Gridiron performance."

The generous salaries paid to the Washington media have allowed journalists to join with the elite on its own terms. The typical correspondent in Babylon sends his kids to private school or public school in an exclusive area, drives a Volvo and goes overseas once every few years and to Martha's Vineyard or the Hamptons every summer.

As Benjamin Bradlee, the *Post*'s executive editor at the time of Watergate, said not long ago, "Reporters are more conservative than the previous generation. And I think there's a very good reason for that. They get paid a hell of a lot better. It's hard to be conservative on $75 a week, but seventy-five grand, you begin to think of the kids and the bank account and the IRA and roll it over and all this stuff." (This comment is somewhat ironic coming from Bradlee. He retired to a seat on the board—and a newly created vice presidency—of the *Post* in August of 1991, which paid him in excess of $1.2 million, including bonuses and stock options.)

Some top correspondents make more in a single speech to industry groups than the average American takes home in a year. ABC's and National Public Radio's Cokie Roberts—sister of DC's most prominent lobbyist, Tommy Boggs, of Patton, Boggs & Blow—pulled in an estimated $30,000 for a 1995 chat with the Junior League of Greater Fort Lauderdale, Florida. JM Family Enterprises, a $4 billion firm, picked up the check. In October 1994, Roberts and her husband, reporter Steve Roberts of *U.S. News & World Report*, netted $45,000 for a joint appearance at a Chicago bank.

Other journalists who make significant income from speeches include Sam Donaldson of ABC ($30,000 a pop), Tim Russert of NBC ($10,000) and David Broder of *The Washington Post* ($7,500).

Cocktail time in Babylon: ABC/NPR screen-queen Cokie Roberts with husband Steve of *US News & World Report*, Cokie's brother and prime influence peddler Tommy Boggs, and Mr. Virtues himself, William Bennett. (Vivian Ronay/Photoreporters)

Back in 1993, when health reform was one of the day's biggest topics, CBS's Lesley Stahl took home roughly $10,000 from Cigna Corp., one of the nation's largest insurance companies.

Figures such as Donaldson and Bernard Goldberg of CBS, one TV producer recalls, are such ardent players in the stock market that they become edgy when they're away from the phone for too long and can't check in with their brokers. In 1992, David Brinkley—who earns somewhere in the neighborhood of $1 million annually—told a business group that the idea of raising taxes on the rich was a "sick, stupid joke".

In 1995 some Republicans pressed for reporters with congressional press passes to disclose sources of outside income. This sensible idea was greeted with howls of protest about intrusions into free speech.

Charles Lewis, a former *60 Minutes* producer who resigned to found the Center for Public Integrity, says, "The values of the news media are the same as those of the elite, and they badly want to be viewed by the elites as acceptable. Socially, culturally and economically they belong to the group of people who they are covering."

The quintessential elite reporter is ABC's Diane Sawyer, the former Junior Miss from Kentucky who, after a brief stint as weather girl at a Louisville station, moved to DC and (thanks to the influence of her father, a prominent Kentucky Republican) got a job at the Nixon White House press office in the early-Seventies. Sawyer was keenly loyal to President Nixon, and when he resigned she flew with the disgraced leader to San Clemente. There Sawyer remained for four years, helping her then-boyfriend Frank Gannon prepare Nixon's autobiography.

In 1978 CBS hired Sawyer to join its national team. Thanks to her cultivation of network decision makers such as William Paley (she

Sam Donaldson on Santa's lap, as Nancy Reagan cheers from the sidelines. Father Christmas duly answered Sam's wish, with over $100,000 in federal subsidies for his sheep ranch in New Mexico. (Library of Congress)

was in close contact with the media mogul as he lay dying), she netted a slot on *60 Minutes* in 1984.

Sawyer signed a $7 million deal with ABC in 1994 to host *Prime Time Live*. While there she has become known for her hard-hitting interviews with such figures as Marla Maples ("Was it the best sex you ever had?" she asked Maples of her activities with Donald Trump) and Charles Manson.

During an episode on social spending, Sawyer berated a welfare mother who was illegally working two part-time jobs in order to supplement her $600 per month welfare benefits. "You know, people say you should not have children if you can't support them," Sawyer sternly lectured her victim. As pointed out by FAIR, the media watchdog group, Sawyer earns every day almost as much as the welfare mom earned per year: $16,700.

Sawyer has dated a number of powerful political figures, including Henry Kissinger and Clinton's assistant secretary of state

Diane Sawyer with Nancy Reagan in the White House. Sawyer began with Nixon's White House (sitting in Henry K's lap), progressed to CBS (ministering to dying mogul Bill Paley), and now is comfortably married to film director Mike Nichols. (Library of Congress)

James Reston: Recently deceased super-pundit of *The New York Times* in whom the condition known as Reston's Syndrome was first isolated. This ailment (easily confused with Lippmannism) is now conspicuously displayed in the person of David Broder, touted as dean of the Washington political press corps. Symptoms include occlusion of the cerebral faculties, suffusion of ego amid belief that the Republic's well-being largely depends upon the keen insights of the pundit. Broder has spent decades in DC all the while oblivious to the total corruption of the political process wrought by big money. In January of 1996 he bitterly attacked PBS's *Frontline* for airing a program which suggested that politicians can be bought by campaign contributions. "The American political system is much more complex . . . than the proponents of the 'auction' theory of democracy understand", the pundit sniffed.

Richard Holbrooke. (The latter's romantic career is highly reflective of the incestuous links between the media and political elites. After splitting with Sawyer, Holbrooke dated Barbara Cohen, the former wife of *Washington Post* columnist Richard Cohen. He later married the ex-Mrs. Peter Jennings. Holbrooke's second wife has described him as a relentless bore, saying his favorite activity is "watching him-

New Yorker editor **Tina Brown and NPR's Nina Totenberg: Brown shuttles the power triangle between New York, DC and Babylon West. She evicted famed Exocet of Ennui Elizabeth Drew from** *New Yorker* **pages but replacements Blumenthal, Kelly and Boyer scamper along, without even the distinction of Drew's dogged devotion to the literal. NPR's producers zealously cleanse its programs of anything resembling radical taint. Back in 1990, pressed to devote its five-minute book section to Noam Chomsky's** *Necessary Illusions,* **"All Things Considered" pre-recorded Chomsky in its Boston studio, then announced at 5 p.m. that the interview would be aired at 5:25. Came 5:25 and the eager listeners heard nothing but solemn music. In the interim a senior NPR executive, hearing the 5:00 announcement, had axed the segment over the protests of the producer. Five years later the show's host Robert Siegel stated publicly, "We wouldn't be interested in airing the views of such media and political critics as Chomsky." A footnote on public radio north of the border:** *Necessary Illusions* **was delivered as lectures, mostly about US media, over CBC.** (Vivian Ronay/Photoreporters)

self being interviewed on TV"). Though now married to film director Mike Nichols, Sawyer still protects her former beaus.

Despite her hefty pay check, Sawyer has never demonstrated any great public appeal. When she left *60 Minutes,* there was no impact on the show's ratings. *Prime Time* was ranked No. 18 in 1993-94, but fell to No. 87 during Sawyer's first four episodes. The program's popularity today remains muted.

ASIDE: MEMORIES OF A NETWORK PRODUCER,
OR HOW NOT TO GET AHEAD IN TV JOURNALISM

NBC News hired Carl Ginsburg as a producer when he was in his mid-twenties. A decade later, having worked at CBS and Fox, he went to ABC's *Prime Time*, which he finally quit in frustration.

According to him, it's almost impossible to get anything on the air that fairly depicts the union movement. During the Bush years, he did a story on the issue of corporations hiring permanent replacements—scabs—for workers on strike, an episode which caused much offense.

Rep. Dick Armey and other members of Congress complained about the piece on the House floor, and said it reflected an anti-corporate bias on the part of the network. Armey and other congressional right-wingers were invited to a meeting with Bob Schieffer of CBS's Washington bureau, and a new piece on striker replacement, reflective of the views of Corporate America, soon aired.

Ginsburg, meanwhile, received a memo from CBS's corporate public relations department which contained a copy of Armey's speech on the House floor. The message was clear enough.

Most of Ginsburg's colleagues were highly conservative on social issues, and scornful of minorities. Ginsburg once suggested to Bob Faw, who has worked for CBS and NBC, that they do a story on how the medical establishment fails to meet the needs of blacks. An angry Faw asked, "Is it lifestyle or poverty?"—in other words, Isn't it their own fault if they eat potato chips and drink soda? "Network correspondents generally embrace Gingrich's view that poverty is habit", Ginsburg says. "They may not like Gingrich—his radicalism makes them uncomfortable—but the underpinnings are the same."

Ginsburg recalls traveling to South Carolina in 1990, one year after Hurricane Hugo had destroyed the area. He and another producer found that many residents had never recovered, and were living in wretched shacks and mobile homes. In a fine display of sensitivity, Ginsburg's colleague and a CBS cameraman, after finishing an interview with a particularly desolate family, asked the husband and wife what local restaurant offered the "best shrimp dinner in town".

Ginsburg moved to *Prime Time* in mid-1994, but retired a year later. The breaking point came when he pitched what he thought was a sure-fire winner about Oshkosh, the Wisconsin manufacturer of the quintessential American product—bib overalls—shutting a home-state plant and moving to a free-trade zone in the Dominican Republic. His proposal included a look at another US company, Liz Claiborne, whose garment factories in Honduras

Lally Weymouth and politico David Keene: Across the world there are brave
men and women who turn ashen upon hearing that Lally, daughter of Kay
Graham and thereby a *Washington Post* op-ed page contributor, is headed their
way. These are the *Post*'s regular foreign correspondents, who know well the
consequences of Her Royal Highness's descent: imperious demands for interviews to be set up with presidents and chief tycoons, the blinding inaccuracy of
her perceptions, tantrums and incessant rudeness, the right-wing dementia and
conspiracies spoonfed to her by her favored advisers, mostly Israeli diplomats
and spies. Weymouth's partner is dingy Eric Breindel, nearly sunk by a heroin
scandal when he worked for Senator Pat Moynihan, rescued by Martin Peretz,
and now installed as editorial page editor of *The New York Post*. Once upon a
time Breindel was married to Tamar Jacoby. He persuaded her to accompany
him and his father on a trip to Europe, thence for a tour of Auschwitz. In Paris
he proclaimed that editorial duties required his immediate return to New York,
but urged Jacoby to continue the trip. She and Breindel père made their way to
Auschwitz. They returned at last to New York. After depositing Breindel senior
in his apartment, Jacoby returned to the nest that she and Eric had made their
own. It was empty, denuded of all traces of Breindel, who had returned from
Paris to decamp with Weymouth. It is hard to say on which of the two, Eric or
Lally, Fate has inflicted the more terrible revenge. (Vivian Ronay/Photoreporters)

used child labor. Both countries' free-trade zones have been supported by the US Agency for International Development with taxpayer money.

Diane Sawyer soon dashed Ginsburg's hopes. "I hear problems, Carl", she said after listening to the pitch. "I'm interested in solutions."

★

THE YOUNG RIGHT WING

In early 1995, James Atlas wrote a cover story for *The New York Times Magazine*, "The Counter Counterculture", which devoted considerable space to such wild and crazy young conservatives as David Brock, Richard Brookheiser and Adam Bellow. Unlike their stodgy elders, today's Beltway conservatives listen to 10,000 Maniacs and Smashing Pumpkins, and advertise themselves as "hip" to popular culture.

Also featured in Atlas's story was Laura Ingraham, a former editor of the *Dartmouth Review*. Like many of her former colleagues Ingraham designed her session at the *Review* to catch the eye of right-wing patrons and win lucrative employment in Washington.

After working as an aide to the Reagan administration's Education Department, she served as Clarence Thomas's law clerk. Ingraham now works at the Washington law firm of Skadden, Arps, Slate, Meagher & Flom. She also is a leading member of the Independent Women's Forum (IWF), the conservative group which is popular with the media and whose members include Wendy Lee Gramm, Senator Phil Gramm's wife.

One of the IWF's top priorities is fighting affirmative action. As part of its campaign, Ingraham penned a *New York Times* op-ed piece which argued that women no longer faced a "glass ceiling", and that "the idea that women are constantly thwarted by invisible barriers of sexism relegates them to permanent victim status."

Ingraham was featured on the cover of the *Times Magazine* wearing a leopard miniskirt. The *Times* implored her to wear the miniskirt in the interest of a story hyping the wild and crazy young right wing.

Over drinks at Washington's Tabard Inn, Ingraham told Atlas about a trip she made in the mid-Eighties to El Salvador. Asked how she spent her time, Ingraham, with "a dry laugh", replied, "subjugating third world nations". A Dartmouth professor who read the article recalled that the *Review* berated university teachers who traveled to El Salvador during the Eighties and suggested that they stay at the "Five Dead Nuns Inn". Ho, ho.

The *Times*'s Atlas didn't mention a stunt the *Review* pulled during Ingraham's years as editor, one of the most reprehensible in its history—and bear in mind that this is a newspaper which thought it uproariously funny to hold a lobster and champagne lunch on the same day that students had scheduled a series of events to combat hunger.

In May of 1984, a *Review* writer, Teresa Polenz, infiltrated a meeting of the newly founded Gay Students' Association (GSA). Polenz, masquerading as a gay student who was questioning her own sexual preferences, secretly taped the meeting. Ingraham and her colleagues published transcripts in the *Review* and sent them to the parents of GSA members.

Accompanying the issue with this story was a "Letter from the Editor" from Ingraham, who called GSA members "cheerleaders for latent campus sodomites" who were "helping frightened gays shed heterosexual peer pressure and act in accordance with their urges". Ingraham also attacked Dartmouth administrators, saying that in supporting the GSA the university was guilty of "jumping on the pink bandwagon".

YOUNG STRUTTER OF THE RIGHT

At the age of 25, Ruth Shalit is one of the most successful of the young, right-wing writers who patrol the opinion pages or sport their prejudices in the Sunday magazines. Shalit has a $45,000 contract with *GQ*, showed up in the *New York Times Magazine* with a cover story on Bob Dole and in late 1995 gained pleasing notoriety with an attack on affirmative action at *The Washington Post*, published in *The New Republic*, where she is an associate editor.

Shalit (pronounced "shall eat") is a hot property in Washington and an emblematic one, too. She has made all the proper moves along a path well trodden by careerists seeking fortune in right-wing journalism. First, attacks on "multiculturalism" or "PC" while at a college newspaper; next, arrival within the Beltway as an aide to a politi-

New York Times Magazine **cover with Laura Ingraham in animal-print miniskirt: The death squads had her hot but not bothered.**

cal figure or for one of the right's think-tanks; then on to work at a conservative publication.

Shalit's story in *The New Republic*, "Race in the Newsroom: *The Washington Post* in Black and White", claimed that black staffers at the newspaper, apparently acting out of racial solidarity, have sought to cover up the failures of the city's political elite. Furthermore, the newspaper's once aggressive "coverage of the social pathologies at the heart of Washington's black underclass—chronic welfare dependence, adolescent childbearing, neighborhood crime and violence—has increasingly given way to puffery".

There are many reasons to criticize the *Post*, a newspaper which in recent years has carefully leached out any tincture of liberalism. But Shalit's piece wasn't about the *Post*. In the tradition of D'Souza and Charles Murray, it was an attack on African-Americans dressed up as social science.

Editors "will end up with a nearly all-white staff", Shalit wrote, if they hire purely on the basis of qualifications". A "newspaper's mandate—to be an arbiter of truth, an enemy of euphemism, a check on social complacency—is directly at odds with the ideology of diversity management, with its ethos of sensitivity and conflict avoidance at all costs."

Yet despite attempts to diversify, the *Post* is still largely a white institution—minority journalists make up roughly 18 percent of its professional staff—in a city which is overwhelmingly black and minority. "Why shouldn't black people be encouraged to write about a black city and black government?" asks Jill Nelson, who chronicled her 1986 to 1990 tenure at the *Post* in *Volunteer Slavery*. "White men have traditionally held a privileged position in the world of journalism. When occasional attempts to level the playing field have been made, white men, and sometimes white women, have freaked out."

Shalit calls herself a "social liberal", and insists that she "tried to be scrupulously fair" in preparing her story. "If any of the goals of affirmative action are to be preserved, affirmative action must be reformed. The only way to do that is to criticize its excesses", she wrote in a letter to *The New York Times* in which she defended the *Post* article.

Scrupulous fairness and candor are not conspicuous in Shalit's resumé. At Princeton University, from which she graduated in 1992, Shalit served as editor-in-chief of the *Sentinel*, a right-wing publication in the tradition of the *Dartmouth Review* and propped up with checks from a variety of reactionary foundations, including the Madison Center, an outfit founded by William Bennett. In addition to Shalit, the *Sentinel* was the testing ground for Ramesh Ponnuru of the *National Review* and David Miller of *US News & World Report*.

In her letter to the *Times*, Shalit distanced herself from D'Souza. But as editor of the *Sentinel*, she published at least one article by D'Souza (in which he attacked Rigoberta Menchu, the Guatemalan Indian who later won the Nobel Peace Prize), as well as a slavish review of his first book, *Illiberal Education*.

PETE WILSON'S RECORD—THE FLIP SIDE

THE NEW REPUBLIC

OCTOBER 2, 1995 • $2.95

Jackson Lears on Christopher Lasch • Alan Brinkley on Ecopolitics

The Washington Post

In Black & White

Race in the
Newsroom:
A Case Study

by Ruth Shalit

Shalit's snow job: 25-year-old rising star in Babylon's journalism circles, Ruth Shalit, like D'Souza, rose to fame with attacks on blacks cloaked as social science; dancing partner of Newt Gingrich.

Shalit herself wrote essays attacking "hand wringing" multiculturalists, that favorite target of the campus right. She also penned an odd article in which she argued that the War on Poverty had been "as clumsy, protracted and casualty-filled as Vietnam", though fortunately the national malaise resulting from the latter had been "buried . . . in the sands of Kuwait".

In 1992, Shalit worked for the Bush campaign. After Bush's defeat by Clinton, Shalit dropped out of politics and soon bobbed up as an intern at *The New Republic*, where she enjoyed the patronage of Fred Barnes, now an editor at Rupert Murdoch's *Weekly Standard*.

A 1994 story in *Mediaweek* reported Shalit's zeal to "rise early on weekday mornings to accompany [Newt] Gingrich on his daily constitutional through the tree-lined avenues of his Capitol Hill neighborhood." The piece also mentioned that she had been the House Speaker's dancing partner at a black-tie event held by the Cato Institute in 1994, as "a cadre of young editorial writers from the *Wall Street Journal* looked on, waiting to cut in".

Shalit's attacks on African-Americans have been unremitting. In 1993, she sped to Harvard after hearing a rumor that an article by a black law school professor had actually been written by his students. The story turned out to be false, but Shalit wrote an article anyway, under the pretense that the "pseudo-scandal" had "energized racial politics across the campus". She also penned a foolish piece on the evils of diversity at the government level, in which she quoted neo-con Ben Wattenberg as saying that the Clinton administration was "turning into a walking billboard for a quota society".

Shalit makes so many mistakes that nothing that she writes can be trusted. Among the dozens of errors in her article on the *Post*: in what her target calls a "nice libel suit", Shalit erroneously wrote that Roy Littlejohn, a city contractor, once "served time" for corruption; she mistakenly claimed that Jeanne Fox-Alston, the *Post*'s director of hiring and recruiting, had formerly worked as a copy editor (one of at least five errors that Shalit makes in regard to job titles and job descriptions). Fox-Alston was one of Shalit's prime targets because of her alleged role in "winnowing out white males"—that oppressed group which holds almost all of the top positions at the *Post*, and whose members have been selected for 123 of 330 newsroom positions over the past nine years. Shalit also falsely stated that the late Herb Denton was part of an equal employment opportunity suit filed against the *Post* in 1972; she charges that Graciela Sevilla, who worked at the *Post* between 1992 and 1995, quit "after less than a year".

Roughly half of the 28 former and current *Post* staffers Shalit talked to say she misquoted them or manipulated their remarks. James Ragland, a black journalist described in Shalit's piece as having "quit [the *Post*] in frustration after the '94 mayoral campaign", and who is quoted as saying that stories "that should get in the paper without any trouble become much more difficult [because of race]. I understand the need to be sensitive, but it goes overboard."

Ragland, now at the *Dallas Morning News*, says he "specifically and directly" told Shalit that he did not quit in frustration, but left because of a highly attractive offer from the *News*. "It was a very tough decision", he says about leaving the *Post*. Ragland says that at one point he had been frustrated by editorial "heavyhandedness", but that the problem was resolved to his satisfaction after he complained.

Citing unnamed sources, Shalit claims that Michael Getler, the *Post*'s deputy managing editor, was keen to hire Douglas Farah (now a correspondent in Central America) because he thought Farah was Latino. "Gee, Doug, everyone is just so excited at the prospect of hiring such a talented Hispanic reporter", Getler is said to have blurted out, only to be crushed when Farah replied, "I'm happy to be a Hispanic reporter if you'd like me to be, but I'm from Kansas."

Both Getler and Farah deny that such a meeting took place. Prior to publication, Shalit called Getler to ask about the meeting. He told her that he had no memory of it or of ever having said anything resembling what she quoted him as saying. He relented when Shalit told him that Farah was her source. But Shalit never talked to Farah, and the latter, in a letter that *The New Republic* refused to publish, wrote, "I could never have said I was from Kansas, as that is simply not true." (Farah was born in Massachusetts.) Shalit claimed in her article that she had unsuccessfully tried to reach Farah, but he says she never called him at the *Post*'s bureau in San Salvador, and that "there was not a single fact about me [in her story] that was true".

At a substantive level, many of Shalit's charges are bizarre. The supposed mastermind behind the *Post*'s plot to cover up for black politicians is Milton Coleman—a man best known to the public for having effectively killed Jesse Jackson's 1984 presidential campaign by publishing Jackson's comments about New York being "Hymietown".

Shalit charges that Coleman is "socially close" to Mayor Marion Barry and other black power brokers, which results in overly sympathetic coverage—a somewhat reckless allegation coming from Newt Gingrich's dancing partner. Of course, many DC journalists and publishers maintain indecently close ties with political leaders, starting with Shalit's boss, Martin Peretz, president of *The New Republic* and an intimate of Al Gore. The *Post*'s former executive editor, Ben Bradlee, was a great friend of JFK, while Katharine Graham is close to Robert McNamara and Henry Kissinger, among others. In Shalit's view, though, it's only black journalists whose social ties are problematic.

The New Republic published only a few of the outraged letters it received from *Post* employees over the Shalit article. Among those it didn't print was this from Warren Brown, an automotive writer.

"Dear Ruth:

"Talk about lousy journalism! Your thinly disguised attack on affirmative action consumed 13 pages. If you had any guts, you could've done the job in one paragraph. To wit:

"'We don't want any blacks, yellows, reds. Not one is as well-qualified as a white, or white derivative, to give America the news. All of this diversity stuff is taking jobs away from deserving white folks.'

"Had you written that, you would've had my respect. Instead, you chose to hide your prejudice behind the veil of 'objective reporting'....

"You've obviously never read a 'pre-diversity' newspaper. I did. I grew up in segregated New Orleans reading the now defunct *New Orleans States-Item* and the still-published *Times Picayune*. Even as a kid, I knew what was going on in those newspapers: Black criminals were clearly identified by race. If there was no racial identification, that meant the perpetrator of the crime was white. Black people never got married, according to those newspapers. But whites got married. You could tell, because their photos and names were in the papers' social writeups. Black people never did anything well, except maybe sing and dance. White people were pretty damned near perfect. But, I suppose you call that kind of journalism 'truth'."

THE FINANCIAL PRESS

Historically, the financial press has been one of the least dignified sectors of the trade, perhaps because business reporters feel more keenly than their colleagues the need to relay the corporate outlook. The financial press isn't perhaps as corrupt as it was a few decades ago. Back then a business wanting to place a story needed only to negotiate the proper price with the editorial staff. But today the chief function of the business press is still to relay the claims of government officials, financial speculators, bankers and so forth.

Morton Mintz, once a very fine reporter for *The Washington Post*, has chronicled the way that "the sense of property" is still amply reflected in the media. A few years back officials from NBC News deleted three sentences critical of General Electric, NBC's owner, from a report on shoddy standards in American industry. Reporters quickly learn that to get ahead, they must toe the line. Mintz recounts the story of Ronald Kessler, a *Post* reporter who in the early Eighties investigated the insurance industry in a series of articles: "In an irrational, hellish process lasting more than three years, [Kessler] was directed to cut the series from ten parts to six, then to three.... Finally, it became a highly compressed single article, published in a typographically repellent format....He later resigned."

By now, there aren't many Kesslers left in the newsroom. The new breed is represented by the *Post*'s Clay Chandler, a man who never met an official source he didn't like, this being broadly reflected in his uncritical reports on Babylon's power brokers. In a profile of Lloyd Bentsen in late 1994, Chandler called the then-Treasury Secretary "a courtly millionaire", a "stickler for order, discipline and hierarchy", and someone who "was behind many of [President] Clinton's triumphs" while having "side-stepped the failures". In one particularly timorous moment, Chandler cautioned that "if Bentsen were to retire, the administration would lose potentially valuable experience".

When Bentsen did resign a few weeks later, Chandler was equally deferential to his successor, Robert Rubin, saying that the transition at Treasury had "the air of a venerated chairman passing the reins of the firm to a trusted junior associate". He described Rubin as a "self-effacing millionaire" who regards "the hurly-burly of Washington politics with the detachment of an anthropologist engaged in field research", and as someone with a "long-standing concern . . . for urban America".

This view of Rubin (net worth: $155 million) as a champion of the underclass, endlessly repeated by Chandler's colleagues in the press, is laughable. Before joining the administration Rubin headed Goldman, Sachs & Co., a Wall Street firm whose financial speculations in 1992 generated pre-tax earnings of $1.4 billion, one-fifth the entire income of the Bronx's 1.2 million people. Rubin's share of that year's haul was $26.5 million.

Over at *The New York Times*, David Sanger is only slightly less craven than Chandler. When Mexico's economy crashed in December 1994, Rubin was vacationing in the British Virgin Islands. The Treasury Secretary's "initial instinct was to let the Mexicans and the market sort it out, and return to the important business of casting for bonefish in the azure waters of the Caribbean", Sanger wrote. "[But Rubin] became convinced that in Mexico the Administration was faced with the most modern of foreign policy crises. No nukes, no troops, just the potential for global financial apocalypse."

Sanger failed to mention Rubin's other interests in Mexico. The Treasury Secretary's 1993 disclosure statement lists 42 firms with which he had "significant contact" while at Goldman, Sachs, of which six were Mexican firms or state agencies, including Mexico's finance ministry. Furthermore, during the last few years, Rubin's old firm was the leading underwriter of Mexican stocks and bonds, marketing $5.17 billion in securities.

Reporting on business is in general equally reverential. A 1993 *New York Times* profile of John Purcell, managing director for emerging markets research at Salomon Brothers, called its subject a "guru on the Third World". The *Times*'s Jeanne Pinder said that "Mr. Purcell's research unit has a reputation for being hot", and that no one questions "the quality of work done" by Purcell's department.

Some of Purcell's clients at Salomon Brothers might dispute that assessment. In mid-1992, Guru Purcell was touting investments in Brazil and predicting that a corruption scandal threatening the regime of Fernando Collor de Mello would soon blow over. "The current situation [is] no more than a blip on the screen", he told investors at a seminar in New York. Collor was soon impeached, shaking Brazilian stock markets.

In the *Times*'s profile, Purcell chided Moody's rating agency for its "fundamental error of pessimism" towards Mexico, saying the agency was taking "a highly conservative stance". Less than a year after Purcell's strictures over Moody's needless pessimism the Chiapas uprising took place, followed at the end of 1994 by the collapse of the peso.

John Liscio, publisher of *The Liscio Report,* a business newsletter, and a former columnist for *Barron's* and *U.S. News & World Report,* describes most business reporters as little more than glorified stenographers. "Most of them are looking to get jobs in outright flackery. They take dictation when they work as reporters and they end up doing the same thing for more money when they move to handling PR for the private sector."

Indeed, not a few economics reporters have moved from the business pages to Wall Street. The most prominent example is Steven Rattner, who swapped the offices of *The New York Times* for the executive suites of Lazard Freres. Rattner is hardly alone. Many of the members of the New York Financial Writers' Association are "associates", meaning they now work outside the journalistic profession, mostly in public relations or on Wall Street.

Even worse, economics reporters rarely talk to anyone besides Wall Street brokers and other officials from the financial sector. One source financial reporters quote constantly is Stephen Roach, the chief economist at Morgan Stanley. According to an article Roach recently penned for the *Financial Times,* the past decade's "wrenching corporate restructurings", which have produced plant closings, layoffs, outsourcing and industry-wide consolidations, "offer nothing but upside for the financial markets". Roach's main concern is to see that American companies keep firing workers. He finds that during the first three months of 1995 US firms fired *only* 97,200 employees, less than half the rate during the same period in 1994 and far fewer than the numbers laid off by Japanese and German firms. Roach spies here a disturbing trend which might signify a "slackening of restructuring by Corporate America". Of course, Roach and other Wall Street "analysts" beloved by reporters serve as adjuncts to their firms' sales forces, and are charged with the task of keeping money flowing into the stock market.

For example: in an early 1995 story from Buenos Aires, Calvin Sims of *The New York Times*—apparently unable to find a local analyst—quoted Salomon Brothers' Larry Goodman as saying that Argentina's economy would grow by 3 per cent that year. This wildly optimistic prediction should be set alongside the fact that Goodman's firm markets Argentine securities, which sell far more briskly if investors believe that country's economy is on strong ground. "If the Yankees are in last place in August, no sports writer will say that they're going to win the pennant because the manager says so", Liscio remarks. "[Wall Street analysts] are salesmen, but the press treats them like prophets." (Incidentally, Argentina's economy sank by 2.5 per cent in 1995.)

MILLIONAIRE JOURNALISTS VERSUS DISABLED CHILDREN

T wo decades after Watergate, the *Post* is a highly conservative outfit. Thomas Edsall, Jr., was once a good journalist with a mind of his own. In the Eighties he wrote a fine account of Reaganism, *The New Politics of Inequality.* But then Edsall seemed to realize that even the barest tincture of radicalism would doom his prospects for career advancement.

By 1995, he was attributing the murderous anger of the alleged Oklahoma bomber, Timothy McVeigh, to the rise of the women's movement and the decline in status of the vaginal orgasm. Men face a poor economic future because of affirmative action, and are being laid off in greater numbers than women. Those who hold a job supposedly live in fear of being unfairly charged with sexual harassment. Hence, men have "a private sense of siege, voiced most often only in quiet tones at lunch or more angrily over beer after work".

But nowhere, Edsall went on, has the "seismic upheaval" been greater than in the area of sex: "In the same year that Timothy McVeigh was born, the pill had just started to sever the linkage between intercourse and pregnancy.... The pill opened for women the same vista of sexual opportunism that had been available to men. At the same time, the 'myth of the vaginal orgasm' ... was replaced by the recognition of the clitoral orgasm, further freeing women seeking such autonomy from dependence on men for sexual satisfaction."

Unemployed and listless, their women locked in the bedroom in a haze of solitary pleasure, American men of the late 20th century are frustrated. They seek relief in one of the few outlets still available: mixing fuel oil with fertilizer and blowing up federal buildings.

The *Post*'s decline is most glaringly illuminated in the evolution of Bob Woodward. Though he carries the portentous title of Investigations Editor, people rarely see Woodward at the paper. His work now largely consists of "insider" reporting, resulting in forgettable books such as *The Commanders* (on the Joint Chiefs of Staff), *The Brethren* (on the Supreme Court), *The Agenda* (on Clinton's economic policies), and *Veil* (on the CIA), which included the famous deathbed conversation with William Casey, regarded by some as having the same relationship to physical reality as the Prince of Denmark's interview with his father in the first act of *Hamlet*.

Woodward's lowest moment thus far may have come with his seven-part series—later turned into a book—on that Augustus Caesar of American politics, Dan Quayle. Woodward co-wrote this series with David Broder in 1991. The two reporters heaped praise on Quayle, mostly from the veeplet's pals. One hard-pressed Quayle aide bravely described the VP's passion for golfing as an intellectual endeavor, it being "not just relaxation [but] a version of Oriental shadow-boxing".

The series produced a flood of good PR for Quayle, a spell only broken after the vice president misspelled the word "potato" at a school spelling bee. The series also showed the depth of political insight of Broder and Woodward, who appear to have concluded that Bush was a certainty for re-election in '92 and Quayle the heir apparent for '96, and thus figured their fawning series would give them an edge on the journalistic competition.

I n the Nineties, Woodward's investigative skills have been deployed largely against the powerless. In early 1994, Woodward and a sidekick, Benjamin Weiser, wrote a front-page story on children's disability, a legal category created in Congress in 1972 as part of the Supplemental Security Income (SSI) program. Requirements were extremely strict. Potential recipients had to be in a hospital or a wheelchair, or possess an IQ under 60. Those with cystic fibrosis, muscular dystrophy, autism and Down's Syndrome were routinely turned down.

The *Post* article zoomed in on Nora Cooke Porter, a state disability review physician in Pennsylvania, "who can barely contain her frus-

Bob Woodward, with Ben Bradlee and Judy Woodruff: In his toughest job since Watergate, Woodward did his best to destroy a federal subsidy helping disabled children. (Vivian Ronay/Photoreporters)

tration as she flips through some of the thousands of applications" for assistance for children who "in her medical opinion, are not suffering from any disability". According to Woodward and Weiser, "children who curse teachers, fight with classmates, perform poorly in school or display characteristics of routine rebellion are often diagnosed with behavioral disorders and therefore qualify for the program's cash benefits".

Parents often spent their children's benefits unwisely, Woodward and Weiser proclaimed virtuously. And while government bureaucrats required an accounting of how the money was spent, they did not have "the resources to scrutinize spending on a large scale".

When the piece appeared, two Wisconsin Democrats, Senator Herb Kohl and Rep. Gerald Kleczka, instantly distributed copies to each member of Congress. A story attacking poor people in the *Post* carries twice the firepower of one in *The Washington Times*, since the former can be introduced with the conclusive words "Even the liberal *Post* says . . ." And when the article bears Woodward's name, the effect is even greater.

The story set off a hue and cry against children's disability, and led to an all-important *Prime Time* report the following October. No fewer than three of the network's millionaire correspondents made haste to beat up on crippled children and steal their crutches: Chris Wallace, chief correspondent for that segment, called it a "taxpayer scam"; Diane Sawyer said it was "a program designed to help disabled children, but parents are helping themselves"; and Sam Donaldson—who receives tens of thousands of dollars of federal agriculture subsidies annually for his New Mexico sheep ranch, ranching being a notorious sump for federal subsidies—marveled at "how easy it is to get on the receiving end of what some are calling 'crazy checks'".

Prime Time's piece opened with a severely retarded white child in a wheelchair, representing a "deserving" recipient in whom the public's money had been prudently invested. The show then moved to the Arkansas Delta, where a variety of white politicians and white school teachers berated black children as frauds. Wallace grilled a poor black woman who found it hard to articulate to the massed inquisitors and technicians why her child needed assistance. Like the *Post*, ABC trotted out Dr. Porter to decry the program's abuses.

Prime Time's attack had a big impact in the capital. The show aired before a congressional subcommittee, and several members cited it in seeking to gut children's disability.

The *Post* and *Prime Time* avoided important facts: children's disability rolls have grown heavily in recent years and now carry some 800,000 children, but the cause is not an explosion of fraud. In 1990 the Rehnquist Supreme Court decreed by a 7 to 2 margin that eligibility requirements were unlawfully tight. Under the new guidelines, more children with severe mental impairments were able to qualify. The Court also ordered Congress and the Social Security

Administration to publicize the program, and thus many parents heard of it for the first time.

For children to get what are, by the standards of today's medical billings, minimal benefits, a doctor must judge them to be in very poor shape indeed. About 60 per cent have mental problems ranging from the grave to the catastrophic; about 25 per cent have severe physical problems; and about 15 per cent have serious neurological or sensory ailments.

Since 1991, more than half a million children—45 per cent of all applicants—have been rejected. In tirelessly publicized Pennsylvania, where Dr. Porter's "frustration" threatens to boil over, 43 per cent of the applicants were turned down. In Arkansas, the rejection rate is 56 per cent.

The *Post*'s and *Prime Time*'s hatchet jobs on the disability program stemmed in part from their heavy reliance on Porter, portrayed in both cases as a doughty friend to the taxpayer. In fact, Porter was fired by the Pennsylvania Bureau of Disabilities Determination because of her unceasing and baseless onslaughts on colleagues. Jonathan Stein, the general counsel for Community Legal Services in Philadelphia who argued the 1991 case before the Supreme Court, alerted Woodward and ABC to Porter's record. But they eagerly relayed her assertions without a word of caution.

Prime Time quoted Porter as saying that the families of disabled children could "buy a Mercedes" with their benefits. Maximum benefits allowed for a single parent are $446 per month, a figure which decreases as family income rises above $13,284 per year. If family income tops $1,907 in any month, the child loses all benefits. Porter also told ABC that "fewer than 30 per cent" of children awarded benefits deserve them. If true, this enormous figure would mean that roughly 600,000 children on the rolls are frauds. Wallace echoed: "If Porter's estimates are anywhere near accurate", then the program is a "massive taxpayer-funded scam". Note the strategic use of the word "if" in this context. As Stein complained bitterly, "Isn't the purpose of [*Prime Time*'s] three-month investigation and the job of such a veteran chief correspondent to ascertain the validity of such an assertion, and not to use the big 'if' as a crutch to buttress the by now demagogic, media cliché of 'taxpayer scam'?"

On Stein's suggestion, *Prime Time* went to Dayton, Ohio, to film

Connie Guyer and her son, Nathan, who suffers from a variety of ailments including Attention Deficit Disorder, depression, hyperactivity and thyroid deficiency. At age 12 Nathan couldn't read, thought he was stupid and was suicidal. Qualifying for benefits enabled Nathan to attend a private school where he learned to read. Now he wants to be a scientist.

Having been burned by journalists in the past, Connie Guyer had serious doubts about working with *Prime Time*. But Jude Dratt, Wallace's producer, assured her that Nathan's story was essential to give a balanced view of the program. "I'm going to be your new best friend", Guyer remembers Dratt eagerly telling her. She says Dratt promised she'd come to Dayton a day before the crew arrived so she could spend time getting to know Nathan. But Dratt never went anywhere near Dayton, and instead sent an assistant on the day of the shoot. Guyer says *Prime Time*'s crew was rude and insensitive: "All they wanted from us was tears and breakdown."

The producers had promised Guyer that they'd let her know when the program was scheduled for broadcast. In fact, the first time she knew it was scheduled was when she saw a blurb in *TV Guide*. She called Dratt, who told her that she still didn't know when the program was going to air, then waffled when Guyer told her she'd seen the *TV Guide* announcement. Sensing a hatchet job, Guyer informed Dratt that she'd never signed a release and didn't want footage of Nathan to be used. Breaking vigorous pledges, *Prime Time* never returned family photographs to the Guyers.

Stein wrote a letter to Jude Dratt in early 1995: "Due to the press of much more important matters at ABC, you and your colleagues are perhaps not aware of the aftermath of your fall 'Prime Time' program in the Congress", Stein began, adding that a bill before Congress would all but eliminate the children's disability program:

"I am sure you and ABC executives must be proud of how instrumental your work has been in bringing down this program in this short span of time. . . . Such recognition can only further your professional careers in TV news and entertainment productions, and give you encouragement to replicate your achievement elsewhere.

"I'm enclosing some narratives of disabled children your program chose to misrepresent, the great majority of children on SSI, who will not be eligible for cash benefits, including eligibility for Medical Assistance, in the future. I do not assume that the loss of necessities of life for hundreds of thousands of such children is of any consequence to you or executives at ABC; I certainly don't assume that there is any news or entertainment value for you in their plight, as there must be other issues that you've moved on to that better address the urgency of keeping *Prime Time*'s ratings up. . . .

"But, if you or Chris wish to respond so I can pass word on to all the parents of cerebral palsy, spina bifida, AIDS, cystic fibrosis, muscular dystrophy, epilepsy, hydrocephalus, mental retardation, missing limbs, blind, diabetic, and cancer children we've talked to, your courtesy of a response—not so much for us but for these parents—will be most appreciated. Your inability to respond will also be most understandable as well.

"The best for future coups in TV journalism."

The dominant mode now at the *Post*'s upper echelons is one of self-congratulation, with endless staff missives about colleagues moving onward and upward.

When the paper's top editorial brass returned from their annual Pugwash meeting in Florida, where they mull over ways of improving excellence at the *Post* and work on their tans, the editors—glowing with sun and health—announced to a meeting of expectant reporters that they were planning to get "really well written stories" on the front page. One reporter then asked whether the editors would share with them whatever great ideas they had dreamed up in sunny Florida. "We just did", said one editor bleakly.

On Foreign Coverage: Apes and People

One incontestable case of genocide since the end of the Second World War is the slaughter of hundreds of thousands of Tutsis in Rwanda during the early months of 1994.

The horror in Rwanda had been building for years, but for the press foreign news is only worth covering if there's a strong US angle. With the end of the Cold War, foreign news editors see Africa's difficulties largely as a depressing distraction. This means that barring brutal warfare, a natural disaster or widespread famine, the continent rarely registers on the American media's screen.

When the misery, disease and death in Rwanda reached a genocidal scale, press attention finally centered on the Rwandans. But for a long time, the media's coverage of the civil war in that country slighted human beings and focused almost entirely on a warmer topic: Dian Fossey's apes.

Warfare broke out in Rwanda in late 1990, when the now triumphant guerrillas of the largely Tutsi Rwandan Patriotic Front (RPF) invaded the country from neighboring Uganda. Their goal was to topple Juvenal Habyarimana's Hutu-dominated government, which was installed in a 1973 military coup. American journalists were mostly unmoved by the dramatic events taking place in the country.

Between January of 1991 and December of 1993, a few months before the recent upsurge in violence, *The New York Times* ran ten stories on Rwanda, half of them brief wire service dispatches. *The Washington Post* didn't have a single story on Rwanda during that period, while *The Wall Street Journal* ran a grand total of four sentences in three one-paragraph filler items.

The press, however, rigorously covered the saga of Rwanda's endangered mountain apes, made famous in *Gorillas in the Mist*, a 1988 movie starring Sigourney Weaver as Fossey, the murdered American researcher. A June 1994 count, which cross-referenced Rwanda with "gorillas" vs. "guerrillas" resulted in a rout by the apes, 1,123 to 138. Ninety-one of the references to the humans came after April 6, when the downing of Habyarimana's plane outside Kigali touched off the terrible crisis that then dominated headlines.

The clearest way to demonstrate the press's ape obsession is to compare events in Rwanda during the 1991 to 1993 period with the coverage of the country provided by American newspapers.

Events, 1991: George Bush increased US aid to Rwanda to $15 million, up from $9 million the previous year. Habyarimana's government received far more important support from France, which deployed combat troops to Rwanda after war with the RPF began. The French also rushed in advisers, helicopter parts, mortars, and munitions. The war led to increased human rights violations. "Dozens of members of the minority Tutsi ethnic group, including possible prisoners of conscience, were detained", says Amnesty

The Giant of Karisimbi, a silverback gorilla stuffed by Akeley and now in the American Museum of Natural History. In the American press, a gorilla was worth one million Rwandans. (American Museum of Natural History)

International's annual report for 1991. "There were reports of torture and 'disappearances'. Hundreds of extrajudicial executions by members of the security forces and vigilante groups were reported." Seeking to defuse the crisis, Habyarimana announced a series of political reforms, amending the constitution in mid-year to replace the existing one-party state with a multi-party system. Nine new political parties formed in anticipation of elections scheduled for 1992.

Press coverage, 1991: Despite the outbreak of warfare, journalists early in the year reported hopeful signs about Rwanda's future. The cause for optimism? Scientists had reported an increase in the population of mountain gorillas to 306, up from 242 in 1981. A brief dispatch in the *Orlando Sentinel Tribune* on January 20 said conservationists were "heartened by the most recent census of mountain gorillas,

The Dirigible of Drivel. Unusually swollen specimen of *Homo sapiens.* Note the steady degradation from *Gorilla savagei.* Limbaugh says he's the champion of the ordinary Joe, but he speaks for the elites. He's a safe demagogue, lunging about on the end of his chain, singing hymns to the innocence of the tobacco companies and assuring the small business people that the Reagan tide lifted them in the Eighties along with the super-rich. He attacks Clintonites but on issue after issue—welfare, military spending, crime—they're all in sync, which is why Limbaugh and the right have to invent or recycle all the personal gossip about Clinton to show there's a devil in the White House rather than someone who's doing basically what they want. (Terry Gydesen/Impact Visuals)

the animals slain scientist Dian Fossey tried to protect". The *St. Louis Post-Dispatch* noted the same encouraging trend on April 17, when a renowned ape researcher mentioned it during a lecture at a local university. Neither paper mentioned there was a war in Rwanda.

Optimism turned to gloom in mid-year: "Observers fear the gunfire is disrupting [the gorillas'] routine and threatening [their] long-term welfare," cautioned a May 26 story in the *Atlanta Journal and Constitution.* In the one ray of hope the newspaper said that while the war had shut down tourism at Rwanda's Kagera National Park, "gorilla tours still are available where the park enters into Zaire".

Events, 1992: Casualties mounted, with human rights groups reporting roughly 2,000 civilians killed in the fighting and hundreds of others raped or tortured. Western weaponry poured in, mostly from France but also including $2.3 million in arms bought from the United States. Mass demonstrations early in the year led Habyarimana to appoint opposition leader Dismas Nsengiyaremye as Prime Minister. The latter's national unity government was shaken in November when Justice Minister Stanislas Mbonampeka resigned his post, citing a lack of cooperation from security forces.

Press coverage, 1992: Anguish reached fever pitch in mid-year, when a silverback known as Mriti, Weaver's co-star in *Gorillas in the Mist*, became the first ape casualty of the war. On May 28, *The Chicago Tribune* lauded the victim as "a magnificent, gentle animal with many human characteristics". *The New York Times* also mourned Mriti, "the leader of a family of rare mountain apes that Western tourists spend thousands of dollars to view close up". *The Christian Science Monitor* ran an 800-word obituary, lamenting that the "needless snuffing of [the ape's] short, noble life leaves a void we will not soon see filled".

The year's only major story on the war in Rwanda and the country's complex political scene was a December 13 *New York Times Magazine* piece. Still, it's hard not to wonder if the *Times* would have commissioned the article if not for the fact that its author, Alex Shoumatoff, who is married to a Tutsi, focused on his struggle to save his in-laws from the fighting by bringing them to the United States.

Events, 1993: The UN Special *Rapporteur* visited in April and reported that government forces had murdered some 2,300 civilians since the conflict with the RPF erupted in 1990. The rebel army was reportedly responsible for the arbitrary killing of up to 300 civilians during 1993. In December, rights activist Monique Mujawamariya, who the previous April barely escaped being murdered by government soldiers, visited Bill Clinton in the White House.

Press coverage, 1993: More stories on life in the gorilla zone. *The New York Times* ran a May 17 op-ed piece—its only such offering on Rwanda between 1991 and 1993—warning that Dian Fossey's former gorilla camp, smack in the center of a combat zone, was imperiled. Rutgers anthropology professor H. Dieter Steklis bitterly charged

that protecting the apes was "not high on the world's agenda of problems to solve". "There is not one gorilla to spare", proclaimed the
anthropologist, who suggested that the UN take action "to buffer the
gorillas from the dangerous instability of national politics".

The grave threat to Fossey's camp was also the subject of stories in
Newsweek and *The Houston Chronicle.* The lengthy, angry story in the
latter, written by Scripps Howard's Joseph Verrengia, said that the
remote compound had suffered significant damage during recent
combat which had left scientists "sputtering with rage" and "moved
to tears". Verrengia mentioned the war's human toll in Rwanda—
"The Home of the Mountain Gorillas"—only in writing that "the
hunger and desperation of a million war refugees" had made the
country a less "enticing place for visiting scientists to work". Just as
tragically, the war had "ruined the eco-tourism trade that made gorilla sightseeing . . . one of Rwanda's leading sources of overseas
income". A May 20 Reuters story echoed this sense of priorities. The
report led with the news that 36 apes had been reported AWOL from
the Virunga mountain region following an RPF offensive. The gorillas were also "threatened by land mines planted in the . . . civil war",
the story's author wrote, while noting near the end of the article that
"the conflict has made more than 350,000 people homeless and
ruined the lives of close to one million".

Even when press coverage changed focus in mid-1994, journalists
bungled the story. They largely overlooked the Clinton administration's laissez-faire approach to the crisis, most shamefully in its May
16 decision to prevent UN intervention in Rwanda. In another sensitive move, the administration in mid-June instructed officials to
abstain from using the word "genocide" when discussing the killings
in Rwanda, though with up to 400,000 people murdered by that
time, almost all Tutsi, that's precisely what was taking place. Clinton
feared that the use of the word might fan public passion and increase
pressure on his government to stop the carnage. "Some American
officials acknowledge that the administration's posture lacks candor",
said *The New York Times.* "But many argue that the land-locked
African nation has no ties to the US and no oil or other resources
that would make American intervention worth the cost".

That same logic also helps explain why the press for so many years
treated Rwanda merely as "The Home of the Mountain Gorillas".

CONGRESS

Newt Gingrich: One of the great welfare cheats of all time, from troughs both federal and corporate. His home district in Cobb County, Georgia, is third in receipt of federal subsidies, with much of that for military plants; his treasure chests overflow with corporate money, mostly given in expectation, invariably met, that Gingrich will obtain federal favors and funding for donor. Few firm beliefs, except in greatness of N. Gingrich; at Tulane he was a fiery radical, burning university chief in effigy at protest; life-long philanderer while promoting "family values". Will spout almost any nonsense, whether from the Tofflers or Bill Bennett. Exceptionally eager student of strategy and tactics seminars of Col. John Boyd, innovative thinker and sometime co-guide of the military reform lobby active in the 1970s and 1980s. (Shia photo/Impact Visuals)

THE BEST THAT MONEY CAN BUY

Raising money for the 1972 presidential campaign, Richard Nixon's Committee to Re-Elect the President (CREEP) didn't beat around the bush. CREEP told business leaders what dollar amounts it expected and most came through with these generous sums, sometimes delivered in unmarked packages containing small bills.

These covert donations were entirely illegal and the campaign's list of donors—kept by Nixon's secretary Rose Mary Woods and referred to by White House staffers as "Rose Mary's Baby"—was a tightly guarded secret. Among CEOs who kicked in were industrialist Max Fisher, who gave $125,000 in stock and the same amount in cash, drawn from a safe at his home to "insure greater confidentiality", and Phillips Petroleum chairman William Keeler, whose $100,000 contribution came from a Swiss bank account (he passed the money to campaign officials at a meeting arranged to discuss Phillips' concerns about the Clean Air Act).

Prodded by public indignation in the wake of Watergate, Congress addressed the corrupt campaign finance system in a spasm of law-making. The Federal Election Commission limited individuals to gifts of $1,000 to federal candidates and $25,000 to the national parties. It also created political action committees (PACs), which are authorized to give $5,000.

Scarcely a moment elapsed before the money power took advantage of loopholes which legislators had duly installed in the system. Soon, big donors escaped limits by "bundling" $1,000 contributions from colleagues, family (including dependent children) and friends. Most important, there were no limits on "soft" money going to state political organizations, even if that money was spent to benefit a federal candidate.

Since Watergate, some 4,000 PACs have emerged. During the

Bob Dole: Senate majority leader and presidential aspirant in 1996. As a vice presidential candidate in the mid-1970s he won the hearts of all radicals by (accurately) denouncing the "Democrat wars" of the 20th century. These were the days when the Kansas grain surplus made its profitable way to the Soviet Union, so Dole was no demonologist. Optimistic journalists of an independent cast of mind, like Murray Kempton, have always had a soft spot for Dole, reckoning that somewhere in the Kansas historical memory pool there's a link between Eugene Debs declaring his populist presidential candidacy from the steps of the Girard County courthouse in 1916 and the US senator from the same region, and that Dole will do the good that he can and the harm that he must. Others say that he's a mean-spirited swine. High moment of Campaign '96: briefly denouncing that year's telecommunications bill—one of the greatest corporate handouts of the 20th century, sweeping by vast majorities through Congress and eagerly signed by President Bill—as corporate welfare. Low moment of Campaign '96: returning contribution from the Log Cabin Republicans, a group of gay GOP-ers, on grounds money bore taint of vice and unmentionable practices. By their wings shall ye know them. When Dole flies the friendly skies he is, often as not, born aloft by a jet belonging to the US Tobacco Company, or to banana king Carl Lindner. As Dole once remarked with some frankness, the relationship between money and politics in this country is not conducive to good government. (Clark Jones/Impact Visuals)

1991-92 election cycle, they gave $188 million to congressional candidates; of that amount two-thirds came from business.

Still, PACs represent virtually the only way for labor and public interest groups to get into the game. Individual donations of $200 or more account for about 36 per cent of all contributions to political candidates, versus 29 per cent from PACs. But add gifts from

Pat Buchanan: Rough Beast in liberal lexicon, rattles windows with bigotry catered for religious right, but also speaks to fears and furies of those left high and dry by free-trade capitalism—farmers, victims of plant flight, the beleaguered little folk. Populism's sales rep in '96. (Shia photo/Impact Visuals)

business-linked individuals to corporate PAC contributions: business outspends labor by a ratio of 6 to 1.

Despite the huge sums of money involved, the universe of political fundraising is extremely small. Less than one-third of 1 per cent of all givers put up about half of all political donations. One zip code on New York City's Upper East Side—10021—gives more than each of 24 states. "It's more corrupt, insidious and subtle than the pre-Watergate system", says Charles Lewis, head of the capital's Center for Public Integrity. "In the old days, the corporate baron passed a suitcase full of cash in a smoky bar. Now it's sanctioned and legitimized corruption. Disclosure laws give the patina of legitimacy but the same people still dominate the discussion due to money."

Today, the two major political parties seek and receive funding from identical sources, powerful corporations and wealthy individuals. In 1992, eight men, including Dwayne Andreas of Archer-Daniels-Midland, Lodwrick Cook of Atlantic Richfield and Ronald Perelman of the Revlon Group, donated more than $100,000 to both the Clinton and Bush campaigns.

Until the mid-Eighties, business was more inclined to give money to the GOP than to the Democrats. This changed in part because the Democrats have been moving to the right for two decades, but also thanks to the shakedown tactics of Tony Coelho, the congressman from Modesto, California, who raised vast sums for the Democrats in the late 1980s and early 1990s, abruptly resigned under a cloud of scandal, then re-emerged in 1994 as Bill Clinton's sutler for the mid-term elections. Coelho recognized that the corpo-

Phil Gramm: Doomed also-ran in Campaign '96 for prime reason obvious to all but himself. Gramm is a nasty fellow with a pharaonic belief in his own importance. Whether he's beating up on welfare moms, calling for the death penalty for shoplifting, or exiling federal employees to Alaska for challenging his duck-shoots in eastern Maryland, Gramm really is the vicious brute people once considered Bob Dole to be. (Shia photo/Impact Visuals)

rate world could be a gold mine for his party, and he put the case bluntly to business: if you want access, you're going to have to fund the Democrats, because we are the party of power in Congress.

Even in 1994, business gave more to Democratic than to GOP contenders by a margin of about 52 to 48 per cent. With the Republican sweep of Congress in 1994, the balance is shifting, but the Democrats won't be cut off. As Ellen Miller of the Center for Responsive Politics points out, "The more beholden the Democrats are to business, the more likely they are to side with them on important swing votes."

The current campaign finance system has two important implications. First, virtually the only candidates who stand a realistic chance of winning office are those acceptable to monied interests. Second, the rich are able to buy influence on the cheap.

A few decades back a credible run for Congress cost $30,000. By 1994, the average House campaign cost $516,000 and a run for the Senate took $4.6 million. A presidential bid requires, at a minimum, $20 million.

For political candidates, there's only one place to raise that kind of money: the bottomless pockets of business and the rich. Crusading populists have few resources to draw on. The arms industry outspends peace groups by a ratio of 20 to 1. The oil and gas industry outspends environmentalists by 10 to 1.

Jake Lewis, a long-time aide to the House Banking Committee, says that the cost of campaigning is a huge factor in the demise of candidates willing to step outside the narrow boundary lines of the establishment. "Any candidate that expects to show up on PAC lists is well aware of the need to tailor, if not eliminate, any populist leanings. No big time donors, no TV, no candidacy. It's not a formula that opens the door to any but establishment candidates."

As to the question of money and policy, consider the case of the Fanjuls, a right-wing Cuban-American family that controls the Flo-Sun sugar empire, with immense holdings in Florida and the Dominican Republic. During the past decade, the family has made $1.2 million in campaign contributions, heaping money on politicians from both parties with equal fervor. Alfie Fanjul, one of four brothers, served as co-chairman of Bill Clinton's Florida campaign and raised more than $100,000 for the Democratic candidate. Another brother, Jose, was

vice chairman of the Bush-Quayle campaign in 1988 and in 1995
joined the campaign finance committee of Bob Dole. He has given
$186,500 in soft money to the GOP since 1991. The Fanjuls make a
healthy return on their political investments. Year in and year out,
Congress extends agricultural price supports and other subsidies for
the sugar industry that, according to a study by the General
Accounting Office, net the Fanjuls $65 million annually. "It's too sim-
plistic to say, 'Money in, subsidy out', because the process is more subtle", Miller says. "But the end result is the same."

Charles Lewis puts the case more bluntly: "What's astounding is
how cheap it is to buy influence. A company can give $5,000 in an
election cycle or $50,000 to the party and get itself a tax break or
special rule worth millions. It's like tipping the bellman on the way
to your hotel room."

The failure of Congress to pass any sort of health care reform
during the first two years of the Clinton administration presents a
useful lesson in how powerful interests can block unpalatable initia-
tives. Clinton had come to office promising to change the health
care system by reining in costs and profits, a posture which bought
him overwhelming public support.

Clinton quickly made clear that he would not consider supporting a single-payer system based on the Canadian model, this being
tantamount to Bolshevism to his neo-liberal colleagues and advisers
in the Democratic Leadership Council and, crucially, to the insurance industry. But many in the health care industry looked on the
president's own modest proposal with some nervousness, especially
small insurers and drug companies, as well as employers not eager
to pay for their workers' plans.

During 1993 and 1994, some 660 groups shelled out more than
$100 million to thwart health reform. Organizations with health
care interests funneled some $25 million to members of Congress,
according to a report from the Center for Public Integrity. About
one-third of that amount went to members sitting on one of the five
committees overseeing health care.

The sponsor of the corporate-friendly "Clinton Lite" plan, Rep.
Jim Cooper, raised thousands of dollars from health care companies, including $25,000, mostly from insurance company executives,
during a one-day visit to Hartford, Connecticut. (All to no avail.

Cooper was bounced from Congress in 1994.) The Connecticut Republican Rep. Nancy Johnson, once called a "whore" for insurers by her House colleague, Rep. Pete Stark of California, took in $176,000 from health PACs between 1991 and 1994.

Between 1992 and 1993, 85 members of Congress caroused their way through 181 health care industry junkets in San Juan, Paris, Montego Bay and other pleasure domes. More than 130 members, their spouses or dependent children, had investments in health care companies, most prominently drug makers. Senator Claiborne Pell of Rhode Island, who sits on the Labor and Human Resources Committee, held stock in Bristol-Meyers, Procter & Gamble, Merck, Johnson & Johnson and Block Drug Inc.

At least 80 former members of Congress or the Executive branch work for health care interests, including 23 who left public service in 1993 or 1994. Many of these ex-lawmakers swell the rolls of the 97 lobbying and public relations firms hired to influence the debate on health care. William Gradison was a member of Congress on Sunday, and head of the HIAA—producer of the infamous Harry and Louise ads—on Monday.

Jimmy Carter's press secretary, Jody Powell, and Nancy Reagan's press secretary, Sheila Tate, run the PR firm Powell Tate, which was hired by Bristol-Myers Squibb, RJR Nabisco, T2 Medical Inc., Upjohn and Rx Partners, a coalition of drug makers led by Searle. For $2 million, Powell Tate, according to an internal memorandum, would "sow doubt" about Clinton's early call for price controls on the drug companies. Powell Tate gave media training to drug company executives, set up meetings with national and local reporters, and with administration officials.

ASIDE: WATERGATE FALL-OUT

Money has fundamentally changed Washington, but other factors have also contributed to the stagnant political culture. Jake Lewis worked at the House Banking Committee as a majority staffer between 1965 and 1992, before moving on to Ralph Nader's Center for the Study of Responsive Law.

For eleven years Lewis worked under Rep. Wright Patman, the great

Texas populist representing a dirt poor area of East Texas, who entered Congress in 1929, the year of the Crash. Patman was also the first member of Congress to begin probing into the Watergate affair, earning himself a spot on Nixon's enemies list. When Ford named Nelson Rockefeller as his vice president, Patman tried to block his nomination, portraying Rockefeller, accurately, as an agent of parasitic finance capital.

But the New Deal/Depression-era generation has already hobbled from Congress. "Most of today's eligible candidates came into adulthood after the fears of depression were past and after all the safety nets were in place", Lewis says. "They take government activism as 'routine', not as a crusade." He thinks the current regulatory demolition derby underway on Capitol Hill may ultimately create a public backlash, however, as the safety nets are ripped down.

Unlike most analysts, Lewis believes that both Vietnam and Watergate shifted Congress to the right. From the Great Depression into the 1970s, issues of economic justice loomed large and were the mainstay of many Democrats. But, Lewis says, "the big crop of freshmen that came into the House in 1974 ran on narrow platforms—'I opposed the Vietnam War' and 'I am not a Watergate Republican.' Few had to address economic and social issues. Many of them were moderate or even conservative on economic issues, and many rose to power positions in Congress."

Steve Neal of North Carolina—a grand nephew of R.J. Reynolds—won office as a crusading reformer in 1974. He turned out to be one of the most ardent supporters of banks in the history of the Banking Committee. In 1994, as chairman of the financial institutions subcommittee, he engineered passage of the Interstate Bank Branching Act, legislation that had eluded the industry for decades and was essentially a gift to Hugh McColl of NationsBank, a major source of campaign financing for Neal.

Another interesting case was that of California Democrat Tom Rees, who entered Congress in the 1960s and became a darling of liberals because he never missed an anti-war rally. Inside of Congress he was the point man for the S&L industry. In 1970, Patman introduced a major bill to reform the interlocking arrangements between S&Ls and all the hangers-on of the real estate industry—title attorneys, appraisers, insurers, etc. Lewis recalls: "I remember Rees walking into a caucus of committee Democrats, shaking his finger at Patman and warning, 'This is the gravy for the savings and loan industry and neither you nor anyone else is going to take it away from them so long as I'm here.' And the Patman bill failed."

Henry Gonzalez: The last of the great Texas populists, in the tradition of Wright Patman. (Sharon Stewart/Impact Visuals)

The Banking Committee is unusual in that a radical presence survived there, in the form of Rep. Henry Gonzalez, another Texas populist, until the Republican takeover of Congress in 1994. That resulted in Rep. Jim Leach of Iowa—president of the Ripon Society, a blue blood Republican and a man always capable of garnering a respectful editorial in *The New York Times*—taking over as the new committee chairman.

From the perspective of business, Leach has two distinct advantages. First, he is regarded as a moderate but supports virtually every facet of the corporate agenda: he uncritically supports the Federal Reserve—always a hot target for Patman and Gonzalez—and has sought to gut measures long opposed by bankers, such as the Community Reinvestment Act and the Truth in Lending and Savings Acts.

Second, corporate lenders feel more at ease with such smooth establishment figures as Leach than they do with the Republican ultras elected in recent years, even if the latter may be more outspoken in their support for business. "It's hard on a CEO who makes $2 million a year to meet with [Banking Committee member] Sonny Bono", Lewis says. "Of course, the

CEO will work with Bono if it's going to help the company's bottom line, but he's not going to want to invite him to the club for a drink."

Other developments in the political world also leave Lewis with little optimism: "TV domination has virtually eliminated the town meetings, the open air political debates, and similar gatherings that used to give poorly-funded candidates forums on an equal basis with better-financed opponents. And now, I assume, we will have Internet campaigns which will eliminate more of the low-budget candidates and will further dim the interest of the less affluent, who are not likely to be spending thousands of dollars for equipment to provide access to the cyber revolution."

★

THE GOP STYLE OF RULE

It had been a long day at the Commerce Committee and Rep. Dennis Hastert, a Republican from Illinois, had grown weary of debate. "Where's the National Federation of Independent Business on this bill?" he interjected. "If they're for it, I'm for it."

This sort of frank admission that they are the tools of the business lobby is what distinguishes Republicans such as Hastert from the Democrats, who prefer to work more discreetly on behalf of their patrons.

Newt Gingrich has never been subtle about the link between politics and money. A few weeks before the 1994 mid-term elections, he met with a group of Washington lobbyists and informed them that Republicans would not look kindly upon political contributors who waited to see how the vote went before sending in their checks. Already sensing a mammoth defeat for the Democrats, both the lobbyists and the private interests they represent promptly ponied up. Between October 1 and November 28, the GOP—which had raised far less money than the Democrats since Bill Clinton went to the White House—took in $16.2 million in contributions, versus the relatively paltry $4.2 million which the president's demoralized party garnered.

Gingrich's shameless brand of influence-peddling reached new heights after the Republicans took over Congress and he became Speaker of the House. "Gingrich has come to represent the ombuds-

Rep. Dick Armey of Texas: A leader of the GOP's ultra faction. Armey's life-long mission has been to cut taxes, rules and regulations that impede corporations from most effectively fulfilling their mission of pillage in profit's name. In 1995 he breached House rules by allowing the right-wing Capital Research Center to circulate a letter he wrote on congressional stationery. The letter was addressed to 82 CEOs, and warned them that their companies' contributions to left-wing groups made them de facto supporters of the "expansion of the welfare state". Among the radical groups wreaking havoc with corporate cash were the American Cancer Society, the American Heart Association and the League of Women Voters. Like the hardy Jacobins of old, Armey lived a rough existence when first arriving in the halls of power, shunning Motel 6 in favor of a bed on the floor of the House gym. Once called his gay colleague Rep. Barney Frank, "Barney Fag". When outcry arose, Armey claimed it was merely a slip anyone could have made. (Colburn/Photoreporters)

man for American business", Charles Lewis says. "If you've got a problem with the federal government, go see Newt. That's the message that's being sent out."

As the *Daily Report For Executives* noted in a post-election story about the euphoric mood among corporate lobbyists, "Some [companies] believe Gingrich is driving a locomotive that is leaving the station, and they may as well bundle everything on their wish list if they can get it on the train."

Gingrich is a natural ally of business groups, but the House Speaker gives special attention to the needs of big Republican Party contributors, and especially to donors to Newt's own web of fundraising vehicles: GOPAC, his political action committee; the Progress and Freedom Foundation, his think-tank; and "Renewing American Civilization", Prof. Gingrich's satellite college course.

Roll Call, the newspaper of Beltway politics, examined videos of Gingrich's lectures for "Renewing American Civilization" and found that contributors to Newt Inc. were regularly plugged. Newt told students that HealthSouth, a company which has made $11,000 in contributions to Gingrich-linked outfits, does "a remarkable job in helping people with rehabilitation". For a meager $5,800 Gingrich plugged Hewlett-Packard as "one of the great companies in American history" because "it does very interesting things". In Milliken & Co., whose owner Roger Milliken has shelled out $300,000 to GOPAC, Gingrich descried "the most effective, most productive textile company in the world".

Course donors who give $50,000 or more can become "sponsors", offered the chance to "work directly with the leadership of the Renewing American Civilization project in the course development process". Ford once received a pitch from a course official promising the company that "we'll be talking about your all's experience", a fact which made it "particularly appropriate to have [the company] on board as a sponsor".

Contributors to Gingrich's pet causes can count on more concrete assistance as well. Executives from the Indianapolis-based Golden Rule Insurance Co. contributed more than $115,000 to GOPAC between 1991 and 1993. On October 21, 1994, just weeks before the mid-term vote, the company made a $216,000 soft money contribution to the GOP.

Coincidentally, Gingrich emerged as the chief sponsor of Golden Rule's top legislative priority in the new Congress, a bill which would allow consumers to set up medical savings accounts with pre-tax dollars.

An early target of the House Speaker was the Food and Drug Administration. He called the agency's commissioner, David Kessler, "a bully and a thug", and wants the FDA to dramatically speed up the approval process for new drugs.

Gingrich intervened with the FDA on behalf of at least one firm, Solvay Pharmaceuticals. In July of 1994, then-minority whip Gingrich and a Republican colleague, Rep. Cass Ballenger of North Carolina, wrote to the agency to ask why it had not yet approved Luvox, a Solvay-produced drug used to treat obsessive-compulsive disorder. "If delays are administrative and not substantive, we feel it is an unfortunate event for this company and for the potential patient population", worried these two members of Congress.

Solvay, it turns out, is a generous contributor to the Progress and Freedom Foundation, which receives 10 to 15 per cent of its funding from big drug firms such as Johnson & Johnson and Searle. The Foundation—whose president, Jeffrey Eisenach, is one of Gingrich's closest advisers—also proposes that private industry be given responsibility for many of the FDA's duties. (A report from Public Citizen reveals the bogus nature of the attack on Kessler's agency. It found that the FDA had indeed kept off the US market 47 drugs which had been approved for sale in England, France and Germany, but all of these drugs were later withdrawn because of safety problems.)

ASIDE: NEWT AS HOT YOUTH

Newt Gingrich's hypocrisy when it comes to his promotion of "family values" is no secret. Less well known is that during his college days at Tulane in the Sixties, Newt lived and espoused a McGovern-like philosophy which starkly contrasts with his current ideological posture. We are obliged to Tim Wise of New Orleans, a graduate from Gingrich's alma mater of Tulane, whose report on this matter, which follows, first appeared in our newsletter, CounterPunch.

Few have asked what Newt Gingrich was doing in the Age of Aquarius, other than avoiding service in Vietnam by way of a student deferment, and composing a fairly tedious dissertation on Belgian educational policy in the Congo. It turns out that Gingrich was an iconoclastic liberal, albeit a Republican, who served as a go-between for campus radicals at Tulane and that school's administration.

Particularly liberal on social issues, Gingrich would regularly complain about how "corrupt and stupid the white New Orleans conservative elite were, and how the city was missing the boat culturally and economically, mainly because of the racism of the old-timers", according to Gingrich's long-time friend, David Kramer. Gingrich's own children were enrolled in Head Start at a local pre-school and Newt himself was a staunch supporter of efforts to bring the poor into the mainstream, particularly blacks.

Gingrich consorted openly with members of Students for a Democratic Society, and led a movement in favor of the campus paper's right to publish nude photographs. In this role, Gingrich led a 700-strong march to the home of the university president, protesting censorship by the administration. Tulane's chief was hung in effigy. Other Gingrich-led demonstrations included protests at the New Orleans offices of Merrill Lynch, a local bank and a department store, all of which had executives who sat on the Tulane Board of Administrators.

According to a fellow graduate student, Blake Touchstone, now an associate professor of history at Tulane, Gingrich and two other graduate students "took over the campus protest movement when they saw the undergrads weren't doing such a great job". One of those in Gingrich's inner-circle was Eric Gordon, an SDS activist known around campus as "Eric the Red".

Kramer, now a professor at the Free University in Berlin, told the New Orleans *Times-Picayune* that Gingrich was the "spokesman for student rebellion". His photo fight concerned the right of a campus journal, *Sophia*, to publish photos of nude statues with enlarged genitals, along with the sculptor himself—also in the buff. Many students opposed Newt's stance, and a number fired off vitriolic letters to the editor, slamming the "radicals" for expressing their disagreements through "angry protests". A group co-founded by Gingrich, Mobilization of Responsible Tulane Students (MORTS) went on to publish a broader campus political platform which advocated, among other things, the abolition of compulsory attendance and student control of all dormitory regulations, including the right to spend the night in opposite-sex dorms. MORTS soon faded away as a campus force, but students involved in its founding—including Gingrich's friends, Kramer and Bill Rushton—were instrumental in the formation of the Tulane Liberation Front, which led a week-long occupation of the school's student center and called for a "cultural revolution" in America.

Gingrich's most pronounced "countercultural" tendencies surfaced in the area of his educational philosophies, which he had a chance to put into practice in the Spring of 1969. It was then that Gingrich taught a free, non-credit freshman course called "When You Are 49: The Year 2000". Gingrich described his course as one which would probe the likely boundaries of the year 2000 and prepare students "for the world in which they will live", by analyzing and discussing issues of war, peace, racial conflict and the impact of technology on life in America.

Interviewed for the student paper, Gingrich said that he based his teaching method on the concept of "total feedback", that the course would operate without formal notes or lectures, and that exam questions would be given to students two weeks prior to the test, so as to lessen performance pressures and allow better preparation. The problem with universities, said Gingrich, was that they were "bogged down with a lot of useless systems. such as credits and rules, and unrealistic requirements", which he favored eliminating completely. It's easy to imagine what a meal such Gingrich allies as Bill Bennett or the editors of The Wall Street Journal would make of this if Gingrich were a Clinton nominee up for confirmation.

Despite his unorthodox stances, Newt's former colleagues viewed him as something of an opportunist and not entirely trustworthy. "The first time I met Newt", recalls Touchstone, "was in the fall of 1967. A few of us were sitting around the campus pub having a beer and talking about what we would like to be doing in twenty years. Most of us were saying how we'd like to be teaching, or writing a book or something like that. But when we asked Newt, he didn't miss a beat, and said, just as confident as he could be, that he would be a United States Senator from the state of Georgia. It was a very strange moment."

★

Republican House whip Tom DeLay is equally responsive to the needs of business. Before winning office in 1984, DeLay headed Albo Pest Control, a firm which exterminated insects for Houston's wealthy. DeLay developed a distaste for government regulation during his years as an exterminator. He chafed under Environmental Protection Agency rules controlling the uses of pesticides, and federal edicts—such as one which required DeLay to provide his termite crew with helmets when tunneling under houses—protecting workers.

DeLay entered politics with the mission of freeing business from this sort of intrusion. As he once told *The Washington Post*, "I found out government was a cost of doing business, and I better get involved in it."

This stance endeared him to the business crowd, which has lushly funded his political campaigns. For his 1992 run, DeLay hauled in $341,516 in political contributions, about 90 per cent of which flowed from business groups and rich people.

In early 1995, DeLay pushed a bill through the House banning the decree of any new government regulations for 13 months. Coordinating the drive was Project Relief, a corporate group DeLay had set up himself. The group's members included some of the biggest companies in the country, such as Amoco, General Electric and Union Carbide.

To chair Project Relief, DeLay chose Bruce Gates, a lobbyist for the National American Wholesale Grocers Association, a major contributor to DeLay and other conservative Republicans. Another lobbyist, Paul Smith, who works for the nation's motor fleets, assisted Gates. During debate on the bill, Smith sat in Project Relief's War Room pecking out strategies on a lap top computer and relaying them to Republicans on the floor.

Where DeLay is a Jack-of-all-trades, many in Congress concentrate on economic sectors which they oversee from committee posts and from which they can hope to raise immense sums of campaign cash.

Rep. Henry Hyde was elected to Congress in 1974 and soon joined the House Banking Committee. Between 1981—the year he stepped down from the committee—and 1984, Hyde served on the board of Clyde Federal Savings and Loan, an Illinois thrift, an effort which earned him $4,000 annually.

Clyde went bankrupt in 1990, at a cost to taxpayers of about $72 million. Hyde has been sued by the Resolution Trust Corporation for his role in its failure. The RTC has charged Hyde and 11 other former Clyde officers with gross negligence and breach of fiduciary duty.

During Hyde's tenure, Clyde engaged in options trading, and lost $10 million through Refco Inc., the notorious Illinois firm which later took part in Hillary Clinton's commodity trading deals. Clyde abandoned Generally Accepted Accounting Principles (G.A.A.P.) in favor of Regulatory Accounting Procedures (R.A.P.)—a smoke-and-mirrors system which Congress created to allow ailing financial institutions the pretense of solvency.

Hyde has always claimed that he played a minor role in Clyde's affairs, and was but remotely aware of the board's actions. Tim Anderson, an Illinois-based banking consultant, compiled nearly 400 pages of documents regarding Hyde's years at Clyde. The material reveals that the congressman's explanation is entirely deficient.

Hyde not only approved all the steps mentioned above, but also was a prime player in a number of other disastrous moves taken by the thrift. In 1982, Hyde seconded a motion by which the S&L purchased $28 million worth of Eurobonds through a US-owned bank in the Cayman Islands, a place virtually synonymous with shady deals and money laundering.

That same year Hyde also seconded a motion authorizing the thrift to offer bank directors and officials below market rates on mortgage loans. Here Hyde was seconding a violation of the law, since the House Banking Committee in 1978—when Hyde was a member—approved a bill, later passed by Congress, which bars financial institutions from offering directors or officers better credit terms than those they offer to the public.

According to the RTC, Hyde voted in favor of options trading that violated federal law and which resulted in losses of $10 million for Clyde. During Hyde's tenure the S&L also helped finance a $28.5 million beachfront condominium complex in Port Aransas, Texas, a project which later collapsed. Clyde's board, the RTC said, "relied upon information provided and analyzed by a broker who stood to receive a substantial fee" if the project moved forward. The broker in question was J. William Oldenburg, who the Securities and Exchange Commission charged with fraud in 1974 and who was connected to Eureka Federal Savings, a California thrift which allegedly had criminal ties.

Hyde claims he was entirely unaware that Clyde was in dire financial shape when he left the board. This is hard to square with a May 7, 1982, letter, with which Hyde was familiar, from a Federal Home Loan Bank Board agent advising the board that Clyde's position was so precarious that it might be bankrupt within 14 months.

In Congress Hyde has consistently backed the deregulation of S&Ls, lining up with the industry on seven major pieces of legislation during the last decade. That includes his opposition to a 1987 amendment which would have restricted risky loans by S&Ls, and his proposed amendment two years later which would have allowed thrifts to escape raising $6 billion in new capital as reserves against potential losses. The *Los Angeles Times* called the amendment, which was defeated 326 to 94, a device that would "invite a whole new cycle of financial failures".

Hyde was rewarded with more than $115,000 in campaign contributions from banks during the 1980s. More than $7,000 came from the US League of Savings Institutions, the S&L industry's chief lobbying group. Sylvia Miedema, the now deceased former head of Clyde whose estate is also being sued by the RTC, pitched in another $5,850.

Hyde was long close to Miedema, who told *Crain's Chicago Business* in 1981, when the congressman stepped down from the Banking Committee, "Of course we'll [S&L executives] miss him. But I'm sure he won't desert us." Hyde certainly didn't disappoint Miedema, whose salary he voted to increase while serving on the thrift's board.

PACKWOOD AND THE PIG BARONS

T hings are no cleaner in the upper chamber of Congress, as seen in the Bob Packwood affair, which reached a Tartuffian crescendo in the fall of 1995 when the Oregon senator was forced to resign after multiple charges of sexual harassment. The departing chairman of the Senate Finance Committee left a priceless bequest in the form of his diaries, which explain in homely detail how a US senator makes his way in the world. The sexual escapades described in The Packwood Diaries exhibit Oregonian self-righteousness at full stretch. Packwood tells one of the female staffers he's been sleeping with that "I was doing my Christian duty by making love to you." He feared she didn't have time for sex outside of the office because she was lonely, working long hours.

Packwood's diaries show the intimate connection between the money corporate lobbyists give over and the legislative stances members of Congress adopt. "We should have them [the NRA] sewn up", Packwood wrote in his diary after voting against gun control in 1992. Two days later, an NRA lobbyist showed him a draft letter that the organization was going to send out supporting Packwood and denouncing Rep. Les AuCoin, his opponent in the November 1992 election, who as a House member had voted for the Brady Bill. "God, is it tough", Packwood exulted.

At another point, Packwood writes of his attempts to secure job offers for his wife, Georgie, whom he was in the process of divorcing. The wily senator hoped to reduce alimony payments by upping her outside income ("I'm skating on thin ice here"). Packwood wanted railcar company owner William Furman to put up money for Georgie. He thought this highly likely since Furman "is eternally appreciative to me" for inserting a $5 million tax break in the 1986 Tax Reform Act which benefited Furman's firm, Greenbriar Companies.

Packwood raised vast sums of money from the finance, insurance and real estate (FIRE) sector, on whose behalf he did most of his legislative whoring. William Roth, the Delaware Republican who succeeded Packwood as Finance Committee chairman, actually raised more money from that sector than did the departing Oregonian. Between 1989 and 1994, Roth took in $348,045 from FIRE PACs, versus the comparatively meager $260,771 Packwood raised.

As he left the Senate to head toward a second career as a lobbyist, Packwood expressed bitterness about his fate. Indeed he might legitimately have felt that the Senate Ethics Committee had scant reason to single him out from his colleagues, except perhaps on the minor business of cleaning up his diaries. Many of them are as sexually predatory as Packwood and all of them depend on the corporate dollar.

Take the two Senators from North Carolina, as fragrant a duo as can be found in Congress: Jesse Helms and Lauch Faircloth.

In the fall of 1995, Helms, head of the Senate Foreign Relations

Committee, introduced the Cuban Liberty and Democratic Solidarity Act. One section of the bill, which has no basis in international law, would allow Cubans who fled after Fidel Castro took power in 1959 and later became US citizens, to advance claims in US courts on property nationalized by the Cuban government. They could even sue foreign nationals and companies which have indirectly benefited from the use of their former property.

The major beneficiaries of this legislation would be the people who most successfully plundered Cuba under the Batista dictatorship which Castro overthrew: Florida-based sugar barons, cattle ranchers and distillers. This is no coincidence. Among those drafting the Helms legislation was Nicolas Gutierrez, who sits on the board of the Miami-headquartered National Association of Sugar Mill Owners of Cuba and whose family had 100,000 acres of land expropriated by Castro, and Ignacio Sanchez, a lawyer for Bacardi Rum Co., which has long been seeking a means to sue Pernod Ricard, a French firm which distills rum in Bacardi's old plant in Santiago de Cuba.

Also backing the legislation was Juan Prado, a retired Bacardi executive, whose family lost $76 million (in 1960 dollars) when Castro took power, and Manuel Cutillas, head of both the US-Cuba Business Council and of Bacardi Rum Co. For this reason, Wayne Smith, the former chief of the US Interests Section in Havana who is now billeted at Washington's Center for International Policy, tagged the Helms-backed legislation as "the Bacardi Claims Act".

Helms's efforts have further endeared him to the fanatical exiles massed in the Cuban American National Foundation, headed by Jorge Mas Canosa. Pleased by the work of the senior senator from North Carolina, Cuban groups in Miami have organized two major fundraisers for Helms, who is up for re-election in 1996, netting him $85,000 and $75,000, respectively. Last May, Radio Marti, which is controlled by the Foundation, gave Helms six minutes to deliver a personal "message to the Cuban people".

Bill Clinton, with his habitual eye to the Florida vote, supported most sections of the Helms legislation, but refused to endorse the Bacardi Claims Act, forcing it to be stripped from the bill before Congress approved it. Expect Helms and Bacardi to try again in the near future.

What Helms is to rum, North Carolina's junior senator, Lauch

Jesse Helms: Great Beast in the liberal lexicon, tobacco's doughty champion, Debbie De Moss's former employer. A paradox of empire: Helms drew anguished squeak from liberal-ish *Nation* **when, amid his war against the State Department, he held up funding for CIA-backed AFL-CIO program to undermine independent unions in Nicaragua and Haiti. "The last temptation is the greatest treason:/To do the right thing for the wrong reason."** (Rick Reinhard/Impact Visuals)

Faircloth, is to pigs. Faircloth holds about $19 million in pork farming investments. Today in North Carolina the hog industry runs the same way chicken production did 30 years ago, when Purdue and other pioneers introduced vertical integration and wiped out a million small chicken farmers across the country.

The pig barons of North Carolina saw a cost advantage for their "right to work" state as against the traditional hog belt of the midwest, where unions and laws against vertical integration and some forms of corporate agriculture still protect the medium farmer. The coastal plain and Piedmont of North Carolina are now pocked by vast pig-factories and pig-slaughter houses, often surrounded by stinking 25-foot-deep lagoons of ordure that sicken the people living round about, poison the water table and impart high levels of nitrogen and phosphorous into such rivers as the Neuse, the Tar-Pamlico and the Albemarle. Ammonia gas burdens the air, just as it does in northern Europe, where open lagoons are banned and animal wastes must be "injected" into cropland rather than sprayed over them, as in US practice.

Such is the swollen empire of pork in North Carolina, whose reeking lagoons surround darkened warehouses of living creatures, trapped in metal crates barely larger than their bodies, tails chopped off, pumped with corn, soybeans and chemicals until, in six months, they weigh about 240 pounds. At that point, the boars are shipped off to abattoirs for slaughter, sometimes by prisoners on work release from a county jail. The sows survive longer—for about two years, or whenever their reproductive performance declines.

It takes eight to ten people to run a sow factory, overseeing 2,000 sows, boars and piglets. A computerized "finishing" farm where the pigs are fattened may just require a part-time caretaker to check the equipment and clean up between arriving and departing cohorts of swine.

The noise in these factories is ghastly, and many workers wear ear pads against the squealing and crashing of the creatures in their cages. When the *Raleigh News and Observer* did a fine series on North Carolina's pig barons in early 1995 (following a pioneering article in *Southern Exposure* in 1992), readers learned they could call the paper's number in Raleigh, 549-5100, enter category 4647 and listen to a recording of this terrible sound.

To insulate themselves from popular outrage or even regulatory surveillance the pig barons have either purchased political protection or gone into politics themselves to write or endorse laws favorable to themselves. Some do both. Most conspicuous in this art is Wendell Murphy, head of Murphy Farms, the biggest pig operation in the country, selling $200 million worth of hogs in 1994. Murphy joined the state legislature in 1982 and soon augmented the steady stream of laws protecting hog and chicken interests. In North Carolina, legislators may make money off the bills or amendments they offer so long as they can assert that such profit-probabilities do not cloud their judgment. Presumably unclouded, Murphy pushed through or supported laws exempting his business from sales taxes, inspection fees, property taxes on feed, zoning laws and pollution fines.

In 1993, after Murphy left the assembly, one of his executives stayed on as a legislator to press successfully for a bill that blocked environmental researchers from getting state agriculture department records on hog farm sites and sizes. In 1991, when Murphy was still installed as tribune for the pig business, the North Carolina legislature brazenly passed Senate Bill 669 allowing the NC Pork Producers Association to collect a hog levy which could be used to lobby state legislators, fight lawsuits and for other purposes prohibited with money derived from the federal check-off.

The pig men of North Carolina have a friend even higher up the political chain in the form of Senator Faircloth, who is part owner of Coharie Farms, the 30th largest hog producer in the country. In Congress he is now ensconced as chairman of the Senate Subcommittee on Clean Water, Wetlands, Private Property and Nuclear Safety.

When challenged that his hog interests conflicted with his new post, Faircloth asked for an Ethics Committee ruling, and that wise body, taking into account that hog factories are poisoning North Carolina's waters, and that hog barons try to exempt all regulators from their private property, ruled that Faircloth had no conflict of interest. Small wonder Packwood feels aggrieved.

At least Faircloth cannot be charged with hypocrisy. In 1993, shortly after his election to the Senate, he celebrated his arrival by inviting lobbyists to attend his swearing-in party at the Hyatt Regency Hotel—at $1,000 per head.

More recently, Faircloth co-sponsored an amendment which will steer a new highway—originally planned to run through Winston-Salem—through Greensboro, NC. By healthful coincidence, Faircloth owns hundreds of thousands of dollars worth of stock in the Greensboro-based Jefferson-Pilot Corporation, which owns a vast tract of undeveloped land near the route of the new highway and plans to build a shopping mall there if Faircloth's amendment is approved.

In 1992, Jefferson-Pilot and its executives contributed $16,600 to Faircloth's Senate campaign. A Faircloth aide, Harris Vaughn, told

Roll Call that any link between Faircloth's investment in Jefferson-Pilot and his diversion of the highway route was "absolutely" coincidental.

PRESSLER: HOW THE LOBBYISTS LAUGHED

Mentally frail and morally inert, Republican Senator Larry Pressler is the telecommunications industry's point man in Congress. He is also a man long and widely derided in Washington as an imbecile of fantastic proportions. Jokes about Pressler have haunted him from the beginning of his congressional career, when he bucked the Watergate crash for Republicans and won a House seat in 1974. Although he claims to be a Rhodes scholar, Pressler left Oxford about halfway through his prospective term there. He took the South Dakota bar exam twice, then prudently declined the third attempt, which would have been his last.

Having won office with the promise that he would serve only two or three terms in the House, Pressler also said he would rebate 10 per cent of his salary to the taxpayers, a pledge thus far unredeemed.

Through the 1970s he led a mostly spectral existence, propelled into fame only by dint of an unflattering front page story by Al Hunt in *The Wall Street Journal*, which noted his obsession with press releases touting his meager achievements ("*New York Times* Carries Pressler Drought Letter"). Hunt also drew attention to Pressler's elasticity of political principle, which from among many examples had him assuring a constituent that as regards choice, he supported the right of individuals to make their own decisions, while simultaneously co-sponsoring a constitutional amendment to prohibit abortions.

Pressler entered the Senate in 1978. Two years later the young senator was summoning the TV cameras to boast that he had been deemed honest by the FBI during the Abscam sting. Those who have viewed the Abscam video tapes secretly made by the FBI say that the funniest parts of the tapes come when Pressler is apparently trying to figure out how to take the bribe he is being offered without going to prison, and when Mel Weinberg, the FBI middle man, proclaims to a second FBI agent dressed up as an Arab sheikh that Pressler will win the 1980 presidential race and that the money will help him do so. This claim is too much even for Pressler, who inter-

Larry Pressler: They called him "Telephone Pole", and they weren't talking about the communications industry. (Library of Congress)

rupts Weinberg to admit that he doesn't expect to win, but that he is running for president because he is unknown and hopes to heighten his visibility.

A major blow to the Pressler presidential bid came amid the roller-skating craze, when *People* magazine unexpectedly cut a long-planned, laboriously organized photo op of the Dakota legislator on skates. Pressler was crushed, and lost heart.

Invariably described as handsome and a sure warm spot in the hearts of South Dakota womanhood, Pressler's amatory career has been meandering. Amid speculation that he was gay, Pressler suddenly opted for the married state, to a South Dakota widow, Harriett Dent. Steve Gobie, former consort of Rep. Barney Frank, told one reporter that he had seen Pressler at a louche rendezvous where he was known familiarly as "Telephone Pole Pressler".

Pressler's colleagues once watched in bemusement as the Dakota senator rose from a meeting and mistook a closet door for the exit. The immured Pressler realized his mistake but thought that the best strategy would be to stand pat, wait until everyone else had quit the room, and then slip out. His plan was foiled when a few colleagues decided to sit him out. Some 15 minutes later, a red-faced Pressler made his exit at last.

Like the tick that waits 20 years for a cow to pass below, then leaps to opportunity, Pressler's moment came with the Republican capture of the Senate in November of 1994. His long years in the Commerce Committee suddenly paid off. Senators senior to himself, such as Ted Stevens, hastened off to other billets. Pressler became chairman of the committee, gaining oversight of all broadcasting, cable and telecommunications regulations, and hence of a $250 billion industry in the midst of internecine warfare and volcanic change.

After taking charge of the committee, Pressler quickly became noted for his efforts to sell Public Broadcasting to Rupert Murdoch. By the spring of 1995, Pressler was aboard a slush express, traveling to Hollywood where Murdoch, Alan Ladd Jr., Sherry Lansing, Ted Turner, Jack Valenti, Lew Wasserman and other powers in Tinseltown had lent their names to an invitation for a $500 per person cocktail party at Paramount, checks payable to "Friends of Larry Pressler". The invitation noted: "As Chairman of the Commerce Committee, Senator Pressler plays a unique role in setting the broadcasting, cable television, telephone and other telecommunications policies that will shape America's communications infrastructure into the next century."

A hilarious though (for obvious reasons) somewhat deferential story in *Cable* described the extraordinary scene in late March 1995, as nearly a hundred lobbyists for the telecommunications and cable industries, plus assorted Senate aides, chortled and roared as the wretched Pressler attempted to preside over markup of the Omnibus Telecommunications Act. "He makes Quayle look like Kissinger", one industry executive lamented to *Business Week*.

Industry newsletters such as *Broadcasting & Cable* used the words "chaotic" and "bizarre" to describe Pressler's unsure grip on the proceedings and what the industry regarded as a sell-out to such Democrats as Ernest Hollings of South Carolina and Bob Kerrey of Nebraska. Senator Bob Dole allegedly fumed at Pressler's maladroitness and threatened to take over the floor management of the bill himself.

ASIDE: THE PASSIONS OF DEBBIE DE MOSS

One of Congress's most infamous and effective staffers in recent years was Deborah Lynne De Moss, a long-time employee of Senator Jesse Helms and known to many as "Death Squad Debbie" because of her close association with Latin American military establishments. De Moss was Helms's chief Latin American specialist for more than a decade and maintains contact with her old office, although she married a Honduran colonel, Hector Rene Fonseca, and moved to Tegucigalpa in 1994.

De Moss springs from one of America's most right-wing families. The Arthur S. De Moss Foundation of St. Davids, Pennsylvania, is named after her father, the former head of the National Liberty Life Insurance Co., who died in 1979. With some $364 million in assets, the foundation offers hefty support to the radical anti-abortion movement, conservative Latin American groups and, naturally, to Jesse Helms. Mark De Moss, Debbie's brother, runs a public relations firm in Atlanta and is a spokesman for the Moral Majority's Jerry Falwell.

De Moss bounded to fame in conservative circles by helping push the Reagan administration to break with Panamanian dictator General Manuel Noriega. De Moss despised the general, whom she met in Panama in the mid-1980s and correctly accused of ordering the murder of opposition leader Hugo Spadafora. Noriega retaliated by having derogatory allegations against her published in the Panamanian press, pulled from a file on De Moss that the CIA prepared for the dictator, a long-time Agency asset.

While championing "conservative democracies" for Latin America, De Moss aligned herself with the region's most extravagant butchers. She was on warm terms with the Salvadoran death squad leader Roberto d'Aubuisson, who former US ambassador Robert White termed a "pathological killer". The Carter administration classified d'Aubuisson a terrorist and denied him a visa, but after Reagan took office De Moss reportedly helped clear up his status so he could again travel to the US. She also served as an informal adviser to d'Aubuisson's ARENA party.

Another of De Moss's heroes was Nicaragua's Enrique Bermudez, the former Somoza dictatorship National Guardsman and contra commander. De Moss proudly kept a photograph on her desk of herself firing off an AK-47 in a contra camp. "She was the Catherine the Great of the contra movement", Larry Birns, director of the Council on Hemispheric Affairs, recalls.

More recently, De Moss devoted considerable time to attacking the government of Nicaraguan President Violetta Chamorro, on the grounds that her administration was under the thumb of the Sandinistas. The centerpiece of her efforts was the so-called De Moss report of 1992, a well-crafted piece of disinformation on alleged Sandinista perfidy riddled with errors and distortions.

The report told the tale of six ex-contras who were said to have been killed in a "brutal massacre" during which Sandinista police officers went "house to house, systematically capturing and assassinating former members of the Nicaraguan Resistance and their friends". Her story was based on an incident in which a number of demobilized contras took over a police station and were killed, along with several unarmed bystanders, in a shootout with army forces sent to recapture the building.

On a lighter note, the report also accused Chamorro of nepotism. This was somewhat ironic as De Moss's sister, Elizabeth, was also hired by the North Carolina senator in the early Nineties and worked on the study as a researcher.

The report's exaggerations were typical of De Moss's tendency to mix fantasy with reality, the resulting stew being remitted to the press. She once accused *The Washington Times* of endangering her life by publishing her home address, saying her stand "against violence and terrorism in Central America" had made her a "potential target of physical mischief", especially as the Sandinistas were known to "murder people in the United States".

However, no one denies De Moss's excellent capacity to obtain information, a skill said to be based on her close ties to intelligence agencies across Central America. Bruce Cameron, a contra supporter who later lobbied for Chamorro, said that during the 1992 debate on aid to Managua, De Moss "had better information than the Nicaraguan government or the State Department. She was days and sometimes weeks ahead of us."

Fonseca, De Moss's new husband, is a close friend of General Luis Alonso Discua Elvir, who was the best man at the wedding. Discua was the first leader of the infamous Battalion 316, which kidnapped and murdered hundreds of leftists in the 1980s. But one person familiar with the Honduran army says Fonseca himself "comes from the progressive sector of the military. That means he's not a known sociopath."

De Moss's 1994 goodbye party in Washington was a hot social affair with more than a dozen senators in attendance, as well as several officials from the Clinton administration. "Everybody knew Deborah and thought she was a terrific girl", says Admiral James Nance, Helms's staff director, in explaining the event's appeal.

★

DUMB-DUMB BULLETS

T he American body politic has always had its share of boobs and incompetents. H.L. Mencken once wrote that since elections produced such dreadful results, citizens should stop wasting their time voting and simply pick their representatives at random from the phone book. Mencken would have had a fine time with today's Congress, especially with the ebullient ferocity of many of the GOP's newest members.

Rep. Sonny Bono's mental shortcomings have long made him a subject of scorn among California politicians. In 1994, the year he won national office, Palm Desert Councilman Walt Snyder derided Bono as a "laughing stock" and Rep. Al McCandless charged that he took "pride in not having studied [the] issues until just a few months ago". True, worse things have been said about political candidates, but then Snyder and McCandless are Republicans who supported Bono in his race against Democrat Steve Clute.

Bono served as mayor of Palm Springs between 1988 and 1992. His aides worked hard to conceal his meager talents. Bono's public relations director, Marilyn Baker, later revealed to the *Los Angeles Times* that she had to rewrite the mayor's agendas into script form so Bono could conduct official business. "For call to order, I wrote 'sit.' For salute the flag, I wrote 'stand up, face flag, mouth words.' For roll call I wrote: 'When you hear your name, say yes'", said Baker, who quit after three depressing months of service.

Bono's legislative director in Washington, Curt Hollman, is charged with the important task of summarizing complex issues in short, simple memos which Bono can comprehend. But Hollman can't watch over Bono during all of his assignments. At one Judiciary Committee hearing Bono complained, "Boy, it's been flying in this room like I can't believe today. We have a very simple and concise bill here, and I think it would be to everyone's pleasure if we would just pass this thing."

On another occasion Bono complained that his colleagues were becoming needlessly bogged down in "technical" matters and legalese. This about the Judiciary Committee, which writes laws and deals with trifling matters such as constitutional protections.

A former TV sportscaster and football player, Rep. J.D. Hayworth of Arizona, like ex-President Gerald Ford, appears to have forgotten his helmet one too many times. At a convention of People for the West!, a group linked to the Wise Use Movement, Hayworth said that logging was a particularly beneficial activity because forests are a fire hazard.

Hayworth's entire political philosophy can be boiled down to "Big government, bad; less government, good." The *Arizona Republic* has said that "substance has never been a strong suit of Hayworth's (even by sportscasting standards)," and that he even has "to read his clichés from a script".

Hayworth's major activity after coming to Washington—and one which invariably sets off waves of anguished head-slapping on the House floor—is his daily one-minute statement. He often reads off a David Letterman-style "Top 10" list, such as his offering on the "Top 10 tactics of the new minority in the post Contract With America

Helen Chenoweth: Idaho's Boadicea; snacks on endangered species, strangles environmentalists with her bare hands. (AP/Joe Marquette)

period". Among the side-slappers were "Hire Freddy Krueger as the new liberal Democrat spokesman" and "Set up a new political action committee–the 'Whine Producers'."

Though dumb, Hayworth is also smooth and relentless. "You can't have a real debate with Hayworth", says one Democratic staffer. "He talks as passionately about his need to take a No. 1 as he does about the need to cut government spending."

"The Greeks and the Romans were homosexuals. Their civilizations did not stand. Did they come in contact with a social disease like AIDS? I don't know the answer. But I wonder." This was Frank Cremeans pondering the enigmas of history during the 1994 campaign against Democrat Ted Strickland. Comments like this prompted the *Dayton Daily News* to call Cremeans "a bad joke" whose election would constitute "a mockery of democracy". Voters from Ohio's 6th district paid heed to such words, and duly selected Cremeans to represent them in Congress.

Cremeans has continued to make bizarre statements since taking up residence in the capital. He once declared his opposition to sex before marriage, saying that "marriage is a very sanctimonious commitment". In an interview with a radio station in Marietta, Ohio, during which he discussed Congress's first 100 days under Newt Gingrich, Cremeans excitedly declared to the show's host, "Just think about it Mike, we're advancing backwards!"

Unlike some of his exuberant colleagues, Cremeans recognizes his limitations. He wisely refuses to answer any substantive questions from the press or public, referring all such inquiries to his chief of staff, Barry Bennett, a prominent Ohio Republican who baby-sits Cremeans. "His handlers can tell him anything and he'll simply repeat it over and over", says one staffer at the House Banking Committee, where Cremeans serves. "He takes direction well but when he tries to think on his feet he quickly gets into trouble."

During her 1994 campaign, Rep. Helen Chenoweth of Idaho held fundraisers where she sold baked Sockeye Salmon, an endangered species. Asked if she believed the Sockeye were truly threatened, she said, "How can I, when you can go in and buy a can of salmon off the shelf in Albertson's?" According to Chenoweth, "It's the white Anglo-Saxon male that's endangered today."

Chenoweth quickly became a legend in Congress. To one group of scientists who testified before the Resources Committee, Chenoweth said, "I want to thank you all for being here and I condemn the panel." At a field hearing on the Endangered Species Act in New Bern, North Carolina, she apologized to a witness, saying, "I didn't understand everything you said. You all talk so funny down here."

Chenoweth blindly attacks any proposal emanating from the White House. She once arrived late to a hearing of the water and power resources subcommittee, and quickly began attacking administration officials who were testifying about a proposed bill which she opposed. The acting chairman, John Doolittle of California, finally cut Chenoweth off to inform her that the officials shared her position.

Unquestionably the dumbest man to serve in the 104th Congress, Nebraska Rep. Jon Christensen, rails against the "liberal elite", which he claims is out of touch with the daily struggles of common folk. Christensen himself has no achievements to speak of, and, prior to his election, lived off the interest income of his wife, Meredith, who springs from a rich Texas clan. After a spell in Babylon the couple's marriage struck fatal rocks, while the Texas heiress was rumored to have found a fresh Rep. to conquer.

After graduating from law school, Christensen twice failed the Nebraska bar exam, finally squeaking through on his third attempt. No law firm would hire him (except for clerking duties), so Christensen was forced to sell insurance. He supplemented his income by peddling lawn fertilizer out of his garage. In a touching display of resumé inflation, Christensen now describes his past positions as "Insurance marketing director" and "Fertilizer holding company executive".

During the 1994 campaign, Christensen held a question-and-answer session at Omaha's Westside High School. Apparently fearful that their man would wither under pressure, Christensen's aides prepared questions in advance and handed them out to students who were volunteers for his campaign, telling them to clutch pens in their hands so the candidate could recognize his more amiable interrogators. Other students learned of the fix, and foiled Christensen's plot by clutching pens in their hands.

During a radio interview in Nebraska, Christensen vigorously attacked welfare recipients, saying he favored cutting all government "hand-outs and subsidies" to "eliminate people's reliance on government". When the host pointed out that his subject had outstanding student loans of between $30,000 and $100,000, Christensen feebly replied, "Well, I wouldn't have been able to go to school if I didn't have a student loan."

Christensen once called a press conference to announce his personal deficit reduction plan, which called for cuts in government spending of $1.5 trillion. When informed by a reporter that $1.5 trillion was the entire budget, Christensen, looking like a deer caught in the headlights, hastily changed topics.

Don Young of Alaska, first elected to the House in 1973, is still its most exuberant practitioner of Dada politics. Head of the House Resources Committee, Rep. Young is best known for his rabid attacks on ecologists. Animal rights advocate Mary Tyler Moore once read a poem about the cruelty of steel-jaw leghold traps before the Merchant Marine subcommittee, where Young previously served. Accompanying Moore was Cleveland Amory, who periodically inserted a pencil in a trap, causing it to snap shut.

The moment was highly charged and Young, as a hunter, trapper and taxidermist, realized dramatic action was required to turn the tide. His solution was to place his hand into a trap he had brought along to the hearing, and then begin to calmly question a witness as though nothing unusual had happened. "I never told anyone, but it hurt like hell", Young later confided to a congressional staffer.

Young also made use of a visual aid during a 1994 hearing during which he waved an 18-inch oosik—the penis bone of the walrus —at Mollie Beattie, director of the US Fish and Wildlife Service. Beattie had suggested that Alaskan Natives should be able to sell oosiks only as handicrafts, not uncarved, a posture which Young derided as a frontal assault on the Native economy. Beattie is the first woman to head the Service, and the hearing marked her debut on the Hill.

In early 1995, a group of students in Fairbanks invited the Alaskan wild man to speak about the GOP's Contract With America. Young expounded on a number of his favorite topics, including the need to slash federal funding of the arts. The government, Young said, has funded "photographs of people doing offensive things" and "things that are absolutely ridiculous". One student asked Young what sort of things he had in mind. "Buttfucking", the congressman succinctly replied, referring to a 1990 exhibit, funded by the National Endowment for the Arts, of Robert Mapplethorpe's photographs in Cincinnati. Young said he was merely "trying to educate" the inquisitive youngsters.

THE DEMOCRATIC STYLE OF RULE

The Democrats are just as beholden to corporate power as the Republicans, and indeed the latter party has a far more populist funding base. In 1993 the GOP raised $29 million in small contributions (under $200) and $9 million in "soft" money. The Democrats took in $16 million in soft money and $8.9 million from small contributors.

Two of the most respected Democratic senators, Bill Bradley of New Jersey (scheduled to retire in 1996) and Christopher Dodd of Connecticut, are shills for, respectively, the drug companies and Wall Street. Bradley's state is home to 10 of the 18 largest international drug companies, which have sales of about $10 billion annually. America's most profitable legal industry, drug companies posted a return on equity of 26 per cent in 1991, a good but not exceptional year. The secret to the cartel's success is price-gouging, with prescription drug prices climbing by 216.4 per cent between 1980 and 1993, versus a general inflation rate of 48.6 per cent during the same period. The elderly, who cover two-thirds of prescription costs out of pocket, are the industry's chief victims.

Bradley is so vital to the drug lords that when Clinton first threatened to crack down on the industry soon after taking office, the pharmaceutical czars traveled to Washington for strategy talks with the senator. Bradley is an especially effective agent because he is widely respected, unlike other industry flacks such as Republican Senators Dan Coats of Indiana and Orrin Hatch of Utah, and he sits on the Senate Finance Committee, one of four committees responsible for health care.

Part of the Jersey Cartel's profits are laundered in the form of generous contributions to political supporters. A 1994 Common Cause study showed that pharmaceutical PACs provided $9.8 million to congressional candidates during the past decade. Bradley's take of nearly $90,000 makes him Congress's fifth biggest recipient of drug money.

Bradley's senate speeches parrot, sometimes virtually verbatim, background material produced by the Pharmaceutical Research and Manufacturers of America, the industry's chief lobbying group. Two standard arguments, both designed to flatter the figure of the cartel's fat profit, are that pharmaceuticals "reduce health care expenditures [by] keeping people out of hospitals" and that price restraints would have a chilling impact on innovation by "reducing incentives for investment".

The latter argument is particularly ludicrous, as the pharmaceutical industry spends about $10 billion a year on advertising and promotion, $1 billion more than it does on research. Furthermore, a good deal of pharmaceutical research is conducted and paid for by the government, which turns its discoveries over to private sector firms for marketing. For years Johnson & Johnson sold Levamisole, a drug used to deworm sheep, for six cents a tablet. After the National Cancer Institute spent $11 million for experiments which determined that Levamisole is remarkably effective in treating colon cancer, the company began charging cancer patients $6 a tablet for the identical drug.

In the fraught year of 1993, Bradley was instrumental in gutting all efforts to rein in the drug industry. A major triumph came when Clinton was forced to abandon efforts to make the government the sole buyer of childhood vaccines, which were to be distributed free to all children. As the drug lords have boosted vaccine prices by a thousand per cent in the last 15 years, less than two-thirds of 2-year-olds receive the full spectrum of recommended immunizations.

Fearing the plan would increase government leverage to restrict prices, the pharmaceutical industry opposed it. Spurred by his patrons' anxiety, Bradley quickly forced a "compromise" with Michigan Senator Don Riegle (who introduced Clinton's proposal in Congress) by which only children covered by Medicaid or uncovered by health insurance would be eligible for free vaccines. That means most children will continue to receive immunizations on the private market, where the average cost for recommended shots is $244, twice as much as when the government buys vaccines in bulk. Hence, the drug industry's profits remain protected.

Bill Bradley: Ask not what he did for his country, ask rather what he did for New Jersey's drug lords. (Library of Congress)

Congress fought a far nastier battle over Section 936 of the Internal Revenue Code, a corporate welfare program which gives American firms operating in Puerto Rico tax breaks worth approximately $3 billion per year. Legislation which Arkansas Democrat Senator David Pryor proposed would have reduced the giveaway to about $600,000 annually.

The drug lords, who run 72 plants in Puerto Rico, led the opposition to Pryor's legislation, arguing that 936 had turned the island into a "showcase of free enterprise" and created good jobs for workers. Unmentioned was that the Jersey Cartel earns three times more in tax breaks than it pays out in wages or that the same pharmaceutical firms championing the Puerto Rican working class have so fiercely opposed labor organizing that only one of the island's drug plants is unionized.

With corporate hysteria mounting, Finance Committee chairman Daniel Patrick Moynihan, another drug cartel ally, assigned Bradley with personal responsibility to gut the bill. The senator did so with vigor, preserving about 70 per cent of 936's tax breaks during backroom negotiations with Pryor.

Bradley also rallied to the drug lords when Clinton threatened to impose some price controls on the industry. Instead, Bradley and the companies pushed non-binding measures such as voluntary price restraints, which can easily be ignored or skirted.

In 1993, New Jersey-based Hoechst made a solemn vow of self-restraint and then hiked its prices by 7.2 per cent, nearly three times the rate of inflation. Since Bradley helped kill Pryor's 1992 attempt to penalize firms that raise prices faster than inflation, cartel members can engage in such price-gouging with impunity.

Bradley defers to the drug companies, even when his own constituents are at risk. Back in the 1980s, Swiss-owned Ciba-Geigy was found to be pumping 4 million gallons of highly toxic waste per day into the Atlantic Ocean from a private pipeline at its dye and resin plant in Toms River, New Jersey. But the senator spurned local residents who sought political support. "During the entire eight years that we were fighting Ciba-Geigy, Bradley never lifted a finger to help us", recalls Frank Livelli, a retired chemical company executive who helped found Save Our Ocean. "He never even responded to our appeals. In fact, one of our people sent [his office] flowers because we thought he'd died."

Dodd of Connecticut, chairman of the Democratic National Committee, was once one of Congress's most liberal members. When money comes calling, though, the senator can be flexible.

A critic of military spending, Dodd almost always favors arms sales made by Pratt & Whitney, a home state firm which generously contributes to his political campaigns. Dodd also has supported military training for soldiers from Indonesia, one of the world's worst human rights violators. The soldiers came to Connecticut for maintenance training for F-16 planes, which Pratt & Whitney sells to the generals in Jakarta.

Dodd has also been highly sympathetic to Wall Street. In 1988, he attended a Beverly Hills conference on Latin American debt sponsored by Drexel Burnham's Michael Milken—this a few years prior to the latter's jail term—and heaped praise on his host, saying, "Mike, the next time you're doing something like this, maybe I could piggyback on it, get you together with some of my colleagues."

For years, the Connecticut senator sought to push through

Chris Dodd (r.), with Senator John Kerry: Took mess of pottage, paid bill in form of securities "reform". (Rick Reinhard/Impact Visuals)

Congress a bill calling for "securities litigation reform", this being code for laws that would make it almost impossible for investors to recover their money when defrauded by financial swindlers.

Dodd and other "reform" backers argued that securities class action suits were exploding in number, and that frivolous suits were chipping away at "capital formation", a mantra for all foes of capital gains and corporate taxes. This ignored the fact that the number of securities suits filed in 1994—290—was less than the number filed two decades earlier—305.

When the Republicans took control of both houses of Congress in 1994, the political field tilted decisively in Dodd's favor. The House quickly passed its version of securities reform, led by Rep. Christopher Cox of California, a lawyer and defendant in a suit filed by investors who say that a real estate fund where Cox worked in the mid-Eighties had swindled them out of their money.

Republican Alfonse D'Amato of New York soon introduced a modified version of a bill Dodd had proposed in the previous Congress. D'Amato and Dodd—who had been chairman of the securities subcommittee in the last Congress—were the two biggest recipients of contributions from business groups pushing the securities legislation, garnering since 1991 $106,150 and $80,300, respectively.

The D'Amato-Dodd measure was drafted mainly by two Senate Banking Committee aides: Courtney Ward, for the Democrats, who had already taken a post at J.P. Morgan when he was working on the measure; and Robert Giuffra, a D'Amato staffer who had previously worked for Sullivan & Cromwell, a New York law firm with close ties to Goldman, Sachs & Co.

They included provisions which prevent investors from suing if they were misled by wildly optimistic "forward looking statements" — corporate predictions of future earnings—even if those statements were made in "bad faith" or with "no reasonable basis [in fact]".

Also working hard on the bill was Dodd's chief legislative assistant on securities reform, Diana Huffman. She is married to Kenneth Levine, a Washington lobbyist whose firm—Wunder, Diefenderfer, Cannon & Thelen—represents American International Group, an insurance outfit that pays out millions annually in securities class action settlements.

Democratic support for the bill was initially tepid, but Dodd lined up at least 10 votes, including those of such liberals as Patty Murray of Washington and Carol Moseley-Braun of Illinois. Dodd carries special weight with colleagues because as head of the DNC, he controls the flow of campaign money which will be made available to Democratic senators up for re-election in 1996.

FAMILY VALUES

Washington has never been known as a city of high ethical standards. In 1974 Rep. Wilbur Mills was caught in a drunken spree with an embarrassing companion, Fanne Foxe. Two years later, Rep. Wayne Hays was found gallantly to have kept the frolicsome Elizabeth Ray on his payroll as a secretary, although she had no known secretarial skills.

These days there's more caution in Babylon. According to Diana McLellan, the long-time DC gossip columnist, "Many years ago [Washingtonians] were unashamed about boozing around and sexual behavior. Now they're a bit more priggish." Still, the exploits of some members of Congress are legend. Strom "Sperm" Thurmond, South Carolina's senior senator, married a 22-year-old beauty queen at the age of 66, and sired his first child three years later. He claims to have a permanent erection, and says he keeps a baseball bat in his office so the undertaker can beat down his member in order to close his coffin lid.

In his glory days, Ted Kennedy cut a broad swath across the capital. A photograph of the Senator aboard a boat with a woman in his lap once prompted Senator Ernest Hollings of South Carolina to remark, "I see that the senator from Massachusetts has changed his views on offshore drilling."

Two Senate colleagues, Christopher Dodd and Daniel Inouye, often accompanied Kennedy on his outings. A waitress at one restaurant on Capitol Hill once entered the upstairs dining room, closed during the lunch hour, to find the senator in intimate colloquy with a lobbyist for Hanes pantyhose. Dodd stood nearby.

Another public official known for his gallantries is Rep. Charlie Wilson of Texas, a legislator best remembered for traveling to Afghanistan in the mid-Eighties sporting Lawrence of Arabia style

Teddy Kennedy: The "last liberal", who destroyed security for workers in the trucking industry; pioneered deregulation and hence catastrophe for workers in the airline industry; sponsored Supreme Court Justice Stephen Breyer. Fond memories of Hanes pantyhose. (Shia photo/Impact Visuals)

vestments in which to accompany the Mujaheddin rebels. Rudy Maxa, formerly the gossip columnist for *The Washingtonian*, recalls browsing in the lingerie at Victoria's Secret in the Georgetown Mall in 1990 and coming upon Wilson holding up a lacy pair of panties and bra for the inspection of a stunning blonde. The woman turned out to be Yana Anastasia Lisitsina, a 24-year-old Soviet folk dancing

Robert Torricelli, his ex-amour Bianca Jagger, real estate exec and publisher Mort Zuckerman and cartoonist Tom Toles: Explosion in a toy factory.
(Vivian Ronay/Photoreporters)

instructor Wilson had met during a trip to Moscow and brought back to the US at his expense. Since Wilson was a member of the Intelligence Committee, Maxa asked if his friendship with Lisitsina had caused any concern. Wilson nervously assured him that his companion's main activity was shopping, and that if Lisitsina was a spy "the Soviets must be absolutely convinced our strategic command center is under Pentagon City", a suburban Washington mall.

The New Jersey Democrat Rep. Robert Torricelli, who broke up with Bianca Jagger in mid-1995, is a man whose extracurricular activities are a frequent topic of conversation in the halls of Congress. One amusing case came in 1990, when Russell Berrie, a multimillionaire New Jersey toy manufacturer, filed for divorce from his wife, Uni, on the grounds that she had had affairs with three men, including Torricelli. The congressman denied the charge, saying that Russell Berrie was simply angry because Torricelli had introduced Mrs. Berrie to her divorce lawyer.

Torricelli's colleagues in Congress tell a different tale. According to one account, Russell Berrie arrived home unexpectedly one day, and found the congressman in bed with his wife. Hot words ensued. Upon his return to the capital, Torricelli set upon legislation aimed at Berrie's business, but House colleagues finally dissuaded him.

As so often happens, those portraying themselves as crusaders for moral values and the Christian Way exhibit the same behavior in private as their more liberal counterparts. Consider Rep. Ken Calvert of California, a stern crusader for heightened morality on the part of the people, especially the licentious welfare moms whose benefits he favors cutting.

In the small hours of November 28, 1993, Officer Jeffrey Bennett of the Corona, California, police force spotted a man, apparently sleeping or unconscious, sitting in the driver's seat of a parked Ford Taurus. After illuminating the Taurus's interior with his flashlight, Bennett, as he later wrote in a police report, saw a woman, whose "head was originally laying on the driver's lap", suddenly sit upright in the passenger seat.

Both of the car's occupants were in a state of disarray. The woman, soon identified as Lore Lindberg, a local prostitute, was clad in a pair of unzipped shorts. Calvert was more formally dressed, but his trousers were in the same state, a condition he sought to conceal with his dress shirt. He started his car and tried to flee the scene, but finally surrendered after Bennett, for the third time, ordered the congressman to turn off the engine.

Calvert claimed that he didn't know Lindberg was a prostitute and that their acquaintance began when she flagged him down in his car as he innocently cruised downtown. Lindberg's account was that the two had met in a bar and that Calvert had offered her a ride home.

Corona law enforcement authorities did everything possible to shield Calvert. The police not only failed to charge Calvert, claiming that there was insufficient evidence to make an arrest, but also declined to make the matter public. It was only in April of 1994, after the local *Press-Enterprise* sued the city to gain access to relevant records, that the Calvert-Lindberg affair became known. Despite his lapse from the family values crusade, California voters re-elected Calvert to a second term in Congress in November of 1994. Lindberg soon returned to anonymity.

Newt Gingrich, although he expresses devotion to family values, has been a poor advertisement for the married state. Back in the early Eighties he abandoned his wife, then showed up at her hospital bed where she was recovering from a cancer operation and flourished a legal pad, dictating stinted terms of divorce.

In *Newt Gingrich: Speaker to America*, a 1995 book carefully ignored by the press, Judith Warner and Max Berley quote Gingrich's former driver, who recalled "dropping him off at a woman's house in the evenings and picking him up at a waffle house the next day". An ex-staffer told the authors that Gingrich's nocturnal activity was "a problem in the '74 [campaign], and it was a problem in '76 and a problem in '78". *Vanity Fair* reported on several women who claimed to have maintained liaisons with Gingrich back in the Seventies, including one who said Newt preferred oral sex because that allowed him to maintain that he had never slept with anyone other than his wife.

Even in 1995, however, Gingrich was widely reported to have indulged his penchant for philandering. He reportedly kept up a torrid romance with a Congressional staffer for the House Agriculture Committee, a 30-ish woman who cut a dashing figure next to the fleshy corpocrat and who had previously worked for a midwestern congressman who is a close ally of the House Speaker.

A few years ago, *The Wall Street Journal* compared lists of donors to Richard Nixon's infamous Committee to Re-Elect the President (CREEP) with contributors to George Bush's 1992 presidential campaign. The newspaper found dozens of overlaps.

• Publisher Walter Annenberg gave $304,000 to CREEP and $200,000 to the GOP between 1988 and 1992.

• Robert Anderson, Atlantic Richfield's chairman in 1972, donated $37,500 to the GOP in the early Seventies—including money run through the 1970 Operation Townhouse, an illegal scheme orchestrated out of a Dupont Circle townhouse in which Nixon staffers solicited huge, secret donations from CEOs. Between 1988 and 1992, Anderson's corporation gave $949,860 in soft money to the Republican Party.

• Dwayne Andreas of Archer-Daniels-Midland gave $25,000 to CREEP; between 1988 and 1992 he personally contributed $300,000 to the GOP and his corporation doled out $770,000 more.

• Max Fisher, the industrialist who worried about "confidentiality" back in 1972, became an honorary national chairman of the Bush campaign's finance committee. He donated $184,050 in soft money between 1988 and 1992.

• Robert Mosbacher, Commerce Secretary under George Bush, gave $24,675 to Nixon's campaign. He also funneled Operation Townhouse money to Bush's 1970 run for a Senate seat from Texas while he served as the head of Oilmen for Bush. (Mosbacher received the money from a Nixon aide in Washington, but signed a letter saying that the money had been raised in Texas.)

It's no wonder that poll after poll shows that roughly three-quarters of respondents believe that Congress cares more about special interests than about the average American. It also explains why huge numbers don't bother to vote. Only abut 20 per cent of the population voted for Republicans in the November 1994 mid-term elections, portrayed nonetheless as an avalanche.

There's been no dramatic shift to the right in American politics. People are cynical and don't vote. The core group of people who do tend to be more conservative. As Ellen Miller says, "Cynicism is the rational response. There aren't real choices."

THE LOBBYISTS

A lobbyist on the way to work, one of 80,000 in Babylon. (Library of Congress)

THE FOURTH BRANCH

The lobbyists massed in Washington are what Percy Bysshe Shelley called poets, the unacknowledged legislators of mankind. Overseeing the crossroads of power like the spirits of old necromancy, these lobbyists dispose the necessary traffic of money and favors.

Influence peddlers have long been a plague on the body politic. In *The Lobbyists*, Jeffrey Birnbaum reports that in 1852 future president James Buchanan wrote to future president Franklin Pierce that "the host of contractors, speculators, stockjobbers and lobby members which haunt the halls of Congress . . . are sufficient to alarm every friend of this country. Their progress must be arrested."

Today they swarm about the capital in ever pullulating numbers. Those able to pay rates of up to $350 per hour may choose among 80,000 such influence peddlers to ensure that their message is heard above the faint rattle of the common folk.

Massed most conspicuously in the office buildings that line the K Street corridor, these hired guns manufacture sympathy for their clients with the help of consulting firms, polling agencies, think tanks and other subsidiary sectors of the capital's opinion-forming industry. They pay academics to prepare "independent" reports which can be trumpeted in the press, hold luncheons where clients mingle with elected officials, even—as one lobbying firm did a few years back—have pizzas delivered to congressional staffers working late on an important bill.

A principal source of lobbyists' influence is the reliance members of Congress place upon them for campaign money, not only to pony up cash themselves, but also to bestir their friends and throw fundraisers. Members of Congress generally don't care to discuss this relationship. However, Martin Schram provided insight into the process in his 1995 report, "Speaking Freely", in which he interviewed dozens of ex-members of Congress about money and politics.

Former Senator Wyche Fowler, a Democrat from Georgia, was among those who spoke bluntly with Schram: "[I would] usually get a list of 30 lobbyists, [and start] calling them, asking them to be on my [fundraising] committee and raise me $5,000 or $10,000 by a specified date. And then when they call and say, 'Wyche, I'd like to talk to you about the agriculture bill or banking bill coming up next week', you say to yourself, 'Well, absolutely.' How can you not?"

Money even rules the ability to attend congressional hearings. Lobbyists now contract with DC firms—which have sprung up to meet demand—that pay people to stand in line and hold places for the influence peddlers. During the mid-1995 congressional debate on the telecommunications bill, a huge line of place-holders formed days in advance in front of the Rayburn House office building.

During the early days of the new Republican regime, lobbyists and corporate groups helped the GOP draft amendments and press for legislative approval of the Contract With America.

• Rep. John Boehner of Ohio held a series of strategy sessions with a group of lobbyists, including, according to *National Journal,* Nicholas Calio and Gary Andres, both of whom worked with George Bush's congressional liaison office; Michael Boland, a former aide to Senator Trent Lott, the majority whip; and James Miller, tax counsel for Bush's Treasury Department.

• A group of business organizations, including the National Association of Manufacturers and a group of chemical manufacturers, wanted to be sure that industry scientists would be allowed to review regulations that directly affect their companies. The GOP swiftly inserted into a regulatory review bill the suggested notion that federal agencies could "not exclude peer reviewers with substantial and relevant expertise merely because they represent entities that may have potential interest in the outcome".

• Three lawyers from Hunton & Williams helped Manus Cooney, staff director for the Senate Judiciary Committee, brief GOP aides on a bill—which they helped write—to strip away regulatory rules. Among Hunton & Williams's clients are more than a dozen firms, including tobacco companies, which had a vested interest in the bill's passage.

One measure of the success of corporate lobbyists, far and away the branch with the most influence in the capital, is the vast amount of corporate welfare money extracted each year by the nation's business sector. The $100 billion allocated for such programs in Fiscal Year 1994—sedately labeled "fiscal incentives" and "export-promotion measures" by business leaders—dwarfs the $75 billion spent during the same period for all social welfare programs. "Politicians are shy about discussing corporate welfare because it's the lubricant that makes this town run", Alex Benes, managing director of the Center for Public Integrity, says. "It's how the contributors to the two major parties cash in."

In real terms, benefits under Aid to Families With Dependent Children (AFDC), the biggest single welfare program and the one subject to most ferocious attack—have fallen by 50 per cent during the past two decades, a period during which the number of Americans living in poverty rose from 11.1 per cent of the population to 14.5 per cent. While welfare recipients—whose lobbyists are few and badly paid—eke out a living on an average of less than $500 in total monthly benefits, recipients of corporate welfare have become swollen with princely dispensations.

Major corporations reap handsome gain from the Market Promotion Program (MPP), which grants money to companies to advertise their products abroad. Past beneficiaries include such cash-strapped companies as Tyson Foods, Dole Fresh Food Co., M&M/Mars and McDonald's. The latter once received nearly half a million dollars to promote Chicken McNuggets.

Seeking to kill the Market Promotion Program in 1994, Wisconsin Senator Russell Feingold pointed to its grant of $3 million to the California Raisin Board. The money was used to produce television ads featuring singing and dancing raisins for broadcast in Japan. Since the merry raisins carolled in English, their message—that raisin consumption is an indicator of hipness—was lost on most Japanese consumers. Feingold's colleagues were in the main unmoved by tales of such boondoggles; only 36 senators joined him in voting to terminate the program, which retained its $90 million in funding.

Virtually every agency of the federal government ladles corporate welfare. The Agriculture Department, which provides $30 billion per year in farm subsidies alone, is the biggest single provisioner. From its coffers the tobacco industry receives a host of government subsidies—including one for research into improved production—worth $400 million annually. Not bad for a crop that kills nearly half a million people per year and adds $80 billion annually to the nation's health bill.

To protect its government handouts the tobacco industry retains a coterie of high-priced Washington lobbyists. The industry is a generous political contributor as well. Tobacco PACs donated more than $2 million to congressional candidates during the 1991-1992 election cycle.

Nearly all of Washington's top lobbyists formerly worked in government. For aspiring lawyers, public service is now merely a brief stop on the journey to a more lucrative career in the private sector. They come to Washington to work for a few years as general counsel to a federal agency, preferably the Internal Revenue Service, the Environmental Protection Agency or the United States Trade Representative. After punching the ticket, they sell themselves to law firms based on their expertise in negotiating the federal bureaucracy. About half of the congressional staffers who worked on the tax reform bill of 1986 went on to become corporate lobbyists.

In 1993, *Washingtonian* ranked the capital's most potent influence peddlers. The top ten included: Stuart Eisenstat, formerly Jimmy Carter's top domestic adviser; Tom Korologos and Bill Timmons of Timmons & Company, both of whom previously were employed in the Nixon White House; Patrick Griffin, a one-time Democratic aide in the Senate who later became Bill Clinton's congressional lobbyist; J.D. Williams, who came to Washington in 1959 as an aide to Oklahoma Senator Robert Kerr; Joel Jankowsky, who first worked in the capital as an aide to former House Speaker Carl Albert; and Lloyd Cutler, former adviser to both Clinton and Jimmy Carter.

Charles Lewis, Benes's colleague at the Center for Public Integrity, calls lobbyists "the investment bankers of the Nineties. There are a lot of young people who dream of becoming a lobbyist. They see it as a way of making a lot of money and being a part of the wheeler-dealer game."

Lewis believes that the ethical standards of lobbyists, never a group known for high moral purpose, have sunk even deeper dur-

6/14/95	$700.00	Jefferson Island Club Don Young of Alaska for Congress	Don Young
Thomas H. Boggs, Jr.			
1/24/95	$500.00	Friends of Senator Rockefeller	John D. Rockefeller
2/15/95	$1,000.00	Nadler for Congress	Jerrold Nadler
2/28/95	$1,000.00	Re-elect Senator Mark Hatfield	Mark O. Hatfield
2/28/95	$1,000.00	Dole for President	Bob Dole
3/2/95	$1,000.00	Friends of John Warner	John Warner
3/7/95	$1,000.00	John D. Dingell for Congress Committee	John D. Dingell
3/8/95	$500.00	Foglietta for Congress	Thomas M. Foglietta
3/21/95	$500.00	Ackerman for Congress	Gary L. Ackerman
3/28/95	$500.00	Louise Slaughter Re-election Committee	Louise Slaughter
3/28/95	$500.00	Billy Tauzin Committee	W.J. (Billy) Tauzin
3/28/95	$500.00	Ed Markey for Congress	Ed Markey
3/29/95	$1,000.00	Arlen Specter '96	Arlen Specter
4/4/95	$500.00	Martin Frost Campaign	Martin Frost
4/5/95	$500.00	Greg Laughlin Campaign	Greg Laughlin
4/27/95	$500.00	Friends of Chris Dodd	Christopher J. Dodd
5/2/95	$1,000.00	The Kerry Committee	John F. Kerry
5/31/95	$1,000.00	Robb for Senate	Charles S. Robb

98600

Tommy Boggs: One of Babylon's top lobbyists. Also a partial record of his firm's political donations for 1995; a dollar here, a dollar there and it adds up to a lot of calling cards. Direct contributions from lobbyists rival the dispensations of rich individuals and political action committees for campaign funding. During the 1991-92 election cycle, lawyers and lobbyists shelled out $44 million, second only to the $71 million from Finance, Insurance and Real Estate. Defense contractors trailed far behind, with a relatively measly $8 million. Between mid-1994 and mid-1995, Patton, Boggs & Blow made political contributions—at the federal, state, city and even county board level—of $70,050.25. Boggs himself tossed in $20,650. (Library of Congress)

ing recent years. "The number of people practicing the trade, the amount of money they make, and their garishness and audacity have all increased", Lewis says. "Some of the things that lobbyists do today—and which they brag about—would have been considered humiliating if exposed twenty years ago."

Some lobbyists are as fixed in their eminence as any Supreme Court Justice. There's Tommy Boggs, of the law firm Patton, Boggs & Blow, generally seen as the capital's most influential lobbyist. He is one of Washington's top political fundraisers, hosting frequent affairs for members of Congress, as well as personally donating huge sums of money to favored politicians. Individual members of Patton, Boggs contributed nearly $100,000 to members of Congress during the first 19 months of the Clinton administration, of which nearly one-quarter came from Boggs himself.

In 1992 *National Journal* did a very critical piece about Tommy Boggs and his law firm. The article said Patton, Boggs & Blow was viewed as "an icon of Washington's mercenary culture", and quoted a critic as saying that "the highest compliment inside Patton, Boggs that one attorney can pay another is that he or she will do anything for money". On *National Journal*'s cover, Boggs posed under the headline, "Ready to cash in on Clinton".

Boggs put a copy of the *National Journal* story on the wall of his office. He saw it as the sort of thing that would bring his firm more business.

Boggs's firm is said to have some 1,500 clients, selected, Boggs once explained—in a fine display of the high moral purpose of his trade—on the basis of "taking the first one who walks in the door".

The prospects of Boggs, a Democrat, soared with Bill Clinton's election. More than a dozen firm lawyers had worked on the man from Hope's campaign, and Ron Brown, a firm partner, became head of the Clinton Commerce Department. Even the downfall of Stephen Sharp—a Patton, Boggs lawyer and former Reagan appointee to the Federal Communications Commission, with backing from the Reverend Jerry Falwell—who was convicted in late 1992 for sodomizing a 12-year-old boy, couldn't dampen the firm's hopes for the Clinton years.

Indeed, the early days of the Clinton regime proved to be highly profitable for Patton, Boggs. The American Bankers Association enlisted Boggs to help push for the repeal of the Glass-Steagall Act, which would allow banks to enter securities markets in full force.

Numerous drug and insurance companies with health-care interests hired the firm. Boggs himself lobbied for the National Association of Life Insurance Underwriters and the Association of Trial Lawyers, the first of which was a leading supporter of a bill to limit legal fees in malpractice suits and the latter of which was that provision's most ardent foe. Things took a turn for the worse for Boggs when the Republicans took control of Congress. Rep. Thomas Bliley Jr., incoming chairman of the House Commerce Committee, reportedly refused to speak to Boggs because of the latter's affiliation with the Democrats.

However, Boggs had prepared for the eventuality of a Republican Congress. Back in September of 1994, when the GOP's prospects were rising, he bought a table at a Gingrich fund-raiser. His firm will no doubt prosper in the years ahead, regardless of who controls Congress and the Executive branch.

Another leading lobbyist is Charls Walker, deputy treasury secretary under Nixon (having previously been chief lobbyist for the Bankers Association) and a man whose life-long mission has been to reduce corporate taxes.

As soon as he left the Nixon administration, Walker began promoting the need for "capital formation". As Birnbaum wrote in *The Lobbyists,* Walker "preached the need for government to create incentives for 'savings and investment'. The rhetoric had all the political sanctity of motherhood, and cleverly masked the deeper intention: to channel more government aid to corporations. Capital formation had its heyday in 1981, when tax write-offs for plant and equipment purchases grew more generous and corporate taxes were dramatically reduced."

Walker's health has declined, but he still is one of corporate America's chief allies. His passion in recent years has been seeking to reduce the tax on capital gains and to introduce a national sales tax (the Value Added Tax, or VAT), which would further shift the tax burden onto consumers and away from business.

Another name that springs to mind is that of legendary fixer Robert Strauss. The ultimate Washington insider, Strauss has served

Robert Strauss: A finger in every pie. (AP/Wide World)

as chairman of the Democratic National Committee, as re-election campaign chairman for Jimmy Carter and as special trade representative under the Georgia peanut farmer. Strauss has also worked for Republican administrations, serving on a presidential commission on Central America formed by Ronald Reagan and as US ambassador to Russia, a post to which George Bush appointed him and which he held from 1991 to late 1992.

After returning from Russia, Strauss rejoined the Washington office of his old firm of Akin, Gump, Strauss, Hauer & Feld. Revelers at Strauss's birthday a few years back sang a tune which illustrates the law firm's self-assurance: "We keep all well-heeled oil men out of trouble, protect each cattle baron's precious rump, recession times we only charge you double, at Akin, Gump."

The country's 19th largest law firm, Akin, Gump's prestige soared to new heights during the first half of the Clinton reign. Among its dozens of clients, many of whom signed up after Clinton took office, have been AT&T, American Airlines, Upjohn, Loral Corp., Westinghouse, Warner-Lambert, Bechtel, Pfizer, Bank of America and several major insurance firms and associations.

Toiling alongside Strauss are Joel Jankowsky, known as the "Wizard of Oz" on Capitol Hill because of his behind-the-curtain role in many deals, and Donald Alexander, a former Internal Revenue Service commissioner and the firm's tax specialist.

Also at the firm is Vernon Jordan, who, even more than Strauss, is Akin, Gump's chief rainmaker. A 1993 article in *Business and Society Review* found that Jordan sat on the board of 10 major firms— American Express, Bankers Trust New York, Corning, Dow Jones, J.C. Penney, RJR Nabisco, Ryder Systems, Sara Lee, Union Carbide and Xerox—of which eight retain his law firm.

Jordan, a friend of the president, who took a leave of absence to serve as chairman of the Clinton-Gore transition team, exerted enormous influence over the selection of presidential appointees.

Strauss also recommended many names, including that of Robert Rubin, first head of the National Economic Council and later of the Treasury Department. In 1991 Strauss rented out the "F Street Club" and hosted a party to introduce Rubin—then a Wall Street superstar owing to his exploits as vice chairman of Goldman, Sachs, but mostly unknown in the capital—to Washington's elite. Among the guests were Pamela Harriman, Katharine Graham, Senator Bill Bradley and other leading capital socialites.

Five Akin, Gump lawyers took jobs in the Clinton administration while seven lawyers now with the firm formerly worked in the federal government or for Congress.

Akin, Gump's influence in the capital is enhanced by its political action committee, the legal industry's most profligate. The firm donated $30,000 to the Democratic National Committee during the first half of 1993 alone; Akin, Gump's PAC, its employees and employees' spouses gave nearly $500,000 to congressional candidates during the 1991-92 election cycle.

Needless to say, Akin, Gump clients have excellent access. In late

Vernon Jordan: An eye on every ball. (Library of Congress)

1993, *The Wall Street Journal* ran a list of 80 business executives who have lunched with the president during the early months of his tenure. At least a dozen had close ties to the law firm, including clients such as John Bryan of Sara Lee, Gerald Levin of Time Warner and Dwayne Andreas, head of the agribusiness giant Archer-Daniels-Midland, who in October of 1993 flew to Washington from Illinois to host Strauss's 75th birthday party.

Akin, Gump–linked firms get special attention from the administration when dark clouds loom on the horizon. John Bryson of the SEC Corp, a firm client, asked the administration for help in obtaining $150 million from Mexico after it pulled out of an energy project in that country. The Commerce Department was soon on the case and Bryson's money was returned, with interest. American Express—one of the corporations on whose board Jordan sits—scored big in winning the federal government's credit card contract away from Diners Club.

The clearest example of Akin, Gump's influence came with its role in promoting US investment in and trade with Russia. The key here was Strauss, who served as ambassador in Moscow and established a rapport with President Boris Yeltsin, whom he reverently described as "one of the three or four greatest men of this century".

To expand ties to Moscow, Strauss set up the US-Russia Business Council (USRBC), whose 38-member board of directors is stuffed with CEOs from clients of Akin, Gump and/or friends of Strauss. In the fall of 1993, the Council used a $250,000 State Department grant to organize a four-day trade fair in Moscow, which Strauss attended. Further assistance for the Council has come from the Commerce Department, which appropriated millions of dollars to establish "business centers" in Russia to help US companies set up operations.

In late March of 1994 Ron Brown traveled to Russia with 28 US business officials and duly announced hundreds of millions of dollars worth of deals. Four of the participants were from firms that are Akin, Gump clients (Westinghouse, AT&T, Enron, Dresser Industries), two were from firms on Strauss's board at the USRBC (Litton Industries, General Electric) and two were from firms Strauss has lobbied for in the past (Rockwell International, Bristol-Myers Squibb).

Such coincidences don't stop there. During the trip, the Overseas Private Investment Council (OPIC), which provides financing and project insurance to promote US exports, announced a $125 million loan guarantee—then the largest in its history—to back a telecommunications project between US West and Russia. OPIC is headed by Ruth Harkin, wife of Iowa Senator Tom Harkin and until recently a top corporate lawyer for Akin, Gump.

Another government agency actively promoting business with Moscow is the Export-Import Bank (Ex-Im), whose vice-chairman under George Bush, Eugene Lawson, is president of the USRBC's

Ruth Harkin, Vernon Jordan and Senator Tom Harkin: The ties that bind.
(Brian Palmer/Impact Visuals)

board of directors. The agency's current president, Kenneth Brody, is an old acquaintance of Strauss from the days when he worked with Robert Rubin at Goldman, Sachs. Brody calls Russia a priority for the Ex-Im, and has said he will "look under every rock" to find money for deals with the country.

In 1993, the Ex-Im negotiated an Oil and Gas Framework Agreement which will finance Russia's purchase of $2 billion in US oil, gas and petrochemical equipment. Since Moscow is a bad credit risk, a special arrangement was made whereby Russian companies were to service the debt with proceeds from oil and gas sales, which were to be deposited in an off-shore escrow account.

A chief beneficiary of the Framework accord could be Dresser Industries, a Dallas-based oil equipment firm which does business with Akin, Gump and which is negotiating a multi-billion dollar deal with Moscow. Company CEO John Murphy, an old Strauss buddy who sits on the board of the USRBC, was one of the lucky few chosen to make the Moscow trip. Murphy, incidentally, is at the same time a member of the Export-Import Bank's advisory committee.

Another corporate participant on the trip was Westinghouse, an Akin, Gump client and board member of the USRBC which signed three deals with public utilities and government agencies while in Russia. "The agreements could give Westinghouse a leg up on its competitors in the region by linking its fortunes with the country's nuclear and electric power businesses", a report in *The Energy Daily* said at the time. "Despite its enormous troubles, [Moscow] could offer Westinghouse fabulous opportunities."

In recent years, "corporate grassroots lobbying" has emerged as an especially fast-growing field. Practitioners use phone banks, letter-writing campaigns and other grassroots tools on behalf of their corporate clients. *Campaign and Elections* magazine reported in mid-1995 that some $790 million was spent on grassroots lobbying during the two previous years, a jump of 70 per cent.

A one-time legislative aide and press secretary to the late Senator John Heinz of Pennsylvania, Jack Bonner is one of the capital's most deft practitioners of grassroots lobbying for corporations. Bonner's firm, Bonner & Associates, opened for business in 1984. Gross billings soared to $7 million within three years, and continue to grow steadily. His clients have included tobacco companies, drug manufacturers and bankers.

Bonner's forte is prodding "white hats"—people with no apparent ties to business groups, preferably respected community figures such as religious leaders—to promote his clients' legislative priorities. Bonner charges up to $9,000 to arrange a personal visit between a "white hat" and a member of Congress. He says that "some guy in a pinstripe suit telling a senator this bill is going to hurt Pennsylvania doesn't have the impact of someone in Pennsylvania saying it."

In 1990, auto makers hired Bonner to oppose an amendment which required the Big Three to build smaller, more fuel-efficient cars. Who, pondered Bonner, could possibly oppose this seemingly unobjectionable measure? The answer: the elderly and the physically handicapped, who have a hard time getting into smaller cars with walkers, wheelchairs and other special equipment.

Bonner arranged a DC press conference, and flew in the head of the South Dakota Easter Seals and an official from a Florida seniors group, both of whom blasted the proposal as an attack on the afflicted. He also recruited the Boy Scouts to the cause, with group leaders endorsing Bonner's position that small cars crumple in crashes and pose a menace to tots everywhere. Scout opposition proved to be the *coup de grace*. The amendment soon died in committee.

Another triumph came the following year, when Bonner helped the American Bankers Association defeat an amendment which would have lowered the astronomical interest rates credit card companies charge. The measure, which passed the Senate with only 14 dissenting votes, appeared headed for sure victory in the House.

Hired at the last minute, Bonner & Associates manufactured a popular revolt against the amendment, arguing—without a shred of evidence—that lowering interest rates would squeeze card issuers, thus causing millions of Americans to lose their Visa and Master Cards, thus decimating the small business sector. The campaign generated some 12,000 phone calls to Congress, which proved crucial in killing the legislation.

Bonner, who was reportedly paid $400,000 by the bankers for his efforts, received an ebullient "thank you" letter from the group's executive vice president, Donald Ogilvie:

"Dear Jack,

"As you say in your ads: 'We help you win.' Well, speaking for the banking industry, you helped us win a big one. It was hard in several days to gain support for an issue that at first blush looked like a good idea to most people. After all, paying less interest on your credit cards sounds great. Nevertheless, Bonner & Assoc. achieved all of our goals.

"Jack, rest assured that the next time the banking industry has a lot on the line with a tough political fight, we'll want Bonner & Associates in there helping us win again."

Grassroots lobbyists are increasingly active outside the capital as well. Addressing a 1994 conference, "Shaping Public Opinion: If You Don't Do It, Somebody Else Will", PR executive Pamela Whitney said that when operating at the community level, she hires local "ambassadors". An ideal candidate would be a woman who had been the head of the PTA.

According to an account in *PR Watch*, Whitney claimed that her outfit could parachute into a community and within two weeks "have an organization set up and ready to go". The key to success, said Whitney, is looking local: "It's important not to look like a Washington lobbyist. When I go to a zoning board meeting I wear absolutely no make-up, I comb my hair straight back in a ponytail, and I wear my kids' old clothes."

Grandma: Public Enemy No. 1 for the corporate world. Here's an advertisement run by the lobbying firm of Davies Communications, which specializes in mounting "grassroots" campaigns for its business clientele.

Speaking to the same conference was John Davies of Davies Communications. His firm's literature claims that it "can make a strategically planned program look like a spontaneous explosion of community support".

Dozens of lobbying firms and business groups emulate and enhance the grassroots techniques of Bonner and other pioneers. Philip Morris and Burson-Marsteller cooked up the National Smokers Alliance, an "independent" pro-tobacco lobby. The corporation provided the Alliance with seed money and lists of smokers whom organizers could recruit to their cause.

The American Bankers Association, fearful that its traditional preprinted mass mailings are easy to spot and hence ineffective, now sends member banks computer disks which let PR department employees mix-and-match paragraphs to form "personal" letters that can be sent on company or individual stationery.

Davies's firm is equally expert at the letter-writing business. He explained at the "Shaping Public Opinion" conference how his tele-marketers produce "personal" letters from real folks: "We want to assist them with letter writing. We get them on the phone, and while we're on the phone we say, 'Will you write a letter?' 'Sure.' 'Do you have the time to write it?' 'Not really.' 'Could we write the letter for you? I could put you on the phone right now with someone who could help you write a letter. Just hold, we have a writer standing by.' [After another Davies employee takes down the letter] We hand-write it out on 'little kitty cat stationery' if it's an old lady. If it's a business we take it over to be photocopied on someone's letterhead. [We] use different stamps, different envelopes. . . . Getting a pile of personalized letters that have a different look to them is what you want to strive for."

"Grassroots" lobbying techniques played a role in killing off health care reform, as specialists created a swell of support to pro-tect insurance companies, pharmaceutical manufacturers and other defenders of the status quo.

At the forefront of the anti-reform effort was the Health Insurers Association of America (HIAA), creators of the aforementioned Harry and Louise TV ads. Made up of 270 insurance companies, the HIAA produced a kit for organizers which includes a "Model Campaign Plan For District Activity", a list of "message points" to

name/company	A / I	90 receipt	·90 expend	91 receipt	91 expend	Organization
McBride, Robert H.	I	0	0	0	0	
Reid & Priest	I	0	0	0	0	·
James Stanton & Assoc.	A	0	0	0	0	·
Winburn, John P.	I	36,000.00	0	270,000	0	tax reform leg HR 3299, 3035
Gold & Liebengood, Inc.	A	125,000	8,350	133,750	9,473	-tb labelling -excise tax -ad restrict.
McAuliffe Kelly & Raffaelli	I	6,000	0	0	0	term. 4/91 -int revenue code
Bergner, Boyette & Bockorny, Inc.	A	0	0	4,000	1,308.35	-reg 7/91 -indoor air leg. in cong.
APCO Associates	A	250	0	0	0	term 10/91 -consumer prod industry leg
Baker, Worthington, Crossley Stansberry & Woolf	I	17,659.50	91.37	3,482.50	89.96	
Bliss, Richard W.	I	3,525	506.01	0	0	term 1/91 -tb advrtising
Knorr, Gene A	I	0	0	0	0	term before 89
Boland, James E.	A	0	0	17,833	1744.01	New York employees:
Dyer, James W.	I	11,175	5,325	0	0	-term 1/91
Greenberg, David I.	I	10,000	4,500	43,500	10,100	-term 1/92
Linehan, Kathleen M.	A	3,937	467.75	11,264	1,062.10	
Maples, Robert Y.	A	2,523.15	644.27	2,051.52	480.39	
Millman, Amy J.	I	2,400	2,825	600	900	-term 7/91
Nicoli, David P.	A	0	0	1,375	0	-reg 10/91
Reese, Robert S., Jr.	A	5,550	3,702.19	12,900	1,909.37	
Scott, Gregory R.	A	2,800.83	997.32	3,963.75	937.11	
Wunder, Diefenderfer, Ryan Cannon & Thelen	A	14,414.29	16,720.55	4,622	326	tax, pension & advertising
Anderson, Fred E.	I	6,000	4,873.53	0	0	term 1/91 -tax legis.
Arnold & Porter	A	1,317.50	.71	8,885	78.24	
Austin, Robb	I	21,600	2,666.16	0	0	-term 1/91
Dave Barrows & Associates	I	4,800	4,008.01	0	0	-term 1/91
Blake, Roy *GT*	A	36,000	2,873.26	12,000	1,765.43	
Bottenberg, John C.	A	15,000	1,935.13	10,833.34	2,001.47	
Clayton, Bill (Capital Consultants) *GT*	I	45,399.99	0	0	0	excise tax leg

Internal Philip Morris document shows partial listing of the nearly 70 firms which lobby for the company. In addition, Philip Morris funds a variety of "independent" front groups and think-tanks to do its bidding. Among the former is the National Smokers' Alliance, which the p.r. firm Burson-Marsteller created with Philip Morris money, and the Oakland-based Independent Institute, which uses tobacco money to crank out studies opposing cigarette taxes. Among the latter: the Washington Legal Foundation, now at the forefront of attack on the FDA's proposed smoking rules. The Foundation's former president, Alan Slobodin, serves as staff counsel to Rep. Tom Bliley, head of the House Commerce Committee and Philip Morris's best friend in Congress.

Carol Tucker Foreman: By day a caped crusader in the consumers' cause; by night (and by day, too, for that matter) a lobbyist for Monsanto and Procter & Gamble. "It puts me in a grey area", she concedes. Like when day is changing into night. (AP/Wide World)

rebut arguments for reform and a sample speech for company execs.

The latter, "Health Insurance: You Can Get It, Keep It and Take It With You," begins:

"Good morning. I am Sidney Garfield, Chief Executive of Provincial Life Insurance. I'm happy to see you all here today. I want to start by saying that I'm not here merely as an insurance company executive nor even as a businessman. I'm here as an American, and I'm also here representing my own family, all of whose members need health care and health-care coverage. My kids get ear aches and they go for their check-ups and immunizations; my wife and I have had our modest share of medical problems; and my parents are senior citizens, with their own special needs. I'm starting by mentioning my family because, when it comes to health care, the old cliché is really true: we are all in this together."

Congress passed a lobbying "reform" bill in 1995, but Republicans exempted disclosure requirements for grassroots lobbyists—who push legislation but don't personally meet with lawmakers—saying such restrictions would stifle free speech. So most citizens still don't know when, and which, private interests are manipulating public debate.

Just as phony as these grassroots "activists" are the many Washington lobbyists who boast publicly about their commitment to consumer causes while they quietly champion the corporate agenda. Consider the case of Carol Tucker Foreman. By day she bustles through the corridors of Washington, lobbying on behalf of the outfit she founded, the Safe Food Coalition. A former assistant secretary of agriculture in the Carter era, she's a familiar sight at congressional hearings, agitating for tougher standards on inspection of meat, poultry and fish products.

But Foreman also discreetly lobbies for Monsanto, the St. Louis-based chemical giant, and Procter & Gamble. She also heads a public policy consulting firm, Foreman and Heidepriem, whose clients include Aetna Life and Casualty—commonly regarded as the mad dog of the insurance pack—and Emily's List, the PAC that puts up money for Democratic women candidates.

The Center for Responsive Politics identified Emily's List as the second largest "ideological/single-issue" contributor in 1992, sandwiched between the National Rifle Association and the National Committee to Preserve Social Security. In 1992 Emily's List unbuckled $6 million.

Foreman has been on the boards of public interest groups, sitting cheek by jowl with some of the most notorious influence peddlers in the capital: at Public Interest with Agriculture Undersecretary Ellen Haas and, until his death, Commerce Secretary Ron Brown; at the Center for Public Policy with Anne Wexler; at the Food Research and Action Center with former Agriculture Secretary Mike Espy and David I. Greenberg of Philip Morris.

With such connections Foreman is a heavy-hitter in Democratic Party fundraising circles. Her brother, Jim Guy Tucker, was lieutenant governor of Arkansas and graduated to the governor's mansion in Little Rock when Clinton went to Washington. Tucker came under a Whitewater-related cloud, in the form of inflated property estimates used to support loans to him from Madison Guaranty Savings and Loan.

One of the press releases issued by Foreman's Safe Food Coalition back in 1993 praised then-Agriculture Secretary Espy's untiring efforts to "overcome the combined effects of inertia, ineptitude and industry influence that permeate Food Safety and

Inspection Service". In due course it turned out that inertia and industry influence were high on Espy's personal list of priorities as Agriculture Secretary, as symbolized in his friendly relations with Tyson Foods, the poultry behemoth of Arkansas.

Foreman's client Monsanto markets the milk-inducing cow drug, recombinant bovine growth hormone (BGH). For some food safety groups BGH is as prime an enemy as cancer-causing pesticides, of which Monsanto is also a leading producer.

Foreman herself won't disclose her hefty retainer from Monsanto. She concedes that "it puts me in a grey area" but says that her relationship with Monsanto "has never been a secret". When her links to the company were revealed in 1994, representatives from at least two members of the Safe Food Coalition—the Consumer Federation of America and the American Association of Retired Persons—said that Foreman's lobbying for Monsanto was news to them.

Grassroots activists for clean food have reported how Foreman uses her status as coordinator of the Safe Food Coalition to inveigle these activists to Monsanto HQ in St. Louis, where they are wined, dined and treated to rapturous disquisitions on the merits of bovine growth hormone by Dr. Virginia Weldon, Monsanto's main PR flack for BGH and named by President Clinton to his Committee of Advisers on Science.

Foreman also lobbies for Procter & Gamble. There her allotted cause is a fat substitute, olestra. The FDA had been reviewing olestra since the mid-1980s. Approved, it meant billions for the company.

As with Monsanto, Foreman's standing as a crusading consumer champion has served her corporate client well. She arranged for activists to attend luncheons P&G held around the country, where well-known chefs whipped up meals cooked with olestra. Dieticians and nutritionists were also on hand to promote the virtues of the product. Prior to FDA approval, participants at these banquets had to sign a statement which frees P&G of liability in the event of any untoward reaction.

Foreign lobbying has been one of the industry's more lucrative sectors, in great part because Third World tyrants spent enormous sums of money in the hopes that a well-coordinated PR campaign will win them favorable media coverage and friends in

Congress. Both of these commodities are vital to the ultimate goal of generating copious flows of American foreign aid.

Foreign lobbyists themselves have perhaps the basest ethical standards of their tribe. Burson-Marsteller signed a deal to lobby for the generals in Argentina in 1977, this being the height of the so-called "dirty war" during which the junta was busy slaughtering 10,000 men and women it accused of "subversion". This was also the period, it turns out, when the military was drugging prisoners and throwing them into the ocean from military planes (also roughly the same time that David Rockefeller was visiting Argentina to congratulate the generals on their commitment to free-market ideology).

The killers paid Burson-Marsteller to combat a "well-financed subversion campaign of international origin", in the words of one of the firm's strategy papers, and to "use the best professional communications skills to transmit those aspects of Argentine events showing that the terrorist problem is being handled in a firm and just manner, with equal justice for all."

Today the world of foreign lobbying is ever more cutthroat. If Hitler were alive, Washington PR firms would battle to gain the right to work with Goebbels in buffing the Nazi image.

The fight to win clients has grown especially fierce because the US has greatly reduced foreign aid with the end of the Cold War. As a result, many countries have given up on hiring lobbyists, since even with a successful PR campaign there is no realistic hope of hitting pay dirt.

Most countries have a harder time winning US aid, and must rely to a greater degree on hired guns. Of course, some countries, by dint of special circumstances, have no trouble extracting vast sums of foreign aid. Even as foreign aid falls off to most of the rest of the world, Israel still manages to pull down some $4 billion in U.S. taxpayers' money annually. The country's willingness to serve as a US agent in the oil-rich Middle East makes Israel an invaluable ally to American governments. Back in the 1960s, Egypt's President Gamal Nasser was high on Washington's enemies list for his role in encouraging Arab nationalism, which was seen as a threat to "stability" in Saudi Arabia and other big oil producers in the region. Israel's smashing of Nasser in the 1967 Six-Day War was rewarded with a significant increase of US aid.

In 1970, when Jordan brutally put down a Palestinian movement in what became known as "Black September", the US feared that Syria might intervene in the conflict. This came at the height of domestic opposition to US involvement in Vietnam and President Nixon didn't dare use American force to counter the Syrians. In a move that was coordinated with Washington, Israel mobilized its armed forces as a warning to the Syrians, who promptly backed off. This move cemented Israel's relationship with the US, and aid levels more than quadrupled very swiftly. More recently, Israel has served as a US surrogate in South Africa and Latin America, most notably in regard to the latter with its training of proxy forces.

Further solidifying ties are the large political donations made by pro-Israel PACs, especially to the Democrats. There are roughly 70 such outfits, and during the 1991-92 election cycle they distributed nearly $4 million to political candidates.

The leaders of these outfits tend to be far more hawkish than Israelis themselves. In 1993, the vice president of the American Israel Public Affairs Committee (AIPAC), Harvey Friedman, was forced to resign after calling Israel's deputy foreign minister, Yossi Beilin, a "little slime ball". Friedman was responding to Beilin's suggestion that Israel should return land on the West Bank and Gaza Strip to the Palestinians.

Thomas Dine, AIPAC's head until 1993, was another extreme hard-liner. He, too, had to step down after making unpalatable remarks, describing some Orthodox Jews as "smelly" and "low class".

AIPAC's influence in terms of US Middle Eastern policy is extreme. Back in February of 1991, amid the Gulf War, Saudi Arabia requested that the US sell it 72 F-15E warplanes. Immense opposition to the sale immediately arose, coordinated by AIPAC. Faced with sure defeat—67 senators soon delivered a letter of opposition to the Saudi deal to Bush—the president backed off.

The deal finally went through the following year, but only after AIPAC acceded to the transaction. According to a report from the Project on Demilitarization and Democracy, many proponents of the deal, especially weapons manufacturers, "insist that [the campaign's] success was due primarily to its private side: an effort to gain Israeli acquiescence by promising Israel additional U.S. military technology, including its own F-15Es. Few political analysts would dispute a

Senate staffer's claim that 'only active opposition from Israel and the US Jewish community can block sales' to Arab nations."

According to the report, McDonnell Douglas, maker of the F-15E, hired Dov Zakheim, a former Pentagon official, to engage in a dialogue with Jewish groups to determine how to win their approval for the deal:

"Supporters of the sale worked energetically behind the scenes within the administration to win for Israel promises of new weapons and continued US government grants to pay for those weapons. Those promises were apparently made in late August, when Israeli Prime Minister Yitzhak Rabin publicly said he did not object to the sale. At that point AIPAC, which had been organizing against the sale with arms control groups, stopped its active opposition and signaled that it would not expect its congressional supporters to block the sale."

Much of what is written about the power of the Israeli lobby in Washington lurches towards paranoia. If the Jewish state had been founded in Timbuktu, as Republican congressman Hamilton Fish Sr. publicly recommended in the 1930s, we very much doubt that $4 billion a year would now be furnished to the young nation isolated in the oil-free Sahara.

All the same, it's fair to rate the lobby as one of the capital's most effective. In 1994, Avinoam Bar Yosef, a correspondent with the Hebrew language newspaper *Ma'ariv*, delightedly described the prominent position of American Jews at the highest levels of the US government, in an account which carried the excited headline of "The Jews Who Run Clinton's Court":

"Every morning at about 6:00 o'clock, several staff cars travel from the CIA center to the White House with senior officers of the American intelligence community, who are about to present to the president and to the four top staffers a PDB—President's Daily Briefing—the term for the most exclusive report in Washington. ...

"[Clinton will] hold a short discussion on the contents of the document with the five other addressees: Vice President Al Gore, National Security Adviser Anthony Lake, White House Chief of Staff Leon

Panetta, Deputy National Security Adviser Samuel ('Sandy') Berger, and National Security Adviser to the Vice-President, Leon Perth. Two of the addressees, Berger and Perth, are 'warm' Jews. They have reached posts that are extremely sensitive for US policies. They are by no means exceptions. In the National Security Council, 7 out of 11 top staffers are Jews. Clinton had especially placed them in the most sensitive functions in the US security and foreign administrations."

Even within the amoral world of Washington lobbying, Edward J. van Kloberg III stands out for handling clients that no one else will touch. In an unsuccessful effort to establish his ethical bottom line, *Spy* magazine in 1992 dreamed up the German People's Alliance. The group's fictitious representative, Sabina Hofer, telephoned van Kloberg to see if he'd be interested in promoting the Alliance's neo-Nazi agenda on Capitol Hill. Among the demands: banning immigration into Germany, increasing the alliance's voice in the US Congress to counter the pro-Jewish claque and reclaiming Poland.

Informed that the group had up to $1 million to spend, the lobbyist expressed keen interest in obtaining the contract. "I believe in many of the tenets that you believe in", van Kloberg purred to Hofer. "So we are not very far apart, my dear."

Van Kloberg's non-fictional clients have included dictators Saddam Hussein of Iraq, Mobutu Sese Seko of Zaire, Nicolae Ceausescu of Romania, and Samuel Doe of Liberia. Van Kloberg's well-remunerated exertions on behalf of the last two came to an abrupt end when they were murdered by their countrymen after long years of brutal rule.

Van Kloberg specializes in representing mid-level African tyrants. In the fall of 1990, he arranged the DC visit of Rwanda's then-President Juvenal Habyarimana. In a series of functions, including a posh reception at the Grand Hotel, van Kloberg touted the stern but wise leader's great popularity among the Rwandan masses. Unfortunately, the trip was cut short when a guerrilla army seeking to topple Habyarimana invaded Rwanda from neighboring Uganda.

With the war causing serious public relations difficulties, the Rwandan regime in late 1990 signed a new one-month deal with van Kloberg. For the sum of $11,000, the lobbyist was to help Ambassador

H.E. Aloys Uwimana "counterbalance any negative influence [that human rights groups] might exert on US policy".

Van Kloberg's contract also called for him to promote "measures undertaken by the Government of Rwanda in the areas of environmental conservation and wildlife management". America's adoration of Rwanda's threatened mountain gorillas made this an especially deft strategy, and one which helped extract US monies for Rwanda. That was the sole interest of President Habyarimana, whose own relatives were widely believed to be involved in the international trafficking of gorillas.

Van Kloberg also arranged a 1991 US tour for King Mswati III and a delegation of leaders from Swaziland, a corrupt regime which had close ties to leaders of South Africa's apartheid government. The group was given a "VIP tour of the Pentagon" and of the National Aquarium in Baltimore, visited Colt Industry's indoor shooting range in Hartford, then flew to the Martin Luther King Center in Atlanta, where Andrew Young offered a special viewing of *From Montgomery to Memphis.*

A former congressional staffer who worked on African affairs says that rarely was van Kloberg of great service to his clients. "He tries to be suave and debonair, but comes across as paternalistic and patronizing", she recalls. "His views on Africans were offensive and racist. I could never figure out why anyone would hire him."

Van Kloberg has also represented a number of Latin regimes, including El Salvador, Nicaragua, Haiti and Guatemala. The latter government is in perennial need of PR help thanks to Guatemala's awful human rights record and appalling social inequities. Since a CIA-organized coup in 1954 overthrew an elected, left-leaning government and set the stage for decades of rule by terror, the military has murdered 140,000 civilians. In an interview a few years ago in the *Harvard International Review*, former Defense Minister General Hector Gramajo described the army's counterinsurgency strategy as providing "development for 70 per cent of the population while we kill 30 per cent".

In January of 1995, the Foundation for the Development of Guatemala (FUNDESA)—a front group of ultra-conservative business leaders who work closely with their government—contracted van Kloberg to conduct a three-month public relations campaign on its behalf. FUNDESA was especially anxious for van Kloberg to "balance the PR campaign implemented by sympathizers" of Jennifer Harbury, the American woman who, shortly before the contract was signed, organized a hunger strike in Guatemala and in the US. She was seeking to pressure both governments to reveal what they knew about the murder of her husband, Efrain Bamaca Velasquez, a guer-

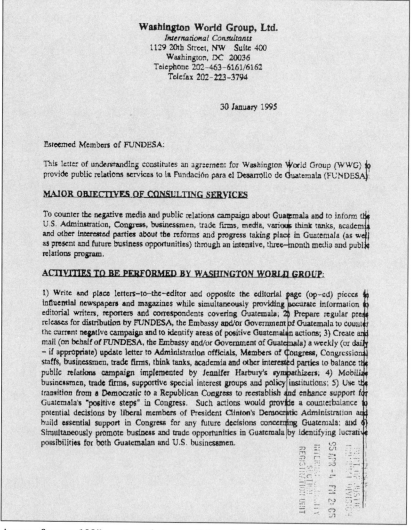

Washington World Group, Ltd.
International Consultants
1129 20th Street, NW Suite 400
Washington, DC 20036
Telephone 202-463-6161/6162
Telefax 202-223-3794

30 January 1995

Esteemed Members of FUNDESA:

This letter of understanding constitutes an agreement for Washington World Group (WWG) to provide public relations services to la Fundación para el Desarrollo de Guatemala (FUNDESA)

MAJOR OBJECTIVES OF CONSULTING SERVICES

To counter the negative media and public relations campaign about Guatemala and to inform the U.S. Administration, Congress, businessmen, trade firms, media, various think tanks, academia and other interested parties about the reforms and progress taking place in Guatemala (as well as present and future business opportunities) through an intensive, three-month media and public relations program.

ACTIVITIES TO BE PERFORMED BY WASHINGTON WORLD GROUP:

1) Write and place letters-to-the-editor and opposite the editorial page (op-ed) pieces in influential newspapers and magazines while simultaneously providing accurate information to editorial writers, reporters and correspondents covering Guatemala; 2) Prepare regular press releases for distribution by FUNDESA, the Embassy and/or Government of Guatemala to counter the current negative campaign and to identify areas of positive Guatemalan actions; 3) Create and mail (on behalf of FUNDESA, the Embassy and/or Government of Guatemala) a weekly (or daily – if appropriate) update letter to Administration officials, Members of Congress, Congressional staffs, businessmen, trade firms, think tanks, academia and other interested parties to balance the public relations campaign implemented by Jennifer Harbury's sympathizers; 4) Mobilize businessmen, trade firms, supportive special interest groups and policy institutions; 5) Use the transition from a Democratic to a Republican Congress to reestablish and enhance support for Guatemala's "positive steps" in Congress. Such actions would provide a counterbalance to potential decisions by liberal members of President Clinton's Democratic Administration and build essential support in Congress for any future decisions concerning Guatemala; and 6) Simultaneously promote business and trade opportunities in Guatemala by identifying lucrative possibilities for both Guatemalan and U.S. businessmen.

A page from a 1995 contract between Edward van Kloberg's Washington World Group and a right-wing business outfit in Guatemala. Van Kloberg netted $75,000 for his efforts to whitewash the human rights record of a government which during the past four decades has murdered 140,000 of its own citizens.

rilla fighter who disappeared in Guatemala in 1992.

Perhaps because blunter tools make "lobbying" in the Third World so persuasive—in Guatemala, for example, a traditional means of influencing press coverage has been bombing opposition newspapers and murdering troublesome journalists—some regimes overestimate the benefits of retaining a DC lobbyist. Van Kloberg's deal with FUNDESA was for $75,000. In return, his firm drafted and placed letters to the editor—signed by Guatemala's ambassador to the US, Edmond Mulet, describing supposed strides toward democracy taking place under the current government—in *The New York Times*, *The Miami Herald* and a few other newspapers. Van Kloberg's firm also produced *Guatemala News*, a three-page newsletter targeted to Congress, the press and business leaders. The publication informed readers that guerrilla groups battling the government had been committing heinous abuses "against the civilian population", by imposing road blocks, collecting "war taxes" from landowners, and by "attacks perpetrated against the electricity grid". *Guatemala News* somehow failed to mention that a few weeks prior to its April 1 publication date, a UN Verification Mission released a report on human rights in Guatemala which detailed 27 extrajudicial executions, eight attempted executions, 10 cases of torture and 72 death threats—all between December of 1994 and February of 1995. The UN concluded that the Guatemalan government "has not guaranteed people's right to safety and security, or to freedom from torture or cruel, inhumane or degrading treatment".

Unfortunately for van Kloberg and his client, the timing for a PR offensive was poor. In mid-March, in the middle of the contract, Rep. Robert Torricelli revealed to the press that Guatemalan soldiers on the CIA payroll had murdered Harbury's husband. Shortly thereafter it was also disclosed that the CIA's Guatemalan assets had been responsible for the 1990 murder of Michael DeVine, an American who ran an inn in the highlands and who apparently had discovered army units illegally logging mahogany. These disclosures produced a flood of denunciations in the American press—which had turned a benighted eye to the previous forty years of carnage.

Van Kloberg defends flacking for thugs by arguing that lawyers represent both guilty and innocent clients, and that he should not be held to a different standard. This contention is wholly specious.

The late Ron Brown: As lobbyist for Patton, Boggs he burnished death squad hirers in Guatemala, the Duvaliers in Haiti. (Shia photo/Impact Visuals)

Unlike suspected criminals, who are locked up pending trial, Van Kloberg's clients hold the reins of power in their nations and pay him to help ensure that they are never held accountable in a court of law.

In the capital, though, van Kloberg's shameful client list has in no way diminished his stature. The *Washingtonian* called him "one' of lobbying's true characters" in a flattering item in 1993, adding that "he maintains friendly relations with Washington's powerful, and his dinners for legislators and opinion-makers at the Jockey Club are legendary."

Over the years the image-fixers at Patton, Boggs & Blow have also tried a hand at buffing Guatemala's image, first in 1980, when General Romeo Lucas Garcia was in the middle of a four-year reign, presiding over the worst period of repression in the country's modern history. By its own count, during the first ten months of 1980 the Guatemalan army executed some 3,000 "subversives".

In the midst of this blood-letting Tommy Boggs signed up a new client, Amigos del Pais, or Friends of the Nation. The Amigos, once described as the "John Birch Society of Guatemala", were a group of landowners who financed death squads and maintained especially tight links to a group of ultra-rightist army officers who called themselves Officials of the Mountain. Robert White, ex-US ambassador to

El Salvador, says that the Amigos paid officers within Officials of the Mountain to carry out their economic program. "When it was necessary, troops would be sent out to break up strikes [affecting members of Amigos] and to weed out those who were deemed trouble-makers", White recalls.

While lethal suppression of labor unrest was the chief aim of the Amigos in Guatemala, the main external priority of the group was improvement in relations with the US, which had deteriorated during the Carter years. Though a Carter-era ban on arms shipments had not materially affected the flow of military aid from the Pentagon to the Guatemalan armed forces, Boggs lobbied with gusto for a public demonstration of forgiveness by the US government, most notably willingness to remit weaponry to the Lucas Garcia regime. Guatemala, Boggs argued, was a nation deserving of sympathy, particularly as it faced "economic, social and insurgent difficulties".

The Reagan regime, installed at the White House in 1981, received the message warmly, although Boggs's paying clients had already earned him the tag "lawyer of choice for Latin American dictators" from Larry Birns of the Council on Hemispheric Affairs. But the Guatemalans still faced problems in Congress, and Boggs, representing a prominent Democratic law firm, was of much use to the Amigos in this regard. He flew about Capitol Hill, meeting with Democratic members of Congress to urge that they ease up on the misundertood generals.

Patton, Boggs also worked for Guatemala in the early 1990s, after yet another terrible period of repression had sullied the nation's image. DeVine, the American innkeeper, was abducted by security forces on June 8, 1990. His corpse was found the following day, his head partially severed by a machete. On September 11, anthropologist Myrna Mack Chang, a supporter of indigenous groups, was stabbed to death as she left her office. On December 2, 13 people, including two children, were killed in Santiago Atitlan when soldiers opened fire on a group of Tzutujil Indians.

A month later Patton, Boggs's David Todd signed a $220,000 annual contract to represent President Jorge Serrano Elias, a civilian who was forced from office in 1993 after he sought to assume dictatorial powers. The contract said the law firm would "provide advice and general guidance about trade, aid and credit issues" and "undertake specific projects on matters involving credit for Guatemala from United States and international lending institutions".

During Serrano's period in office Americas Watch reported that "government forces continued to commit torture, murder and disappearances with impunity". Todd, however, was busy dispatching a steady stream of upbeat chatter about Guatemala to members of Congress and top staffers, lauding the "economic, social and human rights progress" under the Serrano government. On May 16, 1991, Todd distributed a "status report on Michael DeVine", offering the Guatemalan government's point of view on the death of the American innkeeper—an important piece of work for Todd's client, since anger over DeVine's death had led to a reduction in US aid to Guatemala.

Patton, Boggs had also signed a contract with the Sugar Growers of Guatemala, back in the early Eighties. That plum account was signed by Ron Brown.

The head of the Sugar Growers had family ties to the death squads. On the very day that Brown closed the deal—January 19, 1982—the Guatemalan Army "disappeared" religious worker Sergio Berten. On February 13, with Brown now eagerly advancing his client's cause in Washington, Brother James Miller, an American Christian lay worker, was shot to death by masked men as he worked with a group of indigenous students in Huehuetenango. In the four months after Brown began to work on the Sugar Growers' image, more than 2,000 people were killed in what Amnesty International termed "large scale extrajudicial assassinations".

Another client of Brown's during his tenure at Patton, Boggs was Haitian dictator Jean-Claude "Baby Doc" Duvalier. Brown insisted that while he had "apprehensions" about working for Duvalier's regime, he believed he could "do more good than harm". A nine-page memorandum which Brown sent to Baby Doc in 1983 belies this posture, detailing as it does the lobbyist's activities on the dictator's behalf. Not once does Brown refer to Duvalier's notorious human rights record. Instead, he blames *Monsieur le President*'s problems on the American press, which created an "unfair image" of the tyrant.

Here's Brown on Haiti: "We continue to dedicate a considerable amount of time to the improvement of relations between the Republic of Haiti and members of Congress and the American government, with the goal of substantially increasing American aid to Haiti." Early success in this regard, he crowed, "is essentially the result of our Washington team".

While working in Haiti, Brown developed a warm relationship

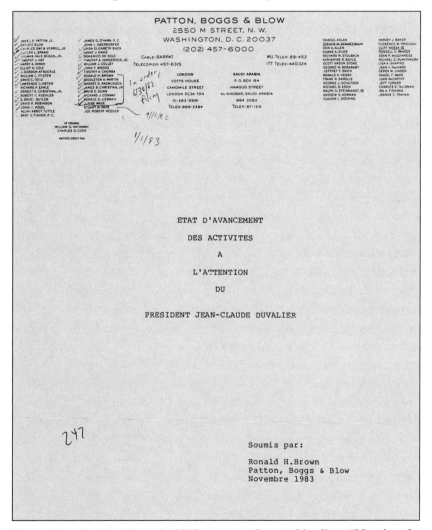

Cover sheet for Ron Brown's 1983 memorandum to his client "Monsieur le President" Jean-Claude Duvalier of Haiti. Brown was then a Beltway lobbyist and the memo, writtten in French, detailed all the marvelous activities he was performing on the bloodthirsty dictator's behalf, namely extracting as much US aid as possible for Duvalier to plunder.

with Lilliane Madsen, who worked as a receptionist at the US embassy in Port-au-Prince and had married into one of Haiti's wealthiest and most conservative families. Madsen traveled in the highest circles of Baby Doc's regime, and was especially close to Michele Bennett, Baby Doc's wife.

By 1993, Madsen was accompanying Brown to official functions, including an Air Show in Paris. She lived in a $360,000 Washington townhouse at 4303 Westover Place, which Brown and his son, DC lobbyist Michael Brown, bought in 1992.

Then there is the case of Herman Cohen, the Bush administration's assistant secretary of state for African affairs who now runs the Global Coalition for Africa, a World Bank-linked outfit which promotes austerity across the continent. Cohen also lobbies for some of Africa's cruelest tyrants.

In promoting himself to clients, Cohen describes himself as "a retired American ambassador who has devoted 30 years to diplomatic work in Africa. He has enormous contacts with the highest levels of government and private sector in Africa" and, in the US, has "rapid access to high officials who are concerned with African affairs". Cohen's perceived "access" is a major selling point to African regimes. In early 1995, Cohen signed a one-year contract with the government of Gabon. Cohen pledged to handle media relations, write a monthly press release and promotional brochure, and prepare a visit to Washington by President El Hadj Omar Bongo. His mission, the agreement said, was to present Gabon as a "politically stable and economically successful country", and to "generate awareness of President Bongo and his national and international accomplishments" including the "very concrete process of democratization and democratic reforms brought about under [his leadership]".

As the ink dried on Cohen's contract, the State Department released its annual report on human rights practices around the globe. According to Cohen's former colleagues at State, the government of Gabon was responsible "for many confirmed extrajudicial killings", and torture in President Bongo's homeland was routine: "Eyewitnesses reported seeing prisoners tied to chairs, doused with ice water, or made to crawl on their stomachs over gravel or sun-baked asphalt. There were other credible reports of security forces extracting confessions by beating the soles of prisoners' feet or by bending or twisting fingers."

As to the "very concrete process of democratization" that has taken place under Bongo, who has held power since 1967, the State Department report said that the December 1993 election in which Bongo triumphed with 51 per cent of the vote was "marred by serious irregularities, including a secret vote count that excluded all but government observers. In Bongo's home region of Haut Ogoue, the number of votes cast for Bongo was greater than the population reported in the 1993 census.

Not long after Cohen began his work for Gabon's supreme leader it was disclosed that some Parisian prostitutes were suing Bongo's tailor, who procured their services for the dictator without revealing that Bongo was widely rumored to be HIV-positive. Bongo paid up to $15,000 per night for his prostitutes. Cohen also charges stiff fees for his services. His contract calls for payments of $300,000.

Another firm which specializes in flacking for African tyrants is Washington & Christian, a black firm with close ties to the Democratic Party. From its work for Nigeria alone the company has made more than $5 million since 1993, when General Sani Abacha staged a coup to deny power to democratically elected Mosheed Abiola. Abacha systematically destroyed every democratic institution in the country.

Not long after Abiola was arrested Washington & Christian produced a report for journalists and members of Congress entitled "The Road to Democracy". This brazen document claimed that Abiola's "election was not 'free and fair' and did not reflect the will of the Nigerian people. Prior to the election, fraudulent acts occurred which could not have been apparent on the actual date of the election, and therefore not known to either the Nigerian election monitors who thought the elections were 'free and fair' based solely on their observations that day." This is curious, since the military announced it would not honor the vote almost as soon as it became apparent that Abiola had won. The report also stated that the Nigerian military "had not only the authority but the duty to annul the June 12, 1993 elections".

The Washington & Christian report concedes that arrests by the military have regrettably taken place, but quickly adds that most of

Henry the K: A nose in every pie, a finger in every nose. (Adriana Lorete)

those imprisoned had been involved in "activities designed to incite Nigerian citizens and create conflicts". In the same vein, the government has been forced to crush press freedom because "developments in the country necessitated certain actions in order to preserve the peace and maintain the stability of the country. The action taken against certain newspapers was taken not as a result of criticism of the Government, but as a result of the anti-state position taken by these newspapers."

A few months after this revolting piece of work, Robert Washington, a partner in the firm, sent out a letter to members of Congress describing dictator Abacha as a devoted democrat. Washington said that when all the facts were marshaled and carefully considered, he was "confident that you and the world will be convinced of the fact, as I am, that democracy will again thrive in Nigeria". He also promised to keep Congress posted on the status of Abiola, whose insistence that he had been rightfully elected—and thus wrongfully deprived of power—Washington described as "offenses against the state".

In late 1995, Nigerian generals executed Ken Saro-Wiwa and eight other human rights activists. This didn't trouble Washington & Christian, which maintained the military as a client.

Nor did the executions trouble the Clinton administration. It had cut off military sales and training to Nigeria before Saro-Wiwa's killing, but that was because of the country's role in the international drug trade, not because of its monstrous human rights record. Clinton sputtered righteously following the executions, even though the US buys nearly half the oil Nigeria exports and could cripple the regime by leading an international oil embargo. But as one administration official intimately involved in the Nigeria situation said during an off-the-record talk last fall, "There is plenty of oil [available on world markets], but there's only so much Bonney Light." He was referring to Nigeria's coveted crude, which is extremely pure and economical to refine.

ASIDE: KISSINGER, STILL VILE AFTER ALL THESE YEARS

In Eastern Europe, the end of the Cold War brought ruin and humiliation for hardline elements, even if many were later resuscitated by the reaction against free market "shock therapy". In the United States, many of the Cold War's most notorious scoundrels maintain their prestige and power.

Al Haig promotes business in China and attacks critics of Peking's human rights record. Elliott Abrams, the butcher of Central America, is a regular guest on the talk show circuit and a resident scholar at the Hudson Institute. Oliver North nearly became Virginia's senator in 1994 and is preparing to try again.

And Henry Kissinger, arguably the most amoral and criminal public official of the post-war era, is not only a respected opinion monger but makes millions as the head of Kissinger Associates consulting firm (for which Goldman, Sachs provided start-up capital). Kissinger's specialty is helping US businesses open doors for CEOs in foreign nations. Lawrence Eagleburger, Brent Scowcroft and other Cold War relics have assisted him in his exertions.

Kissinger is especially adept at helping US companies because as secretary of state and national security adviser he earned the eternal gratitude of so many Third World despots by overlooking or encouraging their abuses. In his biography *Kissinger*, Walter Isaacson described a 1990 trip Kissinger made to Mexico with a client, Robert Day of Trust Company of the West:

"They flew in Day's corporate jet, had a breakfast meeting with the finance minister, and in the course of the day met with every other major cabinet minister. That evening, Day went to a reception thrown for Kissinger by the American ambassador, John Negroponte, who had once been a member of Kissinger's White House staff. On hand were eighty of Mexico's top political and business leaders."

As secretary of state, Kissinger visited Indonesia in 1974 and gave the green light for that country's invasion of East Timor, where one-third of the island's 600,000 people have been killed during the past 21 years. Now, he sits on the board of mining giant Freeport-McMoRan, a company that has befouled the environment across the globe, most egregiously in Indonesia's stolen "province", Irian Jaya.

Other tyrannies on which the former secretary works his magic include Turkey, Singapore, China and Malaysia, whose Prime Minister, Mahathir Bin Mohamad, was a student of Kissinger's at Harvard.

The photographs of Kissinger, seen pondering affairs at a trade conference in Brazil (page 144), originally appeared on the front page of *Jornal do Brasil*, a major Rio de Janeiro daily, on November 13, 1992. The discreet caption which accompanied the photos read: "Nobel Peace Prize winner in 1973, the ex-all powerful secretary of state Henry Kissinger said yesterday that Brazil will be able to enter the NAFTA agreement only in two to three years. At the invitation of the Getulio Vargas Foundation, he participated yesterday in a meeting on Latin America and the new world order, at the Sheraton Hotel, and later lunched at Saint Honore restaurant in the Meridien Hotel."

A few years later, Kissinger's lawyer sent *Jornal do Brasil* a letter saying the former secretary of state would file a lawsuit for damages if the newspaper did not immediately cease and desist from selling the photos. To its credit, *Jornal do Brasil* refused to bow to Kissinger's attempted assault on free speech.

One purchaser of the photos was the advertising agency of Woolward & Partners, which bought the pictures of Kissinger for use in an ad for computer equipment. Woolward & Partners also received a letter from Kissinger's lawyer demanding that it make no further use of the Nobel Peace Prize winner's image.

Here is a man who has been photographed eating lobster with General Augusto Pinochet—a man who oversaw the murder of thousands of Chileans after taking power in a coup sponsored by Kissinger's ex-boss, Richard Nixon—and happily chowing down duck with the rulers of China. Yet it is only these images which Kissinger seeks to keep under lock and key.

★

Attacks on lobbyists were a centerpiece of Bill Clinton's presidential campaign. Candidate Clinton said he intended to "break the stranglehold the special interests have on our elections and the lobbyists have on our government". At the mid-way point of his four-year term, Clinton's call for reform stood as one of the many of candidate Clinton's broken promises.

Clinton did prevent top administration officials from lobbying the government for five years after they left their posts (a similar requirement for retiring members of Congress was dropped). But enormous loopholes in lobbying law remain. Even the five-year ban is pointless, since nothing prevents partners at an ex-official's firm from lobbying or from asking the ex-official for advice. And the 1996 reform bill passed by Congress contains similarly yawning loopholes.

The utter futility of Clinton's pledge, and the shameful ethical standards of the capital's lobbying corps, is perhaps best symbolized in the story of Howard Paster, Clinton's first chief congressional lobbyist. During the 1970s, Paster was a respected member of liberal Babylon, working as an adviser to Indiana Senator Birch Bayh and then as a labor lawyer for the United Auto Workers.

But Paster sold out at the dawn of the Reagan era, taking a high-paying position with the conservative Washington lobbying firm of Timmons and Co. in 1980. Paster worked so hard for his clients—

Lobbyist Frank Mankiewicz with Cokie Roberts: Tobacco and torture OK, though the Papists gave him pause. (Vivian Ronay/Photoreporters)

including oil companies, banks, defense contractors and the NRA—that *The Washington Post* saluted him for "harboring an indefatigable devotion to lobbying for the wealthy and powerful in corporate America".

Paster moved to Hill and Knowlton in 1992, but soon resigned to work for Bill Clinton, that great foe of Washington lobbyists. He lasted less than a year at his post, announcing in December of 1993 that he would return to Hill and Knowlton to serve as president and chief executive officer. Paster had re-entered the revolving door before it had even stopped spinning.

Hill and Knowlton is one of Washington's biggest public relations firms. According to the Center for Public Integrity, Paster's firm earned $14 million between 1991 and 1992 for representing countries that violate human rights, making it the No. 1 company in the "torture lobby". Its clients included:

• Kuwait, which doled out $10 million to drum up public and congressional support for the Persian Gulf War.

• Turkey, whose government routinely uses torture and coughed up $1.2 million for Hill and Knowlton to "lobby Congress and the executive branch on foreign aid". (A top figure working on this account was Thomas Hogg, a Clinton campaign adviser.)

• Indonesia, which paid $3 million for "logistical assistance" in promoting investment and trade with the US.

• China, which although one of the world's worst human rights abusers, paid $163,000 to improve its "overall image in the United States as [a] valued trading partner".

Paster's vice chairman at Hill and Knowlton is Frank Mankiewicz, another pillar of liberal Babylon. Before becoming a lobbyist, he served as campaign adviser for Robert Kennedy and George McGovern, and as the head of National Public Radio.

Neither of these two men ever expressed any ethical concerns about working for the tobacco and firearms lobby at home and the torture lobby abroad. Mankiewicz once did express a slight unease with his firm's work for the Roman Catholic Bishops since, as a good liberal, he is pro-choice. Paster stoutly maintains that he has never done anything "contrary to my principles".

PORK CENTRAL

Folk hero General Colin Powell, seen here with Senator Phil Gramm and ABC's Roone Arledge: As a White House Fellow at the time of Watergate, he absorbed the rudiments of bureaucratic butchery from Fred Malek, a Nixon hit man. He honed those skills under the expert tutelage of Frank Carlucci and Richard Armitage, both notoriously hard players at the Pentagon. Mythic Powell emerged with honor and reputation unblemished from attempted cover-up of the massacre of My Lai; from Iran/contra scandal; from intimate and prolonged association with the Reagan/Bush administrations in their piratical and frequently illegal enterprises. Powell's acclaimed 1995 autobiography, *A Soldier's Life*, gives no evidence that he ever had an interesting idea in his head or entertained a dangerous notion. He complacently reprints portions of his combat diary of 1963, when he was an unofficial leader of a South Vietnamese unit destroying peasant livestock and defoliating crops. The book carefully notes that its hero joined the infamous Americal Division in Vietnam *after* the My Lai killings and then duly supplied an army investigator with the relevant combat report from the Division's files. The real Powell sidetracked an accusatory letter from Tom Glen, a soldier who tried to expose the rampages of Lieutenant William Calley's brigade, and maintained in his own report that "relations between American soldiers and the Vietnamese people are excellent". Powell regurgitates Reagan-era claptrap without remorse, whether it be the Cuban-built "extended airstrip" that justified the invasion of Grenada or the Sandinistas' "exporting" of their revolution. Powell also honors the Gipper's military budgets and notes the advance of inner-city blight in America without reflecting that the two phenomena might be linked. Powell's decision not to enter the 1996 presidential race caused great consternation in Babylon, particularly on the part of pundits—Sam Donaldson, Tim Russert, Charles Krauthammer, Evan Thomas, David Broder, among many—who had encouraged a Powell candidacy. (Vivian Ronay/Photoreporters)

A VISIT TO THE PENTAGON
AND THE NATIONAL SECURITY STATE

In 1976, amid his successful drive for the presidency, Georgia governor and peanut farmer Jimmy Carter told a group of Democrats that "Without endangering the defense of our nation or commitments to allies, we can reduce present defense expenditures by about five to seven billion annually. Exotic weapons which serve no real function do not contribute to the defense of this country. The Pentagon bureaucracy is wasteful and bloated."

In the White House such stern talk quickly gave way to more dispassionate deportment. Carter named Harold Brown, Secretary of the Air Force in the Johnson administration and a one-time government scientist who worked on nuclear weapons development, as his Secretary of Defense.

Carter cited all the usual grave threats the Soviet Union posed to national security. For 1978, the first fiscal year under his budgetary supervision, he requested $112 billion in defense spending, about 25 per cent more than the sum candidate Carter had mentioned. By December of 1977 Carter was publicly declaring that under his leadership, defense spending "has gone up in real dollars, we have compensated for the inflation rate and then added on top of that". By the time he was voted out of office Carter was pledging to spend, in the early 1980s, even more than Reagan actually achieved.

Hoodwinking the public with tales of non-existent security threats is an American tradition dating back for more than a century. Such scares are necessary to the broader purposes of boosting military budgets, the bottom lines of defense contractors, and of stabilizing the overall economy.

As always in wars, military-related theft raged at the War Department after Pearl Harbor. From Wall Street the Pentagon summoned "dollar-a-year men", supposedly patriotic businessmen who would use their executive skills to supervise the procurement system and allocate capital goods. They duly dispatched the goods, to their own firms, thus positioning themselves favorably for post-war production. The day the war ended, the dollar-a-year men burned their files and returned home.

Shortly after the war's end, the aircraft industry, terrified by the prospect of budgetary cuts, spent lavishly to reverse this dreadful possibility. Aided most prominently by Secretary of Defense James Forrestal, a rabid cold warrior who threw himself to his death from a hospital window, and by Secretary of State George Marshall, industry officials promoted the myth that the Soviets were set to seize all of Europe. This succeeded in ratcheting up military spending by an enormous amount, which terrified the Russians and precipitated the Berlin crisis in 1948.

ASIDE: HOW TO KILL PEOPLE

Some time in early or mid-1949, a CIA officer named Bill (surname deleted) asked an outside contractor for input on how to kill people. To infer from the contractor's response later that year, the "performance envelope" required that the Agency's victim appear to have suffered an accidental or purely fortuitous terminal experience.

There's a certain bluff innocence to the letter from Bill's contractor friend, who seems from the style to have been a doctor. The noun-heavy bureaucratic tone of the 1950s is not yet apparent. The timbre belongs more to wartime commando exploits than to the chill advisories that lay ahead, far down the pipeline, in the form of the Assassination Manual furnished to the contras in the early 1980s.

Known CIA murder attempts can be traced at least as early as the Bandung Conference of the mid-1950s, when the Agency made a strenuous effort to blow up Chou En-Lai by putting a bomb on his plane. The bomb went off as planned and the plane fell into the South China Sea; Chou, having dallied in Hong Kong, escaped. The most recent known episode of assassination as an integral part of US foreign policy came with the efforts in

1993 to dispatch Mohammed Farah Aidid of Somalia, said efforts approved by Bill Clinton from his vacation home—the former residence on Martha's Vineyard of Robert McNamara.

The 1949 communication to Bill, which came just two years after the Agency was founded with a charter limiting its activities to gathering and analyzing foreign intelligence, shows assassination policy at a relatively early stage in its process of evolution. Note that two methods favored by the CIA's consultant were already being inflicted on a very large number of Americans in lethal doses. Bill's friend suggests "exposure of the entire individual to X-ray"; or tetraethyl lead "dropped on the skin in very small quantities"—more dramatic than leaded gas, it's true, but not nearly as widely dispersed or so thorough-going in its application.

The memo to Bill follows, virtually in its entirety:

"Dear Bill:

"I regret taking so long to supply you with my thoughts on the problem which you raised when I saw you last. Rather than attempt to organize a logical outline of all the means by which the type of activity you mentioned might be accomplished, I am simply setting down the means that I think might be most efficacious.

"You will recall that I mentioned that the local circumstances under which a given means might be used might suggest the technique to be used in that case. I think that gross divisions in presenting this subject might be (1) bodies left with no hope of the cause of death being determined by the most complete autopsy and chemical examination, (2) bodies left in such circumstances as to simulate accidental death, (3) bodies left in such circumstances as to simulate suicidal death, and (4) bodies left with residua that simulate those caused by natural death.

"There are two chemical substances which would be most useful in that they would leave no characteristic pathological findings, and the quantities needed could easily be transported to the places where they were to be used. Sodium sluoacetate, when ingested in sufficient quantities to cause death does not cause characteristic pathological lesions. . . . Tetraethyl lead, as you know, could be dropped on the skin in very small quantities, producing no local lesion, and after a quick death no specific pathological evidence of the teraethyl lead would be present.

"If an individual could be put in a relatively tightly sealed small room with a block of CO_2 ice, it is highly probable that his death would result and that there would be no chances of the circumstances being detected. It is highly probable, though, that there would be a period of hyperactivity in the course of such a death.

"Another possibility would be the exposure of the entire body to X-ray. When the whole body is exposed, a relatively small amount of radiation is sufficient to produce effects that would lead to death within a few weeks, and it is highly probable that sporadic deaths of this kind would be considered as due to blood dyscrysias.

"If it were possible to subject the individual to a cold environment, he would freeze to death when his body temperature reached around 70 degrees, and there is no anatomic lesion that is diagnostic in such cases.

"There are two other techniques which I believe should be mentioned since they require no special equipment besides a strong arm and the will to do the job. These would be to either smother the victim with a pillow or to strangle him with a wide piece of cloth, such as a bath towel. In such cases, there is no specific anatomic change to indicate the cause of death, though there may be . . . marked visceral congestion which would suggest strangulation along with some other possibilities.

"I hope you will forgive the random way in which I have set these things down....If I can be of any further aid to you, I hope you will call on me."

★

Pleased with its success, the arms industry pressed further. By now Truman's economic advisers, notably Leon Keyserling, had come to the conclusion that the only way for the postwar economy to remain stable was by long-term state intervention in the form of "military Keynesianism": huge state subsidies to the arms manufacturers would take up the slack in the economy and also underwrite long-term research in electronics and other vital sectors. The Korean War offered itself as the first in many national "emergencies" used to justify this long-term policy. The Cold War—chief engine for increased military spending over the next forty years—became irreversible.

None of the money extracted by the war lobby during the build-up to the Korean crisis was used to benefit soldiers serving in Korea. Instead the defense establishment spent mightily on weapons such as the B-47, the first nuclear bomber (useless in Korea where fighter planes were needed), and on vast numbers of tanks which, like the B-47, were sent off to the quiet European front.

Meanwhile, ground forces in Korea were miserably equipped. Half of all US casualties—this category includes the wounded—in Korea were caused by frostbite, because troops weren't supplied with decent boots. US troops would raid Chinese trenches to strip dead peasants from the poorest nation on earth of their footwear. Soldiers desperately needed a good anti-tank weapon, but had only World War II vintage weaponry available.

The next major spasm of threat inflation took the form of the "missile gap", used by John Kennedy to belabor Eisenhower and Nixon and to win the 1960 election. After taking office, Kennedy's Defense Secretary, Robert McNamara, insisted that the US needed 1,000 nuclear missiles to counter the menace posed by the Soviets' nuclear arsenal. This was at a time when the Russians had precisely four missiles.

By 1974, the Pentagon and the arms industry faced a new and highly potent threat. There was a nasty whiff of détente in the air. US involvement in the war in Vietnam was coming to a close. US arms spending had sunk steeply from its late-1960s level; spending for 1975 stood at $230 billion in today's money, a post-Vietnam low.

The Pentagon and its allies rose to the challenge. Within five years the field of battle was covered with dead or dying *détentistas*. A mere handful managed to slip through the encircling cordon of Pentagon shock troops and regroup for a brave but futile guerrilla struggle in the desolate marshes of the Brookings Institution. The Soviet Union was successfully re-demonized, and American arms spending shot up to new levels.

The counter-attack got under way not long after the last Marine had cleared the US embassy roof in Saigon. A key shot came in late 1976, just weeks before Carter's inauguration, with leaked reports of a so-called "Team B" study. That study was prepared by a group of 10 hard-liners—Richard Pipes, Paul Nitze and Daniel Graham, among others—who were given access to classified documents by then CIA director George Bush, who wanted a second opinion on the unsatisfactorily demure assessments of his own CIA intelligence analysis.

The B Team concluded that the Soviets were seeking military superiority over the US and were preparing to fight and win a nuclear war. ("Team A" believed correctly that the Soviets were content with parity and had no intention of launching either a "conventional" or a nuclear attack on the US.)

Though in fact it was demented nonsense, the Team B report won vigorous and sympathetic treatment by the press, particularly the fanatic crew led by Robert Bartley of the editorial pages of *The Wall Street Journal*.

By 1978, President Carter and all major media had largely accepted the concept of US "vulnerability" to a pre-emptive Soviet attack. Early that year *Time* was asking, "Can the US Defend Itself?" The nation's leading defense experts, the magazine reported, were in broad agreement on a number of key matters: "The Soviet Union's continuing nuclear and conventional military build up is increasingly ominous and may jeopardize the delicate balance of power that has deterred nuclear war. . . . Disarmament negotiations like the SALT may not be capable, by themselves, of preserving the US-USSR balance." Carter crumbled. The MX missile—lovechild of Harold Brown—won the day.

Time discussed a supposedly enormous gap in conventional forces between NATO and the Warsaw Pact, and quoted William Hyland, former Kissinger aide in the National Security Council, as saying, "The fact that the Soviets are ahead or gaining in almost every category [of military power] may have no particular relevance to how a war is actually conducted. But the calculus will surely affect how we are perceived by our allies, the rest of the world and ourselves."

Edward Luttwak, a former consultant to Defense Secretary James Schlesinger and resident expert at Georgetown's Center for Strategic and International Studies, who also had ties to the Northrop aerospace corporation, was even more hysterical. He told the magazine that the time was nearing when Moscow could "say to the West, 'Gentlemen, we are superior in ground forces, we can take most of Western Europe in 48 hours. You cannot checkmate that by strategic nuclear forces for you no longer have superiority. Now we want to collect.'"

The second Cold War was already well underway by the time of the Russian invasion of Afghanistan in 1979, as reflected in press coverage at the time. Prior to the invasion, Afghanistan was the subject of no more than a handful of annual newspaper stories

In December 1973, when détente was near its zenith, *The Wall Street Journal* ran a rare front-page story on the country, titled "Do the Russians Covet Afghanistan? If So, It's Hard to Figure Why." Reporter Peter Kann, now the *Journal's* chairman and publisher, wrote that "great power strategists tend to think of Afghanistan as a kind of fulcrum upon which the world balance of power tips. But from close up, Afghanistan tends to look less like a fulcrum or a domino or a stepping-stone than like a vast expanse of desert waste with a few fly-ridden bazaars, a fair number of feuding tribes and a lot of miserably poor people."

After the Soviets invaded to help prop up a friendly regime, this wasteland swiftly acquired the status of a precious geopolitical prize. A *Journal* editorial following the Soviet takeover said Afghanistan was "more serious than a mere stepping-stone" and, in response, called for US troops in the Middle East, increased military outlays, expanded covert operations and reinstatement of draft registration. Drew Middleton, then a *New York Times* defense correspondent, filed a tremulous post-invasion analysis in January 1980: "The conventional wisdom in the Pentagon", he wrote, "is that in purely military terms, the Russians are in a far better position vis-a-vis the United States than Hitler was against Britain and France in 1939."

The Pentagon agitprop machine went into top gear: on January 3, 1980, George Wilson of *The Washington Post* reported that military leaders hoped the invasion would "help cure the Vietnam 'never again' hangover of the American public." *Newsweek* said the "Soviet thrust" represented a "severe threat" to US interests: "Control of Afghanistan would put the Russians within 350 miles of the Arabian Sea, the oil lifeline of the West and Japan. Soviet warplanes based in Afghanistan could cut the lifeline at will."

A few weeks later, a *New York Times* editorial endorsed Carter's call for a 4.5 per cent increase in military spending for each of the following five years. It also supported the Cruise and Trident missile programs, "faster research on the MX or some other mobile land missile", and the creation of a rapid deployment force for Third World intervention, calling the latter an "investment in diplomacy".

Drew Middleton: Long-time military correspondent of *The New York Times*; **master threat-inflator, feared US, NATO powers weaker than plucky little Belgium; notorious for basing many years of reporting on a single source in NATO's HQ in Brussels.** (AP/Wide World)

This was the Pentagon's most glorious campaign—a dazzling offensive in which waves of credulous and compliant journalists were dispatched to promulgate the ludicrous proposition that the United States was under military threat.

As Andrew Cockburn pointed out three years later in his book *The Threat,* by the late 1970s the armed forces of the Soviet Union were in an unprecedented state of disarray and military ineffectiveness, manned by an ill-trained and drunken soldiery, and directed by a military-industrial bureaucracy even more insatiable and incompetent than its American counterpart.

The overwhelming majority of supposedly expert American journalists, tank-thinkers and other whores of the Pentagon and arms manufacturers spent the better part of a decade writing fearful accounts of Soviet armament, supposedly superior both in technology and number. So it is worth recalling the real state of affairs as outlined in *The Threat:*

    • The tank gap. On this theory Western Europe would be overwhelmed in 48 hours. This conclusion was reached by hyping an ineffective Soviet tank—the T-72, and then establishing its numerical superiority by counting every Russian tank ever made, including those perched on war memorials.

• The missile gap. Paul Nitze, Elmo Zumwalt and the other hawks in the Committee on the Present Danger used to traipse around the TV talk shows carrying a porta-pack of Soviet and US intercontinental missiles. They would brandish the mighty Communist dildos, puissant in length and girth and visibly more potent than the diminutive western instruments. The rampant behemoth of the Soviet silos was the SS-18. These histrionics occluded simple facts: neither size nor number were relevant to the effects of a nuclear exchange. Precise targeting of missile silos—the promise of a "pre-emptive strike"—was impossible for reasons of atmospheric disturbance and gravitational pull. No one could win a nuclear war and those who so claimed were either mad or mountebanks or both.

• The civil defense gap. This was the most preposterous claim of all: that at a given signal from the Kremlin, a large proportion of the population would vanish like moles into subterranean shelters and emerge in the post-holocaust world, presumably to cross the sea and till the irradiated pastures of the midwest for grain on which they might live, until they moved into beach front property in Southern California, welcomed by such film quislings as had survived the McCarthy years.

The "security" context of the 1980 presidential campaign was therefore what the Pentagon whistleblower Ernie Fitzgerald accurately described at the time as "the Joint Chiefs of Staff auctioning off the presidency from the battlements of the Pentagon." Carter and Reagan vied with each other in promising donations to the military, exactly like the Roman legions of old selling the imperial throne to the highest bidder. In fact Carter's pledges for arms spending in the early 1980s were greater than what Reagan actually proposed and won in the continuing arms boom of the early 1980s.

Like Jimmy Carter, Bill Clinton campaigned as a military reformer. He promised that with the Democrats again in control of the White House, the American public would see a big peace dividend as a result of the fall of the Soviet Union.

Les Aspin: First flayed Pentagon boondoggles, later lobbied for the MX.
(Ted Soqui/Impact Visuals)

Clinton's ensuing collapse was every bit as abject as Carter's.

The career of Clinton's first Defense Secretary, the late Les Aspin, tells the story. In 1974, the out-tray at the office of Aspin, then a liberal House Democrat from Wisconsin, was filled with disclosures of Pentagon boondoggles and scandals. By day's end the out-tray would be empty and boondoggles retailed in the press. Ten years later Aspin himself was lobbying for the MX missile on behalf of President Reagan. As Clinton's Defense Secretary, Aspin proposed Cold War levels of spending.

Succeeding Aspin in 1994 was William Perry, who handled R&D for Harold Brown during the Carter years. During that time he killed the B-1 bomber only to replace it with the folly of the B-2. When Perry was hired, journalists lauded him for his work during the Carter years to create Stealth technology, which the military claims played a central role in the Persian Gulf War. In fact, Stealth was irrelevant to the conflict. The Allied victory stemmed above all from the fact that the Iraqi army enjoyed the largest mass desertions in history, with between 125,000 and 175,000 soldiers prudently departing the front before ground combat began. Saddam Hussein had stuffed the front with segregated units of Shi'ite and Kurd troops, so when it became clear that they were merely cannon fodder, most returned to their villages. Some 25,000 troops remained to confront 400,000 Allied soldiers when the ground war began.

John Deutsch: Now chief spook, partner with William Perry (r.) in unusual business arrangement. (Shia photo/Impact Visuals) (Dept. of Defense)

The US-led force could have walked in with swords.

Perry, along with John Deutsch, now head of the CIA and formerly in the Pentagon, and Paul Kaminski, Deutsch's replacement after he moved to the Agency, are part owners of Cambridge Research Associates of McLean, Virginia. In 1995 this firm received an $800,000 contract to develop 21st-century ground aircraft. The three men were the first top Defense Department officials allowed to hold investments in a military contractor, even though they have authority over billions in procurement money.

Predictably, under Clinton the weapons systems designed to counter the Soviet "threat"—the C-17 transport plane, first proposed in 1981; the E-8A JSTARS reconnaissance plane (1983); the F-22 fighter (1982); the MILSTAR communications satellite (1983); the Trident II nuclear missile (1979)—continue on their imperious path.

The system today is more corrupt than ever, because the weapons being produced are so pointless. According to Pierre Sprey, a former Pentagon analyst who quit in disgust, "The theft at the Pentagon has become much more open with the end of the Cold War. It's all about dollars and keeping companies afloat. Before there was a passionate belief among at least some people at the Pentagon that there really were threats to national security. Nobody believes that anymore. If you tried seriously to discuss threats to national security today—from countries like North Korea and Iraq—people at the Pentagon would laugh in your face."

One way that the war lobby maintains high levels of arms spending is through its control of Congress. Defense PACs gave members of Congress $7.5 million between 1993 and 1994. Weapons contractors are careful to put their dollars in the pockets of members of key congressional committees. From 1993 to 1994, the 42 members of the House National Security Committee took in $1.2 million, about one-third of the total amount distributed to all 435 members of the House.

The same pattern holds true in the upper chamber. Each member of the Senate Armed Services Committee received an average of $108,528 from defense PACs between 1989 and 1994.

Do such investments pay off? In June of 1995, Republicans in the House approved an additional $553 million in funding for the B-2 bomber, more than the Pentagon had requested and despite an Air Force study which showed that the B-52 could be upgraded for a fraction of the cost of the B-2, and serve until 2030.

Contractors and Pentagon procurement bureaucrats are also careful to spread subcontracts for weapons programs as broadly as possible. In September of 1992, when Congress considered stopping production of the F-16, lobbyists for the plane's manufacturer, General Dynamics, distributed a political atlas of F-16 vendors to every member of Congress. The atlas showed, in dollar terms, the supposed economic impact the F-16 program had in every state, and in every congressional district, across the country.

Now that there's no Soviet Union, national security threats are more difficult to contrive, but when all else fails the threat of inflation can still be an effective tool with Congress. The F-22 fighter offers an especially revealing instance.

A $70 billion program, the F-22 was specifically designed to penetrate far into Soviet air space, a need now obsolete. Unsurprisingly, Lockheed, the plane's designer, argues that the plane is still vital because many foreign nations own advanced aircraft—some of them made by Lockheed.

The company's F-22 literature cites threats ranging from Russian

MIG-29s owned by North Korea to F-16s—built by Lockheed—owned by South Korea and Canada. The latter, Lockheed says ominously, might one day turn on the US. Lockheed boasts that the F-22 can stymie the company's own air defense radar systems which it has installed on planes it exports to other countries.

D uring the first two years of Bill Clinton's presidency, no one played a more vital role in ensuring the maintenance of business as usual at the Pentagon than Georgia's senior senator, Sam Nunn, who is retiring in 1996.

Nunn hails from the Carl Vinson clan, which controlled the House Armed Services Committee for fifty years. Under Vinson began Georgia's privileged role as a recipient of military dollars; Warner Robbins, a gigantic Army/Air Force logistics base, was built on land formerly owned by Vinson-related interests.

This back-scratching tradition continued after Nunn became powerful in Congress. During the Eighties, Northrop (Georgia) was competing with Boeing (Seattle) for the contract to develop an anti-radiation cruise missile. Northrop's prototype stank, but through

Sam Nunn, the Senator from Lockheed: Follow the money, aka follow I-75 to Exit 43A.

Nunn the company won out. Shortly thereafter, Northrop surveyed the lower 48 states to decide where to build the missile factory. After all due deliberation the company determined that the very best spot would be in Nunn's home town. Soon, the state of Georgia was constructing Exit 43A off Interstate 75, which led to Northrop's plant. Responding to an allegation in a 1988 Jack Anderson column that his "cronies" may have profited from the rise in land values near the exit, Nunn heatedly denied any such association. According to Anderson, some in the Pentagon had sought a Senate investigation into the whole affair.

In the Senate, Nunn exercised great power through his control of the Armed Services Committee. After the Democrats regained control of the Senate in 1986, he turned it into a personal fiefdom. The committee's professional staffers on the Democratic side are a secretive group of Nunn loyalists so right-wing that the committee has been called "The Last Plantation". Unelected and overpaid, and influencing everything from budgets to strategy, they play a tremendous role in defining military policy.

Nunn's staff director is Arnold Punaro, a political and social Cro-Magnon who for years ran the committee while Nunn made speeches and politicked. A Marine reservist and faculty member at Georgetown University, Punaro loves the Corps and brands as traitors all who would dare cut its funding. "Today there are forces that would rip and tear at [the Marines]", Punaro once wrote. "These forces may be more dangerous than the frontal assault on the Corps's existence [during the Korean War] because they are subtle not direct…and they are led by budget bureaucrats not warriors."

Thanks to Punaro, the Marines fared far better than the other services in fending off enemy assaults on budget and manpower levels. While the Army was cut from 611,000 to 540,000 between 1992 and 1994, Marine Corps levels were barely touched. The Corps rewarded Punaro in 1993 by elevating him to reserve Brigadier General, a most unusual promotion.

A ferocious conservative, Punaro in private speaks ominously of the menace posed by "wide-eyed feminists" and "liberals", the latter being everyone to the left of Nunn. In regard to gays, Punaro once remarked, "We shouldn't just ban them (from military service), we should burn them."

Punaro's No. 2 man was David Lyles, who has since left. He played a key role in rigging the committee's 1993 hearings on gays in the military to ensure that President Clinton would renege on his promise to lift the ban. Lyles spent weeks at the Norfolk Naval Base before the crucial May 10 hearing aboard the aircraft carrier John F. Kennedy, during which 15 of 17 sailors testified that they favored maintaining the ban on gays.

Lyles had screened and selected the witnesses who were plucked from a pool originally suggested by base commanders, who knew exactly what they would say. Later, when senators toured the carrier and crew members spoke spontaneously, a surprising number said they saw no problem with lifting the ban. Nunn, who had promised that the hearings would be fair and balanced, claimed this proved he hadn't sought to stack the deck.

Lyles was exultant with the Norfolk "poll", as was Punaro. The staff director gleefully predicted that the combination of Norfolk and testimony from General Norman Schwarzkopf, then still basking in the glow of the Gulf War, would be "a one-two punch" that would force the "folks at the White House [to] say 'uncle'".

Committee staffer Rick DeBobes, a retired Navy captain and lawyer, previously served as legal and legislative counsel to former chairman of the Joint Chiefs of Staff, Admiral William Crowe. Under Crowe, DeBobes helped cook up the Fogarty Report, the Pentagon's cover-up of the USS Vincennes' 1988 downing of an Iranian Airbus with 290 civilians on board, regarded by all well-informed sources as an astoundingly mendacious document. DeBobes has pushed for the military to play an increased role in interdicting narcotics, a role the Pentagon relishes as it offers a new justification for spending on everything from satellites to Navy bases.

Maintaining the Pentagon's budget in the post–Cold War period is a job Nunn's entire staff takes with extreme seriousness. One increasingly popular ploy is to shuffle money to the Defense Department for non-military activities, such as the construction of a new (Georgia-based) Pentagon center to study military-related environmental pollution. In a kindred disbursement the Army got more than $200 million for breast cancer research. Nunn even talks of using the Pentagon as a sort of national Peace Corps, saying "there will be a much greater opportunity than in the past to use military assets and training to assist civilian efforts in critical domestic areas".

Technically employed by the US government, Nunn's committee staffers are especially diligent in maintaining the money flow to defense contractors and military installations in Nunn's home state. Among the former, Lockheed, the world's fifth largest weapons manufacturer, receives special attention.

Georgia, itself ranking fifth in the nation in terms of military compensation, escaped virtually unscathed from the early base closure decisions that decimated other states, most notably California. Georgia's position was bolstered by Frank Norton, an old crony of Nunn and Punaro who joined the committee's staff in mid-1993. Norton met with local business and political leaders, and plotted strategy which helped preserve Ft. McPherson, Ft. Gillem, Warner-Robbins Air Force Base and the Marine Corps Logistics Center, the four major Georgia facilities deemed vulnerable during that year's round of closures.

W ithin the defense establishment itself, there are some key bureaucrats who also play especially vital roles in maintaining the slush pipe between the Pentagon and military contractors. Andy Marshall, head of the Defense Department's Office of Net Assessment (ONA), was reverently described by Thomas Ricks of *The Wall Street Journal* as someone "struggling to save the US armed forces from becoming paralyzed by their own successes in the Cold War and Desert Storm".

Ricks's 1994 profile opened with a description of a classified Pentagon war game in which the US was pitted against a resurgent China in the year 2020. To the horror of US officials, Chinese troops pitilessly peppered American forces with high-tech weaponry. Satellite-guided anti-ship missiles showered the US fleet, naked and exposed to space-based Chinese surveillance sensors. By sundown the once-proud American armada had sunk beneath the waves of the South China Sea and the Middle Kingdom ruled once more.

According to Marshall, technological advances have made American defense strategy and hardware obsolete. The unstated but unmistakable conclusion is that immense sums of money must be set aside to purchase a new generation of "brilliant" weapons; otherwise, the US is finished. In this instance Marshall was dutifully furnishing an ex post facto rationale to support decisions made by Bill Perry, the top man at the Pentagon. As one ex-Pentagon staffer, who has savored Marshall's gyrations for years, remarked, "Perry's a total shill for the electronics sector so Andy's now whipping up this bullshit about how the US must prepare immediately for 21st-century conflicts."

Marshall has been at the threat-inflation game so long he should be in the Smithsonian. One of the original nuclear intellectuals, he worked in the Fifties with Herman Kahn at the RAND Corp., where he and his colleagues helped concoct the fraudulent "missile gap" for the 1960 election. In 1972 Marshall was brought in to head the newly created Office of Net Assessment, whose specialty was rigging the conventional balance of forces. Ricks's puff piece portrayed its subject—"a legend within [the Pentagon]"—as a man always one step ahead of the competition. "Well ahead of most Sovietologists, Mr. Marshall noticed weaknesses of Soviet society", wrote Ricks. "In 1977, he focused on the environmental and demographic crises that were undermining the Soviet system."

Associates have no recollection of Marshall ever having expressed such views. "Until the very end he was a major promoter of the line that 'The Russians are coming and they're 10 feet tall'", said one ex-Pentagon man. Eternally vigilant, Marshall in November of 1989—after the fall of the Berlin Wall and shortly before Gorbachev's ouster in the Soviet Union—was insisting that high levels of defense spending were as urgently needed as ever. "It's going to take us several years of careful watching and monitoring to see how much change takes place", he said. "I don't think I've ever seen so much uncertainty about the future as there is today."

Marshall's raison d'être collapsed along with the Soviet Union. He now justifies his pay check by advancing the Revolution in Military Affairs (RMA), a doctrine which holds that today's "platforms"—tanks, aircraft carriers and manned bombers—are hopelessly outdated and must be replaced with 21st-century hardware. The arms systems Marshall proposes as solutions are virtually identical to the "superweapons" Perry promoted when the latter oversaw military research in the Carter administration. Such efforts failed, at hideous expense.

Among the more idiotic of Marshall's ideas is that the best way to halt an Iraqi tank attack may be with "a submarine launching from 100 miles away 'brilliant' missiles that zero in on the sound of Russian-built tank engines". Acoustic homing has been contemplated—and rejected as being too easy to fool—since World War II. A missile like the one envisioned by Marshall could be tricked with a pair of $100 speakers playing the taped sound of a Russian tank engine. While Pentagon porkers might be able to get such a weapon to work under laboratory conditions, battlefield noises—artillery barrages, rocket blasts, gunfire—make acoustic homing entirely impractical.

Marshall also claims that "Stealth" aircraft like the B-2 bomber and the F-117 fighter, which the Pentagon claims are invisible to enemy radar—are fearsome weapons which paved the way for more sophisticated advances. One Pentagon veteran who has reviewed classified material calls Stealth "the biggest fraud ever perpetrated on the American public". During the Persian Gulf War, British destroyers picked up Stealth planes from 40 miles away. US radar identified Stealth crafts from five times that distance.

Another of the national security establishment's pork-seeking missiles has been Dr. John Alexander, who until early 1995 was Los Alamos Laboratory's manager of non-lethal defense research. In 1994, *Aviation Week*—bible of the porkers—named Alexander one of its "Aerospace Laureates" for his outstanding efforts.

"Non-lethal weaponry", funded out of the Defense Department's secret $30 billion "black" budget and therefore virtually free of congressional oversight, is a hot topic in the mid-1990s. The Pentagon calls non-lethal defense "a potent new force", allowing commanders to "inhibit an enemy's ability to prosecute a war." A few possibilities are high-power lasers that disorient enemy pilots, electronic gadgets that disable a hostile nation's computer and financial systems, multi-colored strobe lights that nauseate unfriendly crowds, and a sticky goo that renders enemies helpless.

The press reports lovingly on developments in this new field. A 1994 *Newsweek* story exclaimed that a "new generation of nonlethal weapons may help rout mobs, subdue gunmen, even win wars—without killing the innocent".

Alexander plays a central role, although his background reveals

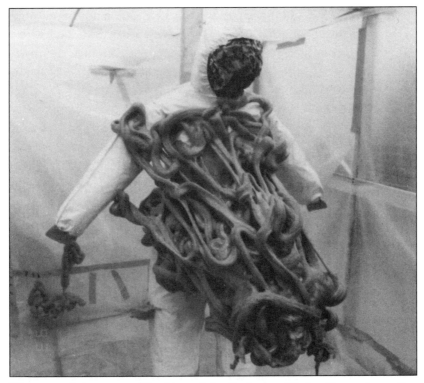

Weapons of tomorrow: Plaything of fertile brain of John Alexander, *enfant terrible* **of the national security establishment, searcher for Atlantis; says jury is still out on whether alien invaders impregnate earthling women aboard their spaceships.** (Sandia National Laboratories)

distinct signs of mental and psychological originality. A thumbnail biography published in his 1980 book, *The Warrior's Edge*, says that this 32-year Army veteran "evolved from hard-core mercenary to thanatologist. As a Special Forces A-Team commander in Thailand and Vietnam, he led hundreds of mercenaries into battle. At the same time, he studied meditation in Buddhist monasteries."

The Australian "New Age" journal *Nexus* reports that in 1971, while an infantry captain based in Hawai'i, Alexander took a trip "diving in the Bimini Islands looking for the lost continent of Atlantis". A man of broad interests, Alexander has also represented the Silva mind control organization, lectured on Precataclysmic Civilizations, served on the board of the International Association for Near Death Studies and conducted ESP experiments with dolphins.

The search for Atlantis apparently on hold, Alexander took time in 1993 to organize a Santa Fe, New Mexico, conference on the Treatment and Research of Experienced Anomalous Trauma. Topics discussed at the conference included ritual abuse, near-death experiences and human contacts with extraterrestrials.

Alexander told the *Albuquerque Journal* that he is deeply concerned because reports of such activities are rapidly growing. "Something's happening that's impacting on the psyche of America", he informed the newspaper. "That's for sure." The Los Alamos director suggested that space aliens may indeed be abducting human beings, but drew the line, albeit hesitantly, when asked whether some female abductees may have given birth to alien children. "Ostensibly, what happens is that impregnation takes place, then the person is brought back aboard ship where the fetus is removed," said Alexander. "But the physical evidence to support this is, in my mind, lacking."

The best guide to Alexander's views on non-lethal weaponry is a 1980 article he wrote for the *Military Review*, "The New Mental Battlefield: Beam Me Up, Spock", in which he discussed "weapons systems that operate on the power of the mind". Alexander argued that telepathic behavior modification, psychokinesis and out-of-body experience (OOBE) travel all have potentially useful military applications, particularly the latter. "The intelligence-gathering capability available through OOBE travel is obvious," he wrote. "When finally developed, this capability could ultimately allow an operator to enter an enemy headquarters at will to observe plans and dispositions." In fact, he said, test subjects in the Soviet Union and China had already used the technique to "penetrate secured areas to retrieve desired data".

Urging full speed on research in the field of "psychotronic weaponry", Alexander said, "Whoever makes the first major breakthrough ... will have a quantum leap over his opponent, an advantage similar to sole possession of nuclear weapons." Alexander recognized that skeptics might consider his ideas to be "ridiculous", but dismissed potential critics by saying that "some people still believe the world is flat".

Many weapons systems investigated by Alexander and his colleagues are far from non-lethal. An article a few years back in the

Institute of Electrical and Electronic Engineers' *IEEE Spectrum* titled "The future battlefield: a blast of gigawatts?" discussed the promising work underway in the area of high-powered microwave weaponry (HPM). In a section on "Troop Vulnerability", Carnegie Mellon University's H. Keith Florig notes that "microwave-induced changes in brain temperature of only a few degrees have been shown to cause convulsions, unconsciousness, and amnesia in rats".

Florig concedes that deployment of anti-personnel microwave weaponry might raise troubling "ethical issues". As he put it, "HPM weapons that merely stun the nervous system temporarily seem, like short-acting chemical agents, to be more humane than lethal force. But HPM weapons that blind, burn, or bake people to death are likely to be viewed as an abhorrent addition to the arsenal."

ASIDE: MURDER AT HOME AND ABROAD

D uring recent years, a few members of Congress have fought a lonely battle in seeking to shut down the School of the Americas at Ft. Benning Georgia, the institution which has provided training for more than 50,000 Latin American soldiers and officers. The closest they came was in 1993, when an amendment offered by Rep. Joe Kennedy which would have cut off the S.O.A.'s $3 million annual funding mustered 174 votes, versus 256 votes rounded up by the school's supporters.

Republican Mac Collins of Georgia, a leading proponent of the school, told his congressional colleagues that the school was a "pioneer in training Latin American soldiers in human rights" and should be evaluated on the basis of its "curriculum, the overall record (of its graduates) and their contribution to the community they serve".

Space limitations prevent a full inventory of community service work performed by its alumni, but in El Salvador alone the S.O.A.'s men were complicit in the 1980 rape and murder of six American churchwomen, the massacre of hundreds of civilians—some of whose brains were scooped out at El Mozote—and the murder of Archbishop Oscar Romero.

Twenty-four academy alumni, including a number of drug traffickers, dictators and all-around thugs, have been inducted into the S.O.A.'s Hall of Fame. One honoree is Bolivian tyrant General Hugo Banzer, who seized power in a 1971 US-backed coup. One of his first acts in office was to offer $115 million in compensation to US companies whose assets had been nationalized by deposed President Juan José Torres—far more than the properties were worth.

The S.O.A.'s curriculum material, Collins's other yardstick, is certainly impressive, reading like a latter day Declaration of the Rights of Man. Current human rights policy was established with Memorandum 91-36 of October 2, 1991, which was signed by then-Commandant Jose R. Feliciano (whose taste in office decor—such as a gift sword and framed letter received from General Augusto Pinochet of Chile—somewhat tarnishes his civil libertarian credentials). The memo states that S.O.A. instructional materials seek to "inculcate a sense of shared responsibility for the preservation of the intrinsic rights of each country's citizens".

The school gives a 24-question multiple choice exam to gauge how well trainees have absorbed their human rights lessons. A few of those questions appear below:

"1. Your squad has three civilians in its custody, one who is a guerrilla. Yesterday the enemy murdered a captured member of your squad. Another member of your unit wants to kill one of the civilians to settle the score. The correct action is:
    a. Execute the guerrilla in retaliation.
    b. Do not execute anyone, but hold the three civilians as hostages until the enemy stops killing prisoners of war.
    c. Protect the civilians and do not injure any of them.

"2. Even though the enemy village is relatively secure, there have been many attacks against your forces at night. Enemy civilians have taken part in these attacks. What should you do?
    a. Take the mayor as hostage until the attacks cease.
    b. Destroy the homes of civilians in reprisal.
    c. Establish an after-dark curfew and punish anyone who violates it.
    d. Make the town pay a large fine.

"3. The squad leader gives an order to cut off the ears of a dead enemy soldier to confirm a body count. You should:
    a. Obey the order but denounce it to your superiors.
    b. Obey the order.
    c. Disobey the order and tell your superiors about the incident.
    d. Order a squad member of lower rank to obey the order."

The exam's final hurdle requires the student to read the following situation and explain in writing what human rights violations have occurred:

"Two weeks of intense fighting have just ended, and Corporal Lima's companero has been killed. Corporal Lima is aching to get revenge. While he is performing guard duty, two unarmed enemy soldiers approach holding up a piece of white cloth as a sign not to fire. The corporal orders them to raise their arms. They obey the order and continue approaching. Corporal Lima shouts, 'Go to hell damned enemies,' and opens fire, killing the two enemies."

For its part, the US bureaucracy rigorously adheres to the rule of law. If the law stands in the way, it can always be changed. Take state-sanctioned murder. Back in the mid-1970s, amid cries for reform provoked by CIA scandals then in the headlines, President Gerald Ford prohibited US officials from murdering political "enemies". The ban was promulgated in Executive Order 11905, which stated that "no employee of the United States Government shall engage in, or conspire to engage in, political assassination."

The order, which has been reissued by all succeeding administrations, seems absolutely to rule out the use of murder as a tool of foreign policy. Since that practice has long been viewed favorably by the government, the Executive Order created a real dilemma for policy makers and intellectuals. As Robert Turner, chairman of the American Bar Association's standing committee on law and national security, once told *The Washington Post*, "The indiscriminate expansion of 'assassination'. . . to encompass every intentional killing of a foreign official risks confusing some highly complex and quite distinct legal and moral issues."

Hence, it became necessary to redefine the word "assassination".

The man charged with handling the job was W. Hays Park, the Army's chief legal officer. Park wrote a Memorandum of Law—published, it seems, only in *The Army Lawyer* in 1989—which sought to clarify "the term [assassination] in the context of military operations across the conflict spectrum".

A Pentagon hack said the memo was "coordinated with and concurred in" by the State Department, the CIA and the Justice Department under George Bush. The House and Senate Intelligence Oversight committees also signed off on it.

Park argued that "the clandestine, low visibility or overt use of military force against legitimate targets, where such individuals or groups pose an immediate threat to United States citizens or the national security of the

United States, as determined by competent authority, does not constitute assassination . . . and would not be prohibited by proscription in [Ford's Executive Order] or by international law." If striking at "a known terrorist" threat involves "too great a risk" for US ground forces, it would even be "legally permissible to employ an air strike against that individual or group rather than attempt his, her, or their capture". (This happened with the Reagan-ordered air raid planned to kill Qaddafi. The missiles from F-111s aimed at his tent missed him but killed his daughter. The Pentagon had prepared a press release stating his death to be an accident. During the war against Iraq up to one-third of all US air sorties at one point were dedicated to the mission of finding Saddam's mobile HQ—a Winnebago—and destroying it and him.)

To sum up, US "enemies" as defined by the president can still legally be dispatched. Having thus paved the way for future non-assassinations, Park's memo then clears the US of wrongdoing for past involvement in the death of individuals who posed "a direct threat to US national security". Of special note here is the 1934 killing of Nicaraguan "bandit leader" Augusto Cesar Sandino by the US-created National Guard, and the 1967 execution of Ernesto "Che" Guevara, who was shot after being captured by Bolivian troops assisted by the CIA.

The Defense Department source denies that Park's memorandum gives the government new authority to bump off foreign political foes. "We had members of Congress wanting to kill people and asking that the [Executive Order] be waived", he said. "You can't waive a law, so we wanted to clear up the ambiguity [about what constitutes assassination]."

Government officials won't comment on if or when the memorandum by Park—who still occupies his Army post—has been invoked. The US has used assassination as an instrument or intended instrument many times since World War II. Castro heads the list of prospective victims. The Park memo merely underscores reality.

★

The pulsing heart of Pentagon pork is the weapons procurement system. Perry and the Clinton administration plan to jack up procurement spending by almost 50 per cent between 1996 and 2001.

Since most of the Pentagon's gold-plated weaponry doesn't work, military bureaucrats are constantly seeking to undermine testing procedures. These, if conducted properly, bring discipline to the acquisitions process by revealing whether the promises made by the sales folks have any merit. Since those promises are generally either wild exaggerations or out-right lies, the Pentagon and contractors routinely seek to rig tests to conceal flaws.

Consider the history of:

• The $500 million Aegis high-tech radar system, which was designed to track and shoot down up to 200 incoming missiles at once. The Navy "tested" the Aegis in a meadow near Exit 4 of the New Jersey Turnpike, where it was charged with the difficult task of monitoring civilian air traffic over New York-area airports.

In another set of tests, the Aegis performed brilliantly, shooting down 10 of 11 drones. It turned out that the system's operators were informed in advance of the path and speed of incoming targets.

In 1988, its first time in combat after being installed on the USS Vincennes, the Aegis successfully bagged an Iranian Airbus with 290 civilians on board. Human and mechanical error led the crew to mistake the Airbus (length: 175 feet) for an F-14 (length: 62 feet), miscalculate its altitude by 4,000 feet and report that the civilian aircraft was descending in attack position when the plane was actually climbing.

• The Maverick air-to-surface missile, used with less than 50 per cent accuracy during the Gulf War, has heat-seeking infrared sensors which "lock on" target. Unfortunately, the sensors are easily distracted. In one test during which the Maverick was supposed to be homing in on a tank, operators discovered that the missile had locked on a distant campfire where two soldiers were cooking beans.

One of the most outrageous pieces of pork in the Pentagon's budget is the C-17 transport plane, staunchly backed by the Clintonites. The chief beneficiary is the McDonnell Douglas Corporation.

The C-17 gained momentum following the Soviet invasion of Afghanistan. The plane's purpose is to rush men and materials to distant wars. The Pentagon initially planned to buy 210 C-17s for $32 billion ($152 million apiece), but in 1990 cut the order to 120 planes for $36 billion ($333 million apiece). In late 1993, the Pentagon announced a further reduction of the program to 40 planes. No cost was given but the price tag is likely to hit $28 billion, or $700 million apiece.

The original justification for the aircraft—confronting the Red Menace—has vanished. But the Pentagon still insists that the C-17 is a "must buy". A 1993 Congressional Research Service report detailed a few of the problems surrounding this wondrous boondoggle.

Officials described the C-17's wings as having "buckled" during an October 1992 "stress" test. A congressional staffer familiar with the program says "the wings didn't buckle, they were destroyed. They ripped like pieces of paper." After McDonnell Douglas spent approximately $100 million on a major redesign—an expense most likely passed on to the Pentagon—a second test was conducted in July of 1993, only to be quickly halted when the wings began to splinter. In a third test conducted two months later, the C-17's left wing cracked in two places. Heartened because the right wing was undamaged, the Pentagon declared this test a rousing success and said no further experiments would be required.

The C-17 also has a mysterious center-of-gravity problem, which makes take-off extremely dangerous unless the plane is fully loaded. When the aircraft is empty, Air Force crews keep two 7,950 pound cement blocs—known as the "pet rocks"—in the craft's forward area to ensure safe take-off. This means that the C-17 will either fly into action pre-loaded with nearly eight tons of cement or advance troops will be forced to tote along two "pet rocks" to load onto the plane after removing its cargo.

Alas, the C-17 is incapable of carrying out its assigned task of forward resupply. The enormous aircraft needs at least 4,000 feet of runway to land, 1,000 more than the Air Force claims. The C-17 cannot come down on a dirt airstrip because its jet engines will "ingest" earth. A used Boeing 747—which can be bought and modified for less than $100 million—can carry three times as much cargo twice as far as the C-17.

The end of the Cold War has made it awkward for the war lobby to justify new weapons programs. So the arms peddlers have been increasingly eager to sell US arms abroad. As of mid-1995, US weapons were being used in 40 regional conflicts underway around the globe.

Under Clinton, the US has exported tens of billions of dollars worth of weapons annually, and holds a 70 per cent share of the world market. In 1994, the four biggest buyers of US weaponry were Israel, Turkey, Saudi Arabia and Malaysia (perhaps explaining why Clinton has opposed an arms sales "Code of Conduct" which would block weapons transfers to nations with poor human rights records).

Clinton has enlisted virtually all sectors of government to the arms export drive. For the first time, diplomatic personnel have been explicitly authorized to offer marketing assistance, once a deal has been approved. In another precedent, industry flacks pitching deals are allowed direct access to foreign officials, a practice that allows bribes and other lures to be offered in more discreet fashion.

The Pentagon handles most arms exports, selling or giving weapons to foreign governments through its Foreign Military Sales department. The State Department oversees the Direct Commercial Sales (DCS) program, by which defense contractors make private sales to foreign military and police forces.

Details about the latter program are hard to come by, since only deals worth more than $14 million must be reported to Congress. In theory, State allows the sale of weapons destined for a "defensive" role. It will not vend arms to an "aggressor" nation.

In practice, State authorizes sales to virtually any nation capable of paying for its purchase. This is not surprising. An advisory panel set up by State to review weapons export policy is dominated by arms industry officials representing the very firms that make the bulk of overseas sales.

Traditionally, much of the DCS trade involved the sale of small arms, but in recent years State has authorized companies to export major weapons systems. During the Clinton years, State has sanctioned the sale of tank engines to Israel, trainer aircraft to Taiwan, and Black Hawk helicopters to Mexico.

The State Department bureau that runs the DCS program is called the Center for Defense Trade (CDT), a more accurate name than the Office of Munitions Control, the agency it replaced in 1990. It approves all but a tiny fraction of the roughly 50,000 export licensing requests it receives from military contractors annually.

In 1994, the Center rejected only 156 of 17,907 requests for Type 5 licenses ("permanent export of unclassified articles"); 45 of 1,903 requests for Type 73 licenses ("temporary export of unclassified articles"); and 8 of 226 requests for Type 85 licenses ("temporary or permanent export or import of classified articles or technical data"). Reflecting the Center's lighthearted attitude, CDT bureaucrats in mid-1992 approved a license for a company that months earlier had been found to have illegally diverted aircraft parts to Iran, which State customarily portrays as Terror Central.

There have been numerous DCS deals with Guatemala, which George Bush formally banned from receiving US military aid in December of 1990, after the Guatemalan army was linked to the death of the American innkeeper Michael DeVine. Ten months after this supposed cutoff, the CDT permitted the sale of $100,000 worth of small arms to government forces.

The flow of weapons to Guatemala, technically prohibited from receiving military assistance, lasted through the remainder of the Bush years and continued after Clinton took office in 1993. Records show that on four occasions during the first half of that year, on February 15, April 20, June 11 and July 13, CDT officials authorized sales of rifles and pistols to Guatemala worth nearly $2 million.

Other countries purchasing arms through the DCS program include El Salvador, Colombia and Saudi Arabia. In the Saudi case, the CDT in 1994 okayed the sale of bodychains used to restrain prisoners. These are banned in most European countries as devices of unusual cruelty.

State offers counsel in regard to Direct Commercial Sales in the form of the Defense Trade Advisory Group (DTAG), a panel of 60, 57 of whom come from the arms industry. The group is headed by William Schneider, a veteran of the military-industrial complex and undersecretary of state for security assistance during the Reagan/ Bush years. One especially enthusiastic DTAG member is Joel Johnson of the DC-based Aerospace Industries Association. Reflecting the judicious approach he brings to the committee, Johnson once said that he "would feel more guilty selling sugar-coated breakfast cereal to kids" than he does about selling weapons abroad.

The three non-industry members of DTAG are two lawyers and Janne Nolan, a polite centrist from the Brookings Institution.

The gung-ho attitude of the 57 arms industry executives on the panel may be explained by the fact that almost all their companies are arms exporters under the DCS program. During 1994 Motorola received 1,127 licenses from State; McDonnell Douglas received 373; and Northrop-Grumman received 125.

OUR S-O-Bs

F oreign policy is essentially an extension of military policy: the motto "Follow the dollars" is generally a faithful guide to the decision-making process.

Take the case of Indonesia. There is overwhelming consensus among the policy-making elites that Jakarta is vital to US national security. "[Indonesia has] a huge population and [is] an important market for US exports", a top Clinton administration official told researchers from the Project for Demilitarization and Disarmament. "[It] has been a very strong supporter of the US [military] presence in the East."

Indonesia's supporters, from Congress to business to the Pentagon, have exerted extraordinary pressure to ensure that Clinton fully maintain America's long-standing alliance with Suharto, who seized power in 1965 and promptly oversaw the execution of an estimated 1 million suspected leftists. The CIA provided thousands of names.

Clinton did reverse Republican policy in some respects. At the UN the administration supported a resolution expressing "deep concern" about the situation in East Timor, a site of brutal human rights violations since Indonesia invaded that island in 1975. The president also angered Suharto by blocking the transfer from Jordan to Jakarta of American-made F-5E fighters.

However, Clinton was careful to preserve the general warmth of Washington-Jakarta relations. He opposed a measure introduced in 1993 by Democratic Senator Russell Feingold of Wisconsin, which would have restricted arms sales to Indonesia and, most egregiously, he skirted a congressional ban on American-paid training of Indonesian troops by allowing Jakarta to pay for its own soldiers' military education in the US.

Senator J. Bennett Johnston, the Louisiana Democrat, retiring at the end of 1996, leads the congressional lobby on Indonesia's behalf. Though publicly defending US ties to Indonesia on strategic grounds, Johnston's real interest is economic, specifically support of

J. Bennett Johnston: What's good for Freeport-McMoRan is good for him (and very bad for almost everyone else). (Shia photo/Impact Visuals)

Freeport-McMoRan, a Louisiana-based mining company with approximately $1 billion invested in Indonesian gold, copper and logging operations.

In January of 1994, Johnston led a group of five senators on a trade mission to Indonesia. The delegation stayed at Freeport's plush headquarters in Irian Jaya, where security forces were accused—in a press conference held the same month—of killing 13 villagers, including women and children. That didn't bother such junketeers as Republicans Alan Simpson of Wyoming and Robert Bennett of Utah, who returned from the trip defending Suharto's regime and saying that the human rights situation in Indonesia was not particularly troubling.

Freeport has paid Henry Kissinger more than $1 million in consulting fees for advising the company on its Indonesian operations. As part of his work, Kissinger in 1991 accompanied company CEO

James "Jim Bob" Moffett to Indonesia to introduce him to top figures in the Suharto regime. It therefore comes as no surprise to
learn that Freeport operates in Indonesia with a free hand and,
according to local human rights activists, grossly exploits its labor
force. Furthermore, peasants told a foreign investigator that company goons forced them off their property, which Freeport wanted, by
chainsawing the stilts of their homes.

Other important Senate backers of Indonesia include:

• Senator Daniel Inouye of Hawai'i, a close friend of deceased
dictator Ferdinand Marcos and a number of other Asian thugs.

• California's Dianne Feinstein, who pressured Clinton to rethink
his veto of the F-5E transfer. Feinstein was acting on behalf of
California-based Eidetics, which saw its plans to sell $1 million worth
of spare parts for the fighters go down the drain when the president
blocked that deal.

Jakarta pays millions annually to lobbying firms, with a major
share going to Burson-Marsteller. But when it comes to direct pressure on Congress and the Executive, the Indonesians rely on US
business, which bears keenly in mind the thought of the $60 billion
Suharto will dole out in infrastructure contracts during the next few
years. US firms also appreciate Jakarta's labor policies, which have
kept average wages in manufacturing down to 28 cents per hour.

Corporate opposition to the Feingold amendment was coordinat-

**Dianne Feinstein: Said murderous Indonesian generals just couldn't get along
without the F-5E. Neither could Eidetics, one of the senator's big campaign contributors.** (Jack Kurtz/Impact Visuals)

ed by the US-ASEAN Business Council and the American League for Exports and Security Assistance, whose members include such firms as McDonnell Douglas, Lockheed, Alliant Techsystems, GE and AT&T. The Council sent its representatives to the offices of every senator with a list of companies in their states that would allegedly be ruined if the Feingold amendment or any sanctions against Jakarta were approved. It also alerted hundreds of companies that deal with Indonesia of the grave threat the amendment posed, thereby provoking a flood of corporate calls to congressional offices.

The business blitzkrieg had a devastating impact and Feingold's supporters dropped out in droves. Bob Dole, who had announced he would back the amendment, abandoned ship when he was squeezed by lobbyists from Boeing, a Seattle-based company with major operations in Wichita.

At the Pentagon, deputy assistant secretary of defense for East Asian and Pacific affairs Stanley Roth, once an aide to former New York congressman Stephen Solarz, works hard to keep Clinton on a tight leash. Roth has had close personal friendships with top Indonesian officials since the late 1970s, when he visited the country at the invitation of the Jakarta-based Center for Strategic and International Studies, an intelligence front for the dictatorship. He's particularly tight with Yusuf Wanandi, a top official at the CSIS who played a key role in secretly lining up US support for the invasion of East Timor.

A final force in the Indonesia lobby consists of international financiers, who have long heaped money on Suharto. Lending was traditionally coordinated by the Inter-Governmental Group on Indonesia, a 14-nation consortium set up shortly after Suharto took power and which included the World Bank and the IMF.

After Indonesian security forces massacred up to 250 unarmed demonstrators in East Timor's capital of Dili in 1991, the Dutch government, which chaired the consortium, said further loans should be tied to human rights conditions. A standoff ensued when Suharto's officials said they would no longer deal with the group.

The solution, arrived at by the World Bank, was to expel the Dutch. The consortium then re-emerged as the Consultative Group on Indonesia and, under that name, loaned Jakarta more than $5 billion in 1994.

Defense Secretary Les Aspin announced his "bottom-up review" of defense spending in late 1993. He termed his request for '94 appropriations "the first post–Cold War defense budget", and sought $1.2 trillion in defense spending for the following five years.

US forces, Aspin said, "will be structured to achieve a decisive victory in two nearly simultaneous major regional conflicts. . . . forces must be sized and structured to preserve the flexibility and the capability to act unilaterally, should we choose to do so."

The conclusion that the US must be prepared to fight two major regional conflicts simultaneously, without help from allies, ignores the fact that the US has not conducted a major war without allies for over a century. But then, the review was not a serious study, but merely a new Pentagon ploy. Once the two-war premise is accepted, significant cuts in military spending become unthinkable.

The US accounts for more than half of military spending on earth. Even assuming that China and Russia became hostile, and were joined in a military alliance by the Pentagon's worst nightmare countries—the "rogue nations" of Iran, Iraq, Syria, North Korea, Libya and Cuba—the enemy coalition would together spend just one-third annually of what the US devotes to its military.

More money gets spent, but fewer weapons get bought. As Pierre Sprey says, "Pacifists should be thrilled with the Pentagon. They buy no hardware, they simply funnel money to weapons contractors. That money mostly pays the salaries of people who write reports and defense lobbyists who extract money from Congress. The amount of money being spent in proportion to the 'threat' involved has never been so out of balance. The Pentagon used to at least offer some sort of justification for the money they spend. Now they don't even bother."

THE GREEN ESTABLISHMENT

Richard Nixon: The greenest president of all. (AP/Wide World)

GREENS AND THE COLOR OF MONEY

C ast your memory back to the days of the Nixon administration, the glory time of American environmentalism. The
country rallied to the cause of cleaning up the nation's
waters and air, preserving its remaining wild lands and rivers, regulating the use and disposal of hazardous chemicals, rescuing wildlife
from extinction.

Remember the first Earth Day: April 20, 1970. It was the brain-
child of a United States senator, Gaylord Nelson of Wisconsin, who
wanted a national teach-in on the environment. Nelson proclaimed
that the environment "was the most critical issue facing mankind".
The teach-in became a media event, orchestrated by a young
Harvard-educated lawyer, Dennis Hayes, who set forth the lofty pro-
tocols of the new movement: "Ecology is concerned with the total
system—not just the way it disposes of its garbage."

That first Earth Day—when millions participated in demonstrations, clean-ups and rallies across the country—has been hailed as
the largest organized event in American history and as a symbol of
rebellion against pollution and the exploitation of natural America.

It didn't take Congress long to get the message. The House and
Senate speedily decreed a new era in environmental law: 1970 saw the
creation of the Occupational Safety and Health Administration
(OSHA) and the passage of the Clean Air and National Environmental
Policy Acts, under which protecting earth, air and water legally became
a priority for all federal agencies. Environmental impact statements, for
example, give "good science" a word in response to corporate projects.
Then in 1972 came the Clean Water Act, the first pesticide regulations,
the Noise Control Act and a series of laws protecting marine mammals
and coastal beaches. A year later Congress authorized the Endangered
Species Act, regulated toxic chemicals and passed new green laws gov-

erning the use of public lands. Throughout the Seventies environmental standards stiffened, with legislation covering everything from the Superfund (to finance clean-up of toxic dumps) to drinking water. The environmental decade culminated in the passage of the Alaska National Interest Lands Act in 1980, which protected about 110 million acres of wilderness, an area larger than the state of California.

In those days Congress was well-stocked with conservationists: Ed Muskie, George McGovern, Jennings Randolph, Birch Bayh and Gene McCarthy. Even in the West, where states were still commonly thought of as resources to be exploited, environmentalism had its champions: Idaho's Frank Church, Montana's Lee Metcalf, Arizona's Morris Udall and Oregon's junior senator, Bob Packwood, an original sponsor of the Endangered Species Act. In his 1970 State of the Union Address Nixon embraced the green theme, proclaiming that "we must make our peace with nature" and reclaim "the purity of its air, its waters, and our living environment. It is literally now or never."

To be sure, that supple politician seized this chance to divert the attention of an increasingly restive middle class from the horrors of his war against Vietnam. Nixon understood that "the environment" could bring together every dreamer green enough to impale an avocado seed on a toothpick and raise it up in the thin light of the Me Decade. The environment might bring the beat legions of the counter-culture together with the heavier left; it could ally those under 30 with those of more august years; it could make friends of radicals, senators, working people and the press. Forthwith Nixon created the Environmental Protection Agency, to which he named William Ruckleshaus as overseer. Ruckleshaus confronted industry polluters—he was the first federal bureaucrat to do so—before being drafted to his short-lived tenure as Attorney General, where he turned on his plucky boss.

In those heady days even the Supreme Court sheltered a radical conservationist, William O. Douglas. Douglas believed that nature should be afforded "rights"; in 1972 he drafted a fierce dissent in the case of *Sierra Club v. Morton*, arguing in forceful and poetic language that wilderness itself deserved standing in federal lawsuits, so that before "priceless bits of Americana (such as a valley, an alpine meadow, river or a lake) are forever lost or are transformed as to be reduced to the eventual rubble of our urban environment, the voice of the existing beneficiaries of these environmental wonders should be heard". Douglas further suggested that conservationists who "have an intimate relationship with the inanimate object about to be injured are its legitimate spokesmen". Thus did Douglas give birth both to environmental law and, though he is rarely credited for it, the deep ecology movement.

ASIDE: THE PRESS AND THE ENVIRONMENT

American newspaper companies own about 1.5 million acres of forest. They manage them on the shortest possible rotations—about 25 years between clearcuts. The production of newsprint in the pulp mills generates millions of tons of toxic waste every year. Only oil and chemical plants produce more.

The Washington Post and The Wall Street Journal, whose editorial positions often share a similar grain, in fact derive physically from the same forests in South Carolina, where the two companies jointly own more than 250,000 acres.

Though the quality of the environment ranks high on almost every American's list of concerns, the mainstream press has never troubled much about industrial threats to the natural world. The problem for honest reporters who would name polluters and rapists of the land is that such stories crash up against a corporate interest. Consequently most newspapers and TV stations prefer to address stories of burdensome regulation, the costs of red tape and of overblown predictions by hysterics, confuted by sober science. Ho-hum stories about global warming and ozone depletion are also popular.

The last time The New York Times had a serious environmental reporter was when Philip Shabecoff had the beat. He did well, but the executive editor of the time, Max Frankel, eager for the usual attacks on regulation, transferred him to the IRS beat. Shabecoff soon quit to edit his own environmental news service, Greenwire, and his place was taken by Keith Schneider, a reporter who had an acute understanding of his editor's desires, best expressed in his memorable hymns to the beneficial properties of dioxin. The best of the current bunch is AP's Scott Sonner.

So, as with the labor movement, and for the same reasons, the environmental movement receives virtually no informed coverage in the corporate press.

★

The 1970s saw the green movement mature as a political force with a permanent DC presence, most notably with the creation of the League of Conservation Voters—an organization later headed by Bruce Babbitt—which, for the first time, tracked the environmental voting records of members of Congress. Eco-lobbyists, operating largely from basements and scruffy offices on DuPont Circle, were considered the leanest and most effective on the Hill.

Meanwhile a more confrontational and grassroots-based faction of the environmental community was beginning to organize, spearheaded by the Arch Druid himself, David Brower. (Brower, named the Arch Druid by John McPhee of *The New Yorker*, was fired by the Sierra Club because he was too radical, founded Friends of the Earth and was dislodged from that job for the same reason.) Using the tactics of the civil rights and anti-war movements, this more radical wing of the environmental movement, mustered in groups such as Friends of the Earth and Greenpeace, used aggressive media campaigns, civil disobedience and direct action against the corporations themselves.

ASIDE: PACKWOOD'S FUZZY BOUNDARIES

In his final Senate speech in September 1995 before he resigned in disgrace, Bob Packwood of Oregon gazed back at the peaks of his political career. At the very top: his environmental legacy. He recounted how he had saved Hells Canyon, on the border of Oregon and Idaho, reputedly the deepest gorge in the United States. This wondrous landmark has been menaced by dams, logging and mines.

One night around the campfire in Hells Canyon, Packwood remembered, he and Brock Evans, an environmental lobbyist (now at Audubon, then with the Sierra Club) had been debating the boundaries of the proposed national recreation area for the canyon.

Bob Packwood: A campfire deal over Hells Canyon. (AP/Mark Wilson)

"Brock laid out a highway map, takes out a laundry pen, and says: 'I think this is where the boundaries ought to be.' And he draws it. But somebody on the trip says, 'What about those minerals down in Idaho?' And he looks and he says, 'All right.' He crosses that line out and draws another up here." This is why there are so few old-growth trees in Oregon wilderness areas. Those lines kept being redrawn to slake the desires of the timber giants, just as they were redrawn to satisfy mining companies with an interest in Idaho.

★

The decade of the Seventies closed with another huge environmental demonstration which was in its own way as prodigious as Earth Day. In the wake of Three Mile Island, 750,000 people gathered on the Mall in front of the Capitol to protest the evils of nuclear power, chanting "Hell no, we won't glow" along with the likes of Tom Hayden, Jane Fonda, Michael Harrington and Barry Commoner, who had decided to run for president on the green platform of the Citizens' Party ticket. The event was organized by Donald Ross, a young protégé of Ralph Nader, who had helped establish a nationwide network of Public Interest Research Groups (PIRGs) on college campuses.

That bright afternoon on the Mall was the last light that shone on the DC-centered green movement. In a decade and a half of Reagan, Bush and Clinton the environmental corps in DC has ripened to a complacent putty. The corporate counter-attack on greens began in the West with the rise of the Sagebrush Rebels, an amalgam of ranchers, corporate executives, free-market economists and right-wing politicians who decried environmentalism as socialism-by-another-name and a backdoor assault on property rights.

The Sagebrush Rebels were ignored until the election of Ronald Reagan, who bowed to the enthusiasms of Joseph Coors—the leading money dispenser of the far right and owner of substantial mineral claims on federal lands—and selected a suite of Sagebrush leaders to fill important posts in his administration. These Reagan rebels, headed by James Watt (who ran Coors's Mountain States Legal Foundation) and Anne Gorsuch, called themselves "the Crazies on the Hill".

Watt, a millennialist Christian and anti-Communist, was given the Department of the Interior, which oversees the management of nearly 500 million acres of public land. He proclaimed he would make the "bureaucracy yield to my blows" and got off to a fast start. Within a matter of months Watt proposed the sale of 30 million acres of public lands to private companies, gave away billions of dollars worth of publicly owned coal resources, fought to permit corporations to manage national parks, refused to enforce the nation's strip mine law, offered up the Outer Continental Shelf oil reserves to exploration and drilling, ignored the Endangered Species Act and purged the Interior Department of any employees who objected to his agenda.

Rebel Watt defended his actions on religious grounds, arguing that conservation of resources for future generations amounted to a waste of "God's gift to mankind".

"I do not know how many future generations we can count on before the Lord returns", Watt warned. Use it or lose it.

Jim Watt: Straight from the book of Genesis; heeded God's word to pillage and subdue. (Jay Mallin/Impact Visuals)

In spite of his ravings Watt held on. He even survived his bizarre attempt to block the Beach Boys, in his fevered mind the incarnation of the counter-culture, even though the group did fund-raisers for George Bush, from playing a concert on the Mall, a stance that provoked an amusing rebuke from Reagan. But like Earl Butz before him, Watt was undone by the racism which welled up invincibly within him. Attacking affirmative action Watt complained that he couldn't set up a panel without out finding "a black, a women, a Jew, and a person in a wheelchair". Although Watt was later indicted on charges that he bilked the Department of Housing, Education and Welfare out of millions of dollars, it was this remark that did him in.

Over at the Environmental Protection Agency Watt's counterpart was Anne Gorsuch, a rough-hewn and ignorant Colorado legislator. Gorsuch, who later married Robert Burford, the rancher and mining engineer Watt selected to head the Bureau of Land Management, surrounded herself with advisers from the pollution lobby, including lawyers from General Motors, Exxon and DuPont. Her objective was to cripple environmental laws passed in the 1970s which, she argued, had created an "overburden" of regulations that had "stifled economic growth".

To lead the toxic waste division of the EPA Gorsuch chose Rita Levelle, a public relations executive with the Aerojet General Corporation, a defense contractor with potentially vast hazardous

Anne Gorsuch: The Artemis of the Sagebrush Rebels. Tossed regs out window, but left high and dry by Uncle Ron. (Library of Congress)

waste liabilities. At her appointment many of the EPA's top scientists and administrators promptly quit.

Gorsuch and Levelle left a miasma of suspended regulations, secret meetings with industry lobbyists, waived fines, and suppressed recommendations of agency scientists. In one piquant case Levelle refused—at the request of Joseph Coors—to enforce new rules which prohibited dumping liquid hazardous waste into community landfills. Coors's breweries disposed of millions of gallons of such wastes near Denver.

The climate of cronyism that infected the EPA in those days had its source in the highest levels of the Reagan administration, which encouraged agency heads such as Gorsuch to pander to its political allies: Coors, Browning-Ferris Industries, Westinghouse, and Monsanto.

Gorsuch's downfall came after congressional investigators requested records of her warm chats with companies under EPA's jurisdic-
tion. At the advice of White House counsel she refused to give over
the documents and was duly cited with contempt of Congress. When
she was called to defend herself, the Reagan Justice Department
refused to accompany her. Gorsuch resigned in disgust. The insipid
and grossly naive Levelle was eventually convicted on charges of
lying to Congress and spent six months in federal prison.

Less heralded, though more sinister, was Reagan's appointment
of John Crowell as assistant secretary of agriculture, a critical position overseeing the operations of the Forest Service, which is one of
the largest agencies in the federal government. As the former general counsel for Louisiana-Pacific, the nation's largest purchaser of
federal timber, Crowell knew his duty. One of his first actions as
assistant secretary was to suppress an internal investigation of his
predatory former employer. Forest Service investigators had concluded that Louisiana-Pacific may have bilked the government out
of more than $80 million by fraudulent bidding practices on the
Tongass National Forest.

Crowell then ordered the Forest Service to double its annual
offering of subsidized timber, much of which was destined for mills
owned by Louisiana-Pacific. He temporarily halted designation of
new federal wilderness areas and squashed scientific reports suggesting that the relentless clearcutting in Washington and Oregon
would wipe out the spotted owl.

Such useful objectives quickly accomplished, Crowell departed
the Reagan administration for more lucrative tenure at a Portland
law firm, which specialized in clients such as the National Forest
Products Association, which have a profound interest in exploiting
the natural resources of the public domain.

The raw ideologues of the Sagebrush Rebellion over-reached, but
their core message took hold: environmental regulations sapped
economic growth. Environmental overkill became the excited talk
of Washington's PR houses such as Burson-Marsteller and lobbying
firms such as Akin, Gump, which plotted a strategy of containment.

Often all that was needed was a kindlier visage. Take the case of
James Watt's replacement as Secretary of Interior, Donald Hodel.
Shortly after Hodel took up his new duties he went hiking in

Rita Levelle: Thought poison pretty, prompted flight of outraged boffins. (EPA)

Yosemite's meadows with David Brower. Brower returned to pro-
nounce Hodel an "honorable man", practically a green. Yet Hodel's
policies at Interior were as pro-industry as Watt's, and far more
effective. During his tenure, the Bureau of Land Management's timber sales hit record levels, as did subsidies for the grazing and mining industries. Hodel was the man who objected to the Montreal
protocol for restricting ozone-shredding chemicals, suggesting that
to avoid skin cancer from increased ultraviolet radiation, people
should simply wear sunglasses, hats and sunscreen.

Watt, Gorsuch, Levelle and Crowell were magnificent villains for
fundraising: direct mail revenues of the top environmental groups
exploded tenfold from 1979 to 1981. Green became the color of
money, and the rag-tag band of hard-core activists who populated
the Hill in the 1970s gave way to a cadre of Ivy-educated lobbyists,
lawyers, policy wonks, research scientists and telemarketers. Executives

enjoyed perks and salaries that rivaled those of corporate CEOs. Jay Hair was pulling down a quarter of a million dollars a year for overseeing the National Wildlife Federation's $80 million budget, and kept his limo engine running at all times, the air-conditioner grinding ozone at full tilt against the moment he emerged from his office on an eco-mission or deal-making sortie.

ASIDE: THE NATIONAL WILDLIFE FEDERATION

The cautious colossus of the environmental movement is a huge organization with more than 4 million members and an $80 million annual budget. It has more political clout in Washington than the rest of the environmental groups combined. Green politics were not always thus. In fact, the National Wildlife Federation used to be a kind of loose, apolitical collection of local hunting and gun clubs.

Jay Hair, a biology professor who served as special assistant to former

Jay Hair (l.): Former Napoleon of National Wildlife; kept air-conditioned car running on sticky days. (Elizabeth Feryl/Environmental Images)

Secretary of Interior Cecil Andrus during the Carter administration, was the architect of National Wildlife's astounding transformation. Under Hair's leadership the Federation's membership doubled and its budget tripled. His strategy was simple: market the Federation as a non-confrontational and corporate-friendly group. Hair created the Corporate Conservation Council, and forged relationships with some of the world's most toxic corporations: ARCO, Ciba-Geigy, Dow Chemical, DuPont, Exxon, General Electric, General Motors, IBM, Mobil Oil, Monsanto, Penzoil, USX, Waste Management and Weyerhaeuser. They receive the imprimatur of the nation's largest environmental group, while the National Wildlife Federation rakes in millions in corporate grants.

The conservation giant shows far less deference to its members. In 1975 Dr. Claude Moore, a long-time member, donated a 357-acre tract of forest land in Louden County, Virginia, to the Federation to be managed as a wildlife sanctuary. The land provided habitat for an extraordinary number of birds. A Smithsonian guidebook called the area a natural gem.

Then in 1986 National Wildlife decided to sell the sanctuary to a developer for $8.5 million and use the money to help pay for the construction of the Federation's new seven-story office building on 16th Street in DC. Outraged, Dr. Moore and other members sued the Federation, alleging it had violated a contract to manage the land as a nature preserve. Moore lost. The land was sold and 1,300 houses constructed on the site.

In the summer of 1995 Hair suddenly resigned from his lucrative post. In a terse note to the press, he cited personal reasons.

★

OUT OF THE WOODS, INTO THE SUITES

O ver at the Audubon Society a lawyer named Peter Berle commanded $200,000 a year. Trimming away at the muscle of the conservation staff, he gloated, "Unlike Greenpeace, Audubon doesn't have a reputation as a confrontational organization."

In the mid-1980s, after the board of directors of Friends of the Earth ousted Brower for being too attentive to grassroots activists, FOE reinvented itself as a more policy-oriented group, closed its regional offices and moved headquarters from San Francisco to Washington, DC.

The Wilderness Society meanwhile passed into the grip of William Turnage, a Yale-educated manager, after the board of directors fired the activist-oriented Stewart Brandborg. Turnage vowed to transform the Wilderness Society into a "mainstream organization" devoted to policy analysis. Within three years, 37 staff members, denounced by Turnage as "young, radical, crusader types", had been forced out, including Dave Foreman, who went on to found Earth First! The greens were replaced by Harvard-educated lawyers such as Peter Coppleman (now a deputy attorney general), conservative economists such as Alice Rivlin (now director of the Office of Management and Budget), and industry foresters such as Jeff Olson, who formerly planned timber sales for Boise Cascade.

ASIDE: WILDERNESS CHIEF CRIES "TIMBER-R-R-!"

The Wilderness Society's recent president was Jon Roush, a millionaire from Montana who was formerly the chairman of the board of the Nature Conservancy, the most pro-corporate of all environmental groups. In the winter of 1995, Roush was caught selling off $150,000 worth of timber from environmentally sensitive lands on his own 800-acre ranch in Montana's Bitterroot Valley. The trees went to Plum Creek, the corporate giant which a conservative congressman from Washington, Rod

Wilderness Society chief Jon Roush leaves his calling card, defends logging of his own ranch as prudent cut. (Jake Kreilick)

Chandler, labeled the "Darth Vader" of the timber industry.

Roush's first gallant reaction to a probing call was to blame it on his wife, whom he was in the process of divorcing. He later claimed that he needed to sell off the timber to pay his property taxes. However, local tax records reveal that Roush owed less than $1,000 a year in taxes on property valued at nearly $3 million.

★

The big environmental organizations were by now well pickled in the political brine of Washington, with freshness and passion gone.

Early in his 1988 campaign George Bush attempted to distance himself from the environmental ethos of Reagan, who had said that if you saw one redwood tree you had seen them all. Bush's strategy was due mainly to the political instincts of Lee Atwater, who closely scrutinized polling data showing that support for green causes cut across class lines: over 70 per cent of the voters wanted more government action to protect environmental quality.

Thus, Bush proudly claimed that he intended to be "the environmental president". He went after Michael Dukakis, governor of Massachusetts and the Democratic nominee, over the dismal condition of Boston Harbor. Bush pledged to support the reauthorization of the Clean Air Act, including provisions aimed at controlling acid rain, and to take action to curb global warming. He actively promoted a plan for "no net loss of wetlands".

Soon after the election Bush followed up these promises by appointing William Reilly, the first professional environmentalist to head the EPA. Reilly had been the director of the Conservation Foundation, a staid environmental group founded by Laurance Rockefeller in 1948 to advance partnerships between industry and government.

"I don't care about the regulations, I want results", became Reilly's mantra at EPA. In practice this meant that Reilly preferred consent decrees to punitive fines and criminal litigation, and voluntary compliance to mandatory regulations. He was also entranced by the notion that economic incentives could be a powerful tool for achieving improvements in air and water quality.

Reilly's primary mission at EPA was to convince environmentalists to get on board the Bush administration's corporate-friendly over-haul of the Clean Air Act. For help, Reilly turned to Bush's favorite environmental group: the Environmental Defense Fund (EDF), a more svelte and modish version of Reilly's Conservation Fund, packed with lawyers, lobbyists and scientists.

Nurtured on generous infusions of corporate grants and dona-tions, the Fund has grown into one of the most influential environ-mental groups in Washington. Operations are directed by Fred Krupp for the brawny sum of $125,000 a year. Krupp is known in some circles as the Michael Milken of the environmental movement, an allusion to the EDF supremo's tireless promotion of the "pollu-tion trading credits" scheme, which allows industrial companies to sell their right to pollute to other companies through the Chicago Board of Trade.

Waggish environmentalists have dubbed Krupp's pollution cred-its "cancer bonds". For his part, Krupp doesn't have much use for grassroots activism, which he sees as tarnishing the reputation of serious environmental groups. Krupp likes to proclaim that "what the environmental movement needs is more scientists and engineers and economists." He prefers to work with such allies of the earth as McDonalds and General Motors, which are cordial to the idea that market mechanisms and technology can resolve nearly every envi-ronmental scruple.

It was precisely these kinds of voluntary and market-oriented approaches which had attracted Reilly and Bush to Krupp in the first place. The whole scheme was laid out in a milestone white paper on so-called free-market environmentalism called "Project 88", which EDF helped write for Senators John Heinz and Tim Wirth. This doc-ument argued that environmental regulations were economically onerous and often counter-productive. Hurt business, stifle econom-ic growth and you deflate corporate interest in environmental quali-ty. Such notions derive from the belief that environmentalism is a luxury concern toward which Americans turn their attention only in times of booming prosperity. The rhetoric of this fake construct is that the best way to protect wildlands, air quality and endangered species is to keep big business running in overdrive.

That such ideas took hold in an era that saw a steady accretion of environmental catastrophes—from Three Mile Island and Love

Canal to Times Beach, Bhopal and Chernobyl; from the listing of the spotted owl and the decimation of commercial fish stocks on both coasts to the wreck of the Exxon Valdez—shows how thoroughly accustomed the mainstream greens had become to the political climate of Washington, DC. Groups such as the National Wildlife Federation and Environmental Defense Fund had lent credence to the notion that environmental quality was a secondary value, that the right to safe drinking water, clean air and functioning ecosystems could be compromised and mediated.

"Project 88" became a bible for Reilly, and many of its key provisions later resurfaced in the final version of the Clean Air Act. Heinz was killed in a plane crash in 1991 and a hefty chunk of his estate went to create the Heinz Foundation, which funnels millions of dollars to such groups as the EDF. Tim Wirth is now ensconced in the Clinton administration as an adviser on international environmental affairs.

ASIDE: WIDOW'S MILLIONS VERSUS BRAINIEST MAMMAL

What have Teresa Heinz, Senator John Kerry, former Senator Tim Wirth and *Delphinus delphis*—dolphins to you—got in common?

Start with free trade. For seven years Mexico has been whining about being prohibited from selling its canned tuna north of the border. The US mandates dolphin-free tuna, requiring methods of fishing that don't snag dolphins as part of the tuna haul. This was one of the great victories of the 1980s, but no sooner was the NAFTA agreement signed than Mexico denounced the US tuna law as a restraint on free trade and demanded its rescission.

Prodded by Mickey Kantor, the chief US trade rep, the White House speedily assented, but said that some national environmental organizations would have to be wheeled forth to provide political cover against assaults from the volatile dolphin lobby. Enter the Environmental Defense Fund, a fanatical espouser of free trade as the salve for more or less everything, vociferously pro-NAFTA in 1992 and a long-time foe of the dolphin protection laws as "ideologically unsound".

The crucial meeting to settle the dolphin's hash took place in the

Mexican embassy in DC in July of 1995. Here US and Mexican government officials hunkered down with executives from the Environmental Defense Fund, National Wildlife Federation, World Wildlife Fund and the Center for Marine Conservation. Carefully excluded were pro-dolphin groups such as Earth Island Institute and the Humane Society. Also shut out were the congressional members and staffers who had framed the 1992 law protecting the dolphin, 7 million of which perished in the eastern Pacific between 1970 and 1992.

The secret session in the Mexican embassy was not auspicious for the dolphin. The conspirators agreed that the 1992 law should be overturned and new statutory language devised which would allow Mexico's dolphin-lethal tuna to roll north into US supermarkets. Staffers from the Environmental Defense Fund and World Wildlife Fund would write the new bill in language congenial to greens, with help from Bud Walsh, an attorney who has labored for the Wise Use movement.

Next came the task of selling dolphin death on the Hill. In the forefront of the lobbying was Tim Wirth, now Undersecretary of State for global environmental affairs. Wirth dispatched handwritten notes to crucial senators, urging them to sign on to the bill and promoting it as a "good package

Teresa Heinz: Ketchup heiress funds "free market environmentalism" following romantic interlude in Rio. Bad news for Flipper. (Vivian Ronay/Photoreporters)

with a sound science/enviro base with Breaux and Stevens as sponsors".

Now, when it comes to environmental matters Breaux of Louisiana and Stevens of Alaska are four-square for rape and pillage, and have long carried water for Don Tyson, Arkansas's chicken-and-fish king. But some were puzzled at Wirth's stance for dolphin death. Early in 1995 Wirth had taken the trouble to leak to *The Washington Post* a memo he'd sent to the White House urging Clinton to stand firm against those around him counseling sellout of Mother Nature.

But the dark side of Tim Wirth's environmentalism goes back to his days in the Senate and his friendship with Senator John Heinz, the ketchup heir, with whom he had drafted *"Project 88"*, the detailed manifesto of "free-market environmentalism", encouraging replacement of federal laws and regulations with cash inducements for corporate pillagers to behave themselves.

After Senator Heinz's death, Wirth was particularly close to his widow Teresa Heinz. Senate staffers suggested that Wirth's proximity to the widow was freighted with more than the melancholy solidarity of the grieved. Some say that when he stood down from the Senate in 1992, Wirth feared malicious rumors to this effect. Wirth has furiously denied such allegations. In any case, the widow Heinz pressed forward into romance with Senator John Kerry of Massachusetts. The tinder ignited at the Earth Summit in Rio in 1992, where they mightily impressed other junketeers, including Senator Larry Pressler, by conversing in French.

Teresa Heinz, the daughter of a Portuguese doctor, was brought up as a child of empire in Mozambique, went to university in South Africa and apparently brought with her to the United States the same ardent veneration for the capitalist system, and indeed for capitalists, as did another import, Arianna Huffington. Teresa made her way onto the board of the Environmental Defense Fund and—in the late 1980s when the EDF was heavily involved in various Amazonian promotions and fundraising endeavors—used to sweep into the Western Amazon in great style, gazing with marked disfavor on the unruly rubber-tappers mustered at the Rio Branco airport to meet her. Frantic EDF staffers would plead with the seringueiros to shed radical buttons lest Teresa conclude that the EDF had fallen into bed with Third World revolutionaries, instead of promoting parks from which Indians and rubber tappers could swiftly be evicted.

Being a member of the Heinz family added clout to Teresa's ideological views, clout in the form of a fortune estimated as between $670 million and

$740 million. Hence the moral crisis of Senator John Kerry. Teresa Heinz lobbied hard for the new death-to-dolphin bill. But her husband (they married in July of 1995) was long a doughty dolphin ally, possibly because this splendid mammal is not profuse on the St. George's Banks, nor on other haunts of the Massachusetts fishing fleet.

If a last-ditch defense of the 1992 law was to be mounted, Kerry was the man to lead it. But the senator had new cares and burdens. When he gave up Morgan Fairchild for Teresa Heinz and joined with her in the refreshments of matrimony, Kerry was asked whether he would use his wife's fortune to stake his political races. Kerry said he wouldn't, unless his opponent also put up his or her own, or family money.

In the last days of 1995 Massachusetts' Gingrich-loving libertarian governor, William Weld, announced he would challenge Kerry. Weld will be a tough opponent, although he prudently called for Kerry to agree to limit spending in the race to $5 million each. Kerry had thus an enormous temptation to turn to his wife for help. His zeal for the dolphin declined markedly. Meanwhile Teresa busily lobbied the Heinz Corporation, whose subsidiary, Star-Kist, is the world's largest tuna processor. Having invested millions in dolphin-safe fishing fleets and having mined excellent publicity for its "dolphin-safe tuna", Star-Kist was loath to see the 1992 law changed. It claimed that the new law will cost the company 6,000 jobs in American Samoa. Nonetheless, Teresa, one of the Heinz Corporation's largest stockholders, pressed Star-Kist to adopt a more cold-blooded attitude toward Flipper.

In December of 1995 Teresa Heinz disbursed the largest single environmental grant in US history: $20 million for an environmental center to promulgate the free-market economics her husband outlined before his decease.

★

The anti-regulatory fervor of the Reagan era also thrived in corners of the Bush administration. One particularly anti-environmental voice was Bush's budget director, Richard Darman, who continually slashed planned spending for national park land acquisitions and hazardous waste cleanups. "Americans did not fight and win the wars of the 20th century to make the world safe for green vegetables," Darman thundered in a memorable lecture at Harvard. In lighter language his boss, Bush, lashed out at

Manuel Lujan: Bush's Secretary of the Interior. No friend to the spotted owl.
(Library of Congress)

broccoli, on the grounds he had been force-fed it as a child.

Meanwhile, over in the vice president's office, Dan Quayle was running the White House Council on Competitiveness, a relay station for the complaints of corporate America. The Council was staffed by a young lawyer from Indiana called David McIntosh, subsequently elected to Congress in 1994, whose function was to review all new federal regulations with an eye toward how much each might impair the profitability of big business. "We're here to listen to the concerns of industry," McIntosh said. "The environmentalists have got the EPA as an audience for their complaints."

A typical example of the Council's chivalry is the case of the Louisiana black bear, an especially rare species that inhabits the backwoods swamps and bayous of the Mississippi delta. On learning that the Fish and Wildlife Service might list the bear as a threatened species, Louisiana-Pacific, Weyerhaeuser and Georgia-Pacific asked the Competitiveness Council to intervene, arguing that the listing of the bear would prove a financial hardship to these multi-billion dollar transnational companies. The Council sprang into action. The listing was delayed for more than two years, while the timber barons clearcut in the last remnants of the bear's habitat.

Meanwhile the pro-development demeanor of the Interior Department, which was now under the control of Manuel Lujan, was only moderately less aggressive than during the frenzied days of Watt. Lujan is a former right-wing congressman from New Mexico with strong ties to the ranching and mining industries. He pushed hard to open the Arctic National Wildlife Refuge to oil drilling, continued Watt's efforts to accelerate exploratory activities on the Outer Continental Shelf, and resisted attempts to charge market prices for cattle grazing on federal grasslands, which under Lujan's tenure amounted to $200 million a year in subsidies to such public lands ranchers as Hewlett-Packard and the agribusiness magnate J.R. Simplot.

Under instructions from Bush, Lujan ordered the Bureau of Land Management to fast track the purchase of the Goldstrike Mine by American Barrick Resources, a Toronto-based company controlled by financier Peter Munk. The way thus lubricated, Barrick purchased the 1,800-acre gold mine on BLM lands outside Elko, Nevada, for the princely sum of $9,500. By the time it is closed, the Goldstrike Mine will yield an estimated $10 billion in gold. In 1995, in consideration for his favors, George Bush was invited to join Barrick's board of advisers.

Lujan also became the first Interior Secretary to challenge directly the Endangered Species Act. Lujan wanted to allow timber companies in Oregon to clearcut ancient forests inhabited by the northern spotted owl, which had been listed as a threatened species. The Interior Secretary fiercely opposed the court-ordered listing of the owl, saying, "If we've a species, I don't see why we have to save a subspecies like the northern spotted owl. Maybe these subspecies just aren't meant to survive. Maybe they just can't adapt to their new surroundings." In an effort to override the Endangered Species Act's prohibition against logging the owl's habitat, Lujan invoked the so-called God Squad, a panel of Bush administration appointees which could vote to "sanction" activities leading to the extinction of a listed species. The God Squad approved the timber sales, but their action was later overturned by a federal court.

ASIDE: SHAKING THE TREE—GREENS AND FOUNDATIONS

Back at the start of the century John D. Rockefeller remarked that "Not even God himself can keep me from giving my money to the University of Chicago." The old bandit's investments duly paid off, and platoons of economists, jurists and academics hymned the free market and invoked inexorable laws which require that some be rich and many be poor.

Philanthropy and its purposes remain the same as when John D. dispensed millions to winch the family name out of the mud. Today the environmental movement receives about $40 million a year from three oil companies which operate through front groups politely described as private foundations. The top two are the Sun Oil Company (Sunoco) and Oryx Energy. (The latter has vast holdings of natural gas in Arkansas, and throughout the oil patch.) The Pew family once entirely controlled the two companies and still has large holdings in both of them; Oryx shareholders recently sued the Pew operation for insider trading.

In 1948 the family set up the Pew Charitable Trust with an endowment now totaling $3.4 billion. In its early days the Trust was vociferously right-wing. Money flowed to the John Birch Society and other anti-Communist crusades, to Billy Graham and population control, an unending preoccupation of the rich.

The necessity of buying liberals impressed itself on the family rather late, in the 1980s. But since then it has more than made up for lost time. Today, Pew Charitable Trusts (now seven in all) represent one of the largest donors to the environmental movement, investing about $20 million a year. But this does not tell the full story of coercion through money. At the head of the Pew environmental sector sits Joshua Reichert. Reichert and subordinates Tom Wathen and John Gilroy allocate Pew money, such as the $1.5 million spent in 1995–96 to buy off vigorous defenders of the Endangered Species Act and ensure a revised and neutered law. They also help direct the donations of other foundations mustered in the Environmental Grantmakers

Tom Wathen (center) and John Gilroy (second from right) of Pew Charitable Trusts: Help dish out $20 million a year to greens. (Elizabeth Feryl/Environmental Images)

Association, which collectively doles out more than $350 million a year. Pew never goes it alone. It always works in coalitions with these others, which means no radical opposition to its environmental policies can get any money. (Notable exceptions include the Turner Foundation, and smaller opponents of the Pew Cartel such as Levinson and Patagonia.)

Meanwhile, the Pew Trusts' endowment is wisely invested in the very corporations that a vigorous environmental movement would adamantly be opposing. In its initial National Forest Campaign, Pew demanded that recipients of grant money agree to focus their attention on government actions; corporate wrongdoers were not to be named. This extreme plan was modified after some recipients balked.

The Charitable Trusts' money increases with the fortunes of timber firms, mining, oil and chemical companies and arms manufacturers. The annual yield from these investments far exceeds the dispensations to environmental groups. Take just one of the seven Pew trust funds—the Pew Memorial Trust. This enterprise made $205 million in "investment income" in 1993 from such stocks as Weyerhaeuser ($16 million), the mining concern Phelps Dodge ($3.7 million), International Paper ($4.56 million) and Atlantic Richfield, which is pushing hard to open the Arctic to oil development ($6.1 million). The income yield from rapacious companies accruing to Pew in this single trust is twice as large as its total grants, and six times as large as all of Pew's environmental dispensations.

Next of the big three in environmental funding is an oil company known as Cities Services (Citgo), which endowed the W. Alton Jones Foundation, based in Charlottesville, Virginia. In the merger frenzy of the 1980s, Occidental Petroleum ultimately took over Cities in a move that saved Ivan Boesky from financial ruin. Alton Jones maintains an endowment of $220 million, and in 1993 gave out $15.7 million in grants. According to its charter, the purpose of the foundation is two-fold: to preserve biological diversity and to eliminate the threat of nuclear war. Alton Jones gives about $14 million a year to environmental causes and uses the same engulf-and-neuter tactic as Pew. This apostle of peace has maintained very large investments in arms manufacturers such as Martin Marietta ($3.26 million), Raytheon ($1.32 million), Boeing ($1.38 million) and GE ($1.4 million).

Alton Jones's portfolio has also gained bulk from bonds floated by Charles Hurwitz's Scotia Pacific Holdings Company, a subsidiary of Maxxam, which is currently embarked on the project of cutting down the Headwaters Grove, the largest patch of privately-owned redwoods in the world. Its 1993 statement to the IRS also revealed $1.4 million in Louisiana-Pacific stock, the largest purchaser of timber from publicly-owned federal forests.

Alton Jones has a position (just under a million in stock) in FMC, the big gold mining enterprise which will soon sponsor dosing an endangered salmon habitat at the Beartrack Mine in Idaho with cyanide, a project greased by Commerce Secretary Ron Brown. Picking up revenue from FMC's salmon destruction with one hand, in 1993 Alton Jones gave about $60,000 to protect the endangered salmon in the same area. The grants went to the most compliant organizations, such as the Wilderness Society and Pacific Rivers Council. At a crucial moment last January, these two groups demanded that a federal judge suspend an injunction they had, to their great alarm, just won. This injunction shut down FMC's Beartrack Gold Mine, from which it expects to make $300 million courtesy of the 1872 Mining Act, whose reform the Clinton administration carefully avoided. When the Wilderness Society's attorneys asked Judge David Ezra to rescind the injunction, he was outraged though had no alternative but to comply. FMC's stock promptly soared, yielding extra money for Alton Jones.

The last of the big three is the Rockefeller Family Fund, run by ex-Naderite Donald Ross, who as of the last filing with the IRS in 1993 was picking up $130,000 a year plus another $20,000 in benefits. The relationship of the Family Fund to oil money scarcely needs stating. Though the Fund dispenses a relatively puny $2 million a year in grants, it exercises great influence by dint of Ross's leadership of the Environmental Grantmakers Association. The Fund also functions as a staff college for foundation executives. John Gilroy and Tom Wathen, both of Pew, learned their trade under Ross's tutelage.

The Rockefeller Family Fund, in its 1993 IRS filing, held $3.5 million in oil and gas stocks, including Amerada Hess (a company convicted of price-fixing, and one of the first to drill on Alaska's North Slope), and UNOCAL, which maintains a cozy relationship to the military dictatorship in Burma.

The Fund also maintains hefty investments in mining companies, including ASARCO, an outfit with a notorious environmental rap sheet whose activities have laid waste to western Montana, easily overwhelming the protests of the Mineral Policy Center, which has conducted a futile campaign partially underwritten by the Fund. The Fund's money is also in FMC and Freeport-McMoRan, whose worldwide operations are on the cutting edge of ecocide and which has a financial partnership with the genocidal Indonesian generals. The Fund's mineral and chemical company holdings exceeded a million dollars on its last filing.

As of 1993 Ross's outfit had a strong position in Weyerhaeuser, the largest private timberland-owning company in North America. The possibility of double-dealing endemic to all foundations with the ability to influence federal policy is nicely illustrated here. The Rockefeller Family Fund was the lead architect of the campaign to protect ancient forests on public lands in the Northwest. Any reduction—actual or prospective—of timber available on public lands sends up the value of privately-held timber tracts. The Fund made a killing out of buying Weyerhaeuser stock low and selling it high, before large-scale logging began again on public lands. The Family Fund was nicely covered because it also had holdings—$237,000—in Boise Cascade, which is the largest purchaser of federal timber sales in the Northwest. Indeed, last year Boise Cascade bought the Sugarloaf tract of 900-year-old Douglas fir trees in southern Oregon's Siskiyou National Forest and is now logging it, courtesy of a released injunction engineered by a deal between the Clinton administration and environmental groups funded and closely supervised by Donald Ross. Ross was the man who hired the Democratic Party hack Bob Chlopak (another former Naderite) to oversee the conversion of a tough national movement to fight Clinton to the death on old-growth forests into a supine coalition which swiftly draped itself in the white flag of surrender.

As an old Nader man Ross presumably should feel some embarrassment at the Rockefeller Family Fund's extensive holdings in the Ten Worst Corporations as listed by *Multinational Monitor,* a Nader operation.

These supposedly nonprofit foundations have their bets beautifully covered. Overseen by Pew, their money has gone to groups brokering the destruction of the Endangered Species Act. As this environmental law expires in all but name, their holdings in mining, timber and real estate ventures soar.

★

At the close of the Bush administration, many high-profile environmental issues, including the fate of the Arctic National Wildlife Refuge and the ancient forests of the Pacific Northwest, remained gridlocked. But a quiet, vital change had taken place. The core idea of conservation and protection, that a strong federal regulatory system represented the best way to protect the American environment, was being quietly refuted by the leaders of the environmental movement.

Many of the old environmental heroes had moved on to strange new positions. William Ruckleshaus now runs Browning-Ferris Industries, the nation's largest solid waste company and sits on the board of the timber giant Weyerhaeuser and the agro-chemical empire Monsanto. Lee Thomas, one of Ruckleshaus's successors at EPA, found an especially remunerative position as an executive in the Atlanta headquarters of convicted federal income tax evader, Georgia-Pacific. Gaylord Nelson, father of Earth Day, joined the board of the Wilderness Society; Donald Ross and Dennis Hayes abandoned the environmental movement for more lucrative positions in corporate philanthropy. The mighty Sierra Club Legal Defense Fund forced its clients to relinquish hard fought legal injunctions as "gestures of goodwill" to its friends and colleagues in the Clinton administration. The promiscuous Bob Packwood, now disgraced, traveled the roads of rural Oregon calling for the repeal of the Endangered Species Act. Corporate criminal Louisiana-Pacific (which pleaded guilty to 16 felonies and misdemeanors in 1995) served as a proud sponsor of the twenty-fifth anniversary celebration of Earth Day.

In the Clinton era, the contours of environmental politics in Washington Babylon have settled into a triangulated landscape, bounded by the Executive Office Building and its agency outlets (where administrative fiats are handed down with devastating finality); the committee rooms of the Congress (where the chairmen of the all important appropriations committees dole out pork and pollution); and the grey mansions of the special interest lobbies, both environmental and industrial, which are stacked along K Street. Daily, the inhabitants of these centers of power determine the levels of lead in the blood of children in south-central LA, the number of Chinook salmon chewed up and spit out by the hydro-electric dams on the Columbia River, the gallons of dioxin flushed into the Mississippi, and the fate of such animals as the grizzly bear, whose habitat can remain protected public land or be transformed into cyanide-laced heap leach gold mines.

At the top of the Executive pyramid now squats Bill Clinton. His interest in environmental matters is, and always has been, opportunistic. Environmental quality and economic progress must advance hand in hand, Clinton counsels. If they don't, well, there will always be time to fix the damage to the earth later.

ASIDE: THOMAS FOLEY

P residing over the House of Representatives through the late 1980s and early 1990s was Tom Foley, who hails from the Inland Empire region of eastern Washington. Foley was the principal architect of the anti-environment policies coming out of the House over the past ten to fifteen years. First as chairman of the powerful Agriculture Committee and later as one of the most autocratic speakers of the House in this century, Foley shilled for the Northwest timber, mining, aluminum and defense industries, which stocked his campaign war chest with hundreds of thousands of dollars. Foley's legacy of destruction is written across the landscape: radioactive contamination at Hanford, destroyed wild lands in Idaho and Montana and numerous endangered species, headlined by the northern spotted owl, hundreds of stocks of Pacific salmon and the grizzly bear.

As speaker he assigned key committee chairs and dictated the legislative agenda of the House, determining which bills received hearings and which languished despite broad popular support.

One of Foley's biggest and most reliable campaign contributors was Plum Creek Timber Company, a limited partnership which owns 2.1 million

Tom Foley: Former Speaker, his name will endure wherever grizzlies and salmon die or where radioactivity enhances nature's temple. (Rick Reinhard/Impact Visuals)

acres of timber land and is the second largest American exporter of raw logs to Japan. Foley fiercely defended Plum Creek's interests from attacks within his own party by Oregon Rep. Peter DeFazio and Rep. Pat Williams of Montana, who wanted to stem the flow of log exports and save 20,000 millworker jobs in the United States. Foley threatened to sanction the impudent congressmen and retaliated by refusing to bring legislation they had sponsored to the floor for votes.

★

When Clinton came to DC, he brought Mack McLarty, formerly with the natural gas behmoth ARKLA Inc. and a golfing pal of the tycoons of Arkansas, with him as chief of staff. Along with the corporate lobbyist Vernon Jordan, McLarty played a decisive role in choosing Clinton's cabinet, including Leon Panetta and Alice Rivlin at OMB, Babbitt at Interior, Ron Brown at Commerce, and former Gore staffers Carol Browner as head of EPA and Katie McGinty as supervisor of the White House Office of Environmental Affairs. All were cut from the pro-business, anti-regulation cloth spun by the Democratic Leadership Council. In a move that was later to yield useful dividends, the Clinton transition team also stocked the administration with a cluster of 24 top-level staffers culled from the ranks of DC-based environmental groups. At the head was George Frampton, former president of the Wilderness Society, picked as assistant secretary of interior.

It didn't take McLarty long to exert his veto power over environmental policy. The administration's initial budget request to Congress included a provision to reform federal policies governing gold mining and subsidized grazing and timber sales on public lands. Widely supported by greens, the provision would have protected millions of acres of forest and grassland from clearcutting and mining and saved the federal treasury nearly a billion dollars a year. Instead, it set a firestorm in the public lands states in the West. A group of Western Democrats, led by Senators Max Baucus of Montana and Ben Nighthorse Campbell of Colorado (who later skipped to the Republican side of the aisle), wrote an angry letter denouncing the provision and threatening to launch a filibuster against it on the Senate floor. McLarty invited the senators to the White House where he obediently agreed to pull the measure from the budget request. (Bruce Babbitt, whose office had drafted the proposal, found out about McLarty's deal-making the next night at a cocktail party. His unlikely informant was Jay Hair, still the head of the National Wildlife Federation. "The son of a bitch", Babbitt raged. "He didn't have the fucking courtesy to ask me about it or even to tell me what he had done."

McLarty's cave-in occurred on the eve of the first-ever presidential summit on environmental issues: the Presidential Conference on Northwest Forests, held in Portland, Oregon, on April 2, 1993. The timber summit, as it came to be known, had its roots in the controversy over the northern spotted owl and the clearcutting of ancient forests on federal lands in the Pacific Northwest.

The spotted owl, which lives only in old-growth trees, had been listed as a threatened species in 1990. The following year William Dwyer, a federal judge in Seattle, halted all logging on 6 million acres of old-growth forest in Oregon, Washington and California.

The judge cited the government for a "systematic disregard" of the nation's environmental laws. The timber industry bellowed that the injunction was going to put them out of business and throw 100,000 millworkers and loggers out of work. Environmentalists responded that the decease of the owl would be just the beginning of a larger annulment of old-growth-dwelling species, including dwindling stocks of Pacific salmon—all threatened by logging. The most puissant predators in the forest, Weyerhaeuser, Georgia-Pacific and International Paper, which owned their own highly productive lands, were not affected by the injunction and in fact had seen their earnings soar.

During his campaign swings through the Northwest, Clinton promised that within 90 days of taking office he would convene a summit to resolve the "timber crisis" once and for all. "I want to produce a legal plan for managing these forests", Clinton assured voters, "and get the logs rolling back into the mills." So on April 2 Clinton summoned his top cabinet officials, corporate executives, millworkers, loggers, economists, bureaucrats, the Cardinal of Seattle, forest sociologists, academic and agency scientists and mainstream environmentalists to Portland.

ASIDE: KNIGHT IN GREEN ARMOR

How is power really leveraged? Read Bob Packwood's diaries. The private record of this disgraced Oregon senator and number one recipient of political action committee dollars from the timber industry—$390,000 since 1991—tells the whole story.

Packwood told the chief lobbyist for the National Lumber Wholesalers Association that if the Lumber Wholesalers wanted him, Packwood, to gut the Endangered Species Act, a hefty contribution was needed. Money duly flowed into Packwood's campaign treasury—and he attacked the spotted owl.

Packwood is a Republican. Democrats are no different. The leading recipient in the House of timber industry money is Norm Dicks, from Washington.

As the Republicans took over Congress at the end of 1994, green groups cried tremulously that foxes were in charge of the coop. They were partially right. At the Senate Interior Committee, chaired by Frank Murkowski of Alaska, Mark Rey became chief of staff. In his previous job, Rey was the top lobbyist for the American Forest and Paper Association, a $60 million a year lobbying giant. Under his watch the rewriting of the nation's environmental laws began.

The green groups looked in desperation to the White House and the veto power which was all that stood between nature and the corporate predators. But the mighty veto sword stayed in its scabbard. Clinton and his number two, Al Gore, did nothing. The truth is that the fox had been in charge of the coop long before November of 1994.

Consider the recent career of Peter Knight. From 1979 to 1991 Knight worked as chief legislative aide for Senator Al Gore. Then he was chairman of the vice-presidential campaign that designated Gore as electoral flypaper for the green vote. Knight duly became the vice chairman in charge of personnel for the Clinton-Gore transition team, overseen by deal-maker extraordinaire Vernon Jordan, who counts among his innumerable obligations to the corporate sector the duties of lobbyist for the timber industry. Knight later emerged in shining armor as a lawyer-lobbyist for the Washington law firm Wunder, Diefenderfer, Cannon and Thelen. Among this firm's prime clients, with whom Knight deals on a regular basis, are Manville of asbestos fame, the solid waste giant Browning-Ferris Industries and two of the nation's largest timber companies, Riverwood and Kimberly-Clark. The firm also represents the American Forest and Paper Association, where Mark Rey once toiled to make the wild woods safer for the chainsaw.

★

The timber summit itself was a piece of theater designed to allow Clinton to demonstrate his affection for nature and to show that he "felt the pain" of laid off millworkers. At the same time he humbly deferred to the true source of millworkers' economic woes: Weyerhaeuser vice president Charlie Bingham, who commands the exportation of billions of board feet of raw logs to mills overseas. Bingham and Clinton had known each other for years.

At the close of the day, Clinton bragged of taking the conflict "out of the courtroom and into the conference room", and promised that his administration would produce a "scientifically credible and legally responsible" plan within 90 days. The goal of the plan was to provide a sure supply of timber to Northwest mills and to protect the federally-owned habitat of the spotted owl and Pacific salmon stocks.

Insinuated into every line of Clinton's screed was the promise that the whine of the chainsaw would be sacrosanct, immune from even modest attempts to slow the frenzied pace of the cut or the export of raw logs. And so it came to pass.

Forest Service chief Jack Ward Thomas: The biologist clicked his heels.
(Elizabeth Feryl/Environmental Images)

Clinton swiftly assembled a task force of federal scientists, headed by Forest Service research ecologist Jack Ward Thomas and forester Jerry Franklin, who also happened to be a board member of the Wilderness Society. The scientists devised eight options for the president to consider. None of them permitted enough logging to satisfy Clinton's political objectives. Clinton and Babbitt instructed the scientists to concoct another alternative, the infamous Option Nine.

While Option Nine reduced the amount of logging allowed on national forests, it failed to set aside any permanently protected old-growth forest preserves, and permitted clearcutting in the most ancient groves and in the most vital spotted owl and salmon habitat. In fact the environmental analysis accompanying Option Nine admits that this strategy places hundreds of species at increased risk of extinction, including the spotted owl, marbled murrelet, and dozens of stocks of Pacific salmon and steelhead.

The scientists working on the project were prohibited from talking to the press, and Thomas promptly shredded documents which revealed the fake science behind Option Nine.

Months later, Clinton picked Thomas as the new chief of the Forest Service. Leaders of the DC environmental groups dutifully claimed Thomas's appointment as a major victory, despite his role in the development of Option Nine.

Thomas is known as a brilliant ecologist, but also as an arrogant and mean-spirited quisling, dating back to his days managing a Forest Service research station in eastern Oregon, called the Starker Forest. The Starker was supposed to be immune from large-scale logging. Here stood one of the last stands of old-growth ponderosa pine in the Blue Mountains; it had become a Mecca for scientists studying the ecology of old-growth systems. As chief research ecologist Thomas managed the land and decided who could conduct studies. When research money began to dry up in the 1980s Thomas secretly sold an area of prime forest to Boise Cascade, which promptly clearcut it. When scientists protested, Thomas threatened to kill their research projects and ban future studies on the forest.

Within months of assuming his post in the Clinton administration, Thomas approved the biggest timber sale in the modern history of the Forest Service. The so-called Prince of Wales timber sale on the

Tongass National Forest in southeast Alaska called for the clearcutting of thousands of acres of ancient forest and the construction more than 100 miles of road into a fragile and previously roadless landscape. Louisiana-Pacific, the buyer, had been strongly opposed by numerous biologists and geologists within the Forest Service.

In the spring of 1994, Thomas fired two Forest Service whistle-blowers. Ernie Nunn and Curtis Bates had stood up to the timber and mineral companies in Montana, and first ran into trouble back in 1990, when they signed a letter which described the Forest Service as dominated by the whims of the extractive industries and out of touch with the environmental concerns of the American public. That letter sparked such a revolt inside the Forest Service that the Bush administration attempted to sack the dissident forest supervisors. This Republican bid failed, rebuffed by congressional hearings and public outcry. Four years later, with a Democratic president and a Democratic Congress, Thomas moved swiftly and with impunity to fire Bates and Nunn.

Despite these outrages, many of the big green groups remained locked in necrotic embrace with the Clinton administration. The Sierra Club's Carl Pope, a long-time friend of Al Gore, hailed the Option Nine plan as "a fair and reasonable compromise". The

Hattie Coons Babbitt and Bruce Babbitt, Clinton's Interior Secretary: "Not Babbitt the Rabbit!" cried Edward Abbey. Breaks strikes, makes water run uphill, cuts old-growth, extinguishes species in a single bound. (Shia photo/Impact Visuals)

National Audubon Society's Brock Evans, long touted as the best environmental lobbyist on the Hill, pronounced it "a shaky victory".

The Clinton administration floated a draft version of Option Nine before the public. Then Bruce Babbitt called on environmental leaders to annul the very injunction they had won in Judge Dwyer's courtroom against logging in spotted owl habitat. As a "gesture of goodwill" to the Clinton administration, Babbitt demanded that the environmentalists accept various timber sales in ancient forests. If they refused, Babbitt said, the administration would ask Congress to overturn the injunction with what's known as a sufficiency rider, a tactic of the Reagan/Bush years. With such a rider, Congress stipulates that a law is "sufficient", overriding all relevant previous laws and regulations and immune to future challenge in the courts.

Lawyers for the Sierra Club Legal Defense Fund (the self-proclaimed "dream-team" of environmental law firms) forthwith coerced its clients into giving over several thousand acres of old-growth forest, and then, months later, the Dwyer injunction itself.

Grassroots greens vigorously resisted this surrender. But the Defense Fund, which holds a near monopoly on nonprofit environmental lawsuits, threatened to abandon any clients who refused to go along with its advice. One of the strange pathologies afflicting contemporary environmentalism is that a conservation group without a law firm behind it suffers extreme pangs of institutional impotence. "The problem was that SCLDF's arguments stemmed from political, not legal, judgments", says Oregon environmentalist Larry Tuttle, "and they were shaped in large measure by their own economic self-interest (i.e., their right to sue and reap hefty attorneys' fees from the government), not the future of the spotted owl."

Eventually, the environmentalists, pummeled by their own attorneys, collapsed, and in the spring of 1994 the cutting of ancient forest resumed for the first time in four years. Things had indeed been better with George Bush and gridlock.

Bruce Babbitt's role in this deal of shame shocked many greens. He had been president of the League of Conservation Voters, and many had seen him as the green chevalier of the Clinton administration. The stab in the back should have surprised no one.

Babbitt comes from a big-time ranching family fed and fattened on the western traditions of cheap water, free range and unregulated mining. When mineworkers in Arizona walked off the job citing unsafe and unfair working conditions at the Phelps Dodge silver mine in the early Eighties, then Governor Babbitt called in the National Guard to crush the strike on behalf of the corporation, which had long planned the confrontation in consort with the University of Pennsylvania's Wharton School as a test case for breaking strikes and unions with permanent "replacement workers".

Babbitt also strong-armed federal park officials in order to secure approval of a resort complex on the rim of the Grand Canyon. The resort was owned by a long-time friend and political contributor.

But Babbitt is perhaps most notorious for his single-minded pursuit of Colorado River water. The multi-billion dollar Central Arizona Project channeled millions of acre feet of precious water onto cotton fields absurdly located in the Arizona desert to assuage the thirst of real estate czars in Phoenix and Tucson. While Babbitt supported mighty water allocations to his state, he opposed them for his neighbors, vigorously objecting to water claims made by California and Utah. These western water battles brought Babbitt into the embrace of Richard Carver, a commissioner in Nye County, Nevada. Carver is now a key leader of the "county supremacy" movement, which asserts that the federal government does not have the right to own land. Carver has promoted his cause at gatherings of far right groups throughout the West, most notably at the Jubilation, organized by the racist Posse Comitatus.

In August of 1994, Carver ignited a war with the federal government when he mounted a bulldozer and constructed an illegal road on the Toiyabe National Forest, nearly running over two Forest Service employees. Carver, who claims that he and Babbitt are close friends, threatened to shoot anyone who tried to stop him. Although harassment of a federal employee is a felony, punishable by a $250,000 fine and up to 10 years in prison, six months passed and the federal government took no action. Finally, only a civil suit was filed, and that against the Nye County government itself, not Carver. Local BLM and Forest Service rangers think Babbitt intervened with the Department of Justice investigation on behalf of his friend Carver.

Ron Arnold (in beard) with David Brower (the Arch Druid): Ahab of the Wise Use movement; worked for Sierra Club, spends life seeking revenge.
(Elizabeth Feryl/Environmental Images)

ASIDE: THE WISE USE MOVEMENT

A s the environmental movement went corporate, the corporations went grassroots. Beginning in the late 1980s timber and mining companies began funneling millions of dollars into front groups. People for the West!, for example, claimed to represent loggers, ranchers and miners displaced by environmental lawsuits and regulations. These groups charged that environmentalists "worshipped trees and sacrificed people".

Leaders of the anti-green Wise Use movement are Ron Arnold, the man James Watt picked to write his biography, and right-wing direct mail operator Alan Gottlieb. Arnold lifted the term "Wise Use" from Gifford Pinchot, one of the heroes of the early conservation movement. "'Wise Use' was an expressive and catchy term", Arnold says. "Plus, it was short enough to fit in newspaper headlines, just like 'ecology'."

The 1980s and early 1990s were a time of big layoffs in the timber industry. The cause was automation of the mills and increased raw log exports to Japan; yet Arnold was able to shift blame for the economic and social restructuring of the West to "environmental ideology".

Gottlieb says: "This anti-environmental movement brings in much more of a response than any other issue, including gun control." Gottlieb and Arnold's mailing list now contains at least 3 million names and is growing rapidly. The Wise Use movement has numerous supporters in the US Congress, including Senators Craig, Burns, Stevens, Thomas and Slade Gorton, and Representatives Linda Smith, Vucanovich, Cubin, Condit and Tauzin, a turncoat Democrat from Louisiana, who stalled reauthorization of the Endangered Species Act and introduced property rights legislation in the 102nd Congress. Idaho Rep. Helen Chenoweth was a Wise Use adviser and says the grizzly bear's only use is killing wolves.

★

Other friends of Babbitt haven't fared nearly so well. Take Jim Baca, who comes from one of the oldest Hispanic families in the Southwest and who served for several years as the lands commissioner for the state of New Mexico, where he acquired a reputation as a progressive and hard-nosed conservationist. But Baca's anti-cattle grazing stance earned him the enmity of ranchers across the West. Over the objections of the National Cattlemen's Association and the American Mining Congress, Babbitt chose Baca to oversee the BLM, the agency in charge of administering about 250 million acres of public lands in the West—lands long viewed as the private dominion of cattle ranchers and gold mining companies.

Baca tried to make ranchers pay market rates for the use of public grasslands. (Currently, ranchers pay less than a fifth of rates charged on private and state lands—a $200 million a year subsidy.) Then he went after the gold companies. Baca became a vigorous advocate for the repeal of the 1872 Mining Law, which allows gold mining companies to claim title to public lands for as little as $2.50 per acre and then pay no royalties on the billions of dollars of minerals they remove. Baca fought for an 8 per cent royalty on the mining of all public minerals and an end to the transfer of federal lands to mineral companies. Finally, Baca became the first BLM director openly to advocate the need for more wilderness. He supported setting aside nearly 20 million acres of high desert and mountain country in Utah, Idaho and Oregon as wilderness, closed to logging, mining and grazing.

This ran Baca athwart very powerful interests, many in the Democratic Party. Baca's most prominent opponent turned out to be the Governor of Idaho, Cecil Andrus, former Secretary of the Interior and a former employee of the Wilderness Society, where Baca had once served as a director. In December of 1993, Andrus attacked Baca in a letter to Babbitt, pronouncing: "My friend, frankly, you don't have enough political allies in the West to treat us this shabbily." Later, Andrus, who after retiring as governor joined the boards of two mining companies, threatened publicly, "It's either Baca or Babbitt, one of them's gotta go."

A few days later Babbitt announced in *The Washington Post* that Baca had been transferred from his BLM post to a new vague role as policy adviser to Babbitt. There was a problem. No one had told Baca about the move and he resisted, publicly.

"I thought Babbitt at least owed it to me as a long-time friend to explain why I was being ousted", Baca said. "I wanted him to ask me for my resignation personally." Babbitt, chastened by criticism from the press, held off for a month. Then he called Baca to his office and asked him either to accept the transfer or tender his resignation. Baca resigned. A month later, as he contemplated a run for governor of New Mexico, Baca said, "Babbitt can't stand up for his principles, because he has no backbone."

The Baca debacle was eerily reminiscent of a similar purge of federal land managers during the Bush administration, when John Sununu engineered the removal of regional directors of the National Park Service and Forest Service who had stood up to the timber, mining, and oil and gas companies which wanted increased access to the public lands adjacent to Yellowstone Park. This firing of the federal land managers sparked roars of protest from environmentalists, prompting congressional hearings and stories in the press and on TV. However, the national environmental leadership remained curiously silent following the removal of Baca.

The man Babbitt chose to replace Baca, Mike Dombeck, was

much friendlier to ranching and mining interests. Six months after his appointment Dombeck wrote a secret memo to Bruce Babbitt outlining a plan that would have seemed radical during the tenure of James Watt. As a budget-cutting measure, Dombeck advised Babbitt that the BLM could either return over 110 million acres of public lands to the states or sell them off to the highest bidder. An attempt earlier in the century to dispose of public lands and resources had sent former Secretary of Interior Albert Fall to prison in the Teapot Dome scandal.

Babbitt's right hand man at Interior is Tom Collier. Before joining the Clinton administration Collier and Babbitt worked together at the DC law firm Steptoe and Johnson, where their clients included many of the same companies they are now in charge of regulating at Interior, including Burlington Northern, Canyon Forest Village Corporation, Aluminum Companies of America, Yavapai-Prescott Tribe, Canadian Forest Industries Council, Sealaska, and the Forest Industries Committee on Timber Taxation and Valuation. One of these companies previously represented by Collier and Babbitt is Norwegian Cruise Lines, which owns a permit from the Interior Department for cruise visits into Glacier Bay National Park. For years the company and Alaska Senator Frank Murkowski pressured the National Park Service to increase the number of cruise visits permitted into the narrow fjords of Glacier Bay. The Park Service resisted, fearing adverse affects from the huge ships on orca and grey whales and other marine life. In fact, Park Service scientists were hoping to curtail the number of cruise ships permitted in the bay, if not ban them outright. Then Babbitt and Collier intervened, overruled Park Service biologists and managers, and raised the number of cruise visits—leading to millions in profits for their former clients.

ASIDE: THE SENATOR, THE FILM STAR AND A BIG GOLD MINE

In late 1995 letters from Robert Redford dropped softly into the mail boxes of A-list Hollywood liberals. The 10-paragraph missive flailed at Republicans for their plans to rape the environment and concluded with an urgent plea to send money to Senator Max Baucus, Democrat of Montana. By letter's end, Redford had managed to convey the impression that Baucus was up there with John Muir and Rachel Carson as a guardian angel of green America.

Redford wrote, "It's important to rally around key leaders who share our commitment to maintaining the integrity of our public lands and the safety of our land, air, water and food."

If Baucus needed a star to rouse sympathetic liberals, Robert Redford was certainly the ideal man to pitch his virtues. Redford lives on a ranch in Utah's Wasatch Mountains and funds environmental causes through his Sundance Foundation. Since he filmed Norman Maclean's trout-fishing novel *A River Runs Through It* in the early 1990s, the Sundance Foundation has given large amounts of money to Blackfoot Challenge, an organization set up to protect and restore Montana's Blackfoot River, the stream that runs through Maclean's book.

In a 1995 speech before the National Press Club, Redford spoke out passionately against the mining companies: "I can only believe that their bottom lines will win out over the health of our lands and our people. I've already seen enough bright orange rivers with no fish, thanks to mining companies who swore their operations were safe, like the Blackfoot, for example, in Montana."

Yet Max Baucus, the beneficiary of Redford's fundraising, is an unrepentant self-described "friend of mining" who stands to profit personally from what is being heralded as the largest open-pit gold mine in North America—which will be located in the headwaters of Redford's beloved Blackfoot River.

Phelps Dodge, the colossus that will operate the mine, says that roughly a billion tons of dirt and rocks will be gouged and blasted out, crushed, dumped into heaps, and then saturated by water laced with cyanide, a process that leaches small flecks of gold from tons of rock. When the mine, known as Seven-Up Pete, is tapped out it will leave a hole in the earth a square mile across and 1,000 feet deep. In 12 years, when the gold runs out, the companies will leave behind cyanide-sodden dirt for all eternity, just a few feet from what will by then doubtless be the lifeless waters of the Blackfoot River.

A large portion of the land belongs to the Sieben Company, an 80,000-acre sheep ranch owned by the Baucus clan, for whom the dead crater will represent a pretty trough of lucre, since the Sieben Ranch will take home 5 per cent of the value of any minerals extracted. Phelps Dodge and its minority partner, Canyon Resources, the Colorado-based mining company,

Max Baucus: A River Ran Through It, Gold Was On It. A nice letter from Robert Redford.

expect to gross at least $4 billion from the big gold mine.

The Sieben Ranch is managed by the senator's brother, John Baucus, Jr., who also serves as president of the Montana Wool Growers Association. Max Baucus maintains a financial interest in the ranch and receives regular dividend checks from the company. Given the amount of boodle due to be collected by the Baucus family, it is not hard to understand why Baucus has never uttered a cautionary word about Seven-Up Pete, despite widespread outrage from ranchers, environmentalists and business leaders across Montana.

It is harder to understand why Redford is raising money for Baucus. Redford knows first-hand the threat to the Blackfoot. When he came to Montana to film *A River Runs Through It*, the river had been debauched by logging and by a mine run by ASARCO, a multinational company headquartered in New York. Few trout swam in the Blackfoot, and clearcuts so scarred the river's canyon that Redford shot many of the film's scenes on the Yellowstone and Gallatin rivers further south.

Over the past few years, though, the Blackfoot River has begun to heal, thanks largely to the aggressive work of local environmental groups, such as the Clark Fork Coalition and the Montana Environmental Information Center. These organizations have forced ASARCO finally to begin a cleanup of its toxic mine site. Now, just as some cutthroat and bull trout runs have returned, progress is endangered. Already exploratory excavations at the Seven-Up Pete site have resulted in the dumping of millions of gallons of arsenic and lead-contaminated water into the Blackfoot.

Across the length and breadth of Congress it is impossible to uncover a more tenacious front-man for the mining, timber and grazing industries than Max Baucus. It was Baucus who led the effort that crushed the Clinton administration's timid effort to reform federal mining and grazing policy and terminate below-cost timber sales to big timber companies subsidized by the taxpayers.

Nothing new here. Back in 1990, Baucus provided the decisive vote in the Senate killing a bipartisan effort to place a moratorium on the sale of mineral-rich federal lands to multinational mining companies for $5 an acre. Baucus also has a deep personal interest in the present perquisites of the western ranching industry. The Sieben Ranch is one of the largest sheep operations in North America and enjoys an exceptionally close and profitable relationship with public grazing lands adjacent to the ranch and administered by the US Forest Service. Here, Baucus sheep graze for only 22 cents per animal per month, less than a fifth of the going rate on private lands.

One of the grazing permits held by the Sieben Ranch is in the Helena National Forest. This wild landscape is home to the threatened grizzly bear, fewer than 800 of which now survive in the Lower 48. The Baucus family ranch holds one of Montana's only remaining sheep grazing permits in critical grizzly habitat. This is an unhappy situation for the bears, since they like to eat sheep, and when they do, the ranch manager calls in the government hunter, who duly shoots the perpetrator with sodium pentathol and exiles the bear to another area. If the bear returns, as it often does, it is either captured and placed in a zoo or, more typically, killed. That's why sheep grazing permits have been denied in other federal forests in Montana occupied by grizzlies. Fish and Wildlife documents show that there have been four non-natural deaths of grizzlies on the Sieben Ranch allotment since the mid-1970s, making it one of the most lethal zones for grizzlies in the Northern Rockies.

Redford describes Baucus as one of the "key leaders who share our commitment to maintaining the integrity of our public lands". Try telling that to Rep. Joe Kennedy of Massachusetts. In 1993, when Kennedy considered co-sponsoring the Northern Rockies Ecosystem Protection Act, which preserves all wildland and wildlife habitat on public lands in Montana, Idaho and Wyoming, Baucus played hardball. Kennedy had told members of the Alliance for the Wild Rockies that he would support their bill. Baucus, using his power as chairman of the Public Works Committee, threatened to withhold funds for the cleanup of Boston Harbor until Kennedy backed off.

Baucus has also criticized the Alliance's use of celebrities, such as Woody Harrelson and Glenn Close, to promote its ecosystem bill. "National money, glitz, and glamour are reaching into Montana", the man who has Robert Redford as a fundraiser warned in June of 1992. "These interests, mostly based out of California, are doing all they can to see that Montana's 12 year civil war over wilderness issues continues on and on."

Baucus scarcely needs money from Hollywood liberals. In his last re-election run in 1990 he was the second-largest recipient of PAC money in the Senate: $1.86 million in a state with fewer than 500,000 registered voters. What Baucus needs from Redford is political cover. The big question is, why was Robert Redford providing it for him? Redford was close-mouthed. An employee suggested that his rationale might be that Democrats rape the environment less harshly than Republicans, although this quaint idea grows harder to believe as old-growth forests, protected by court order in the Bush years, now buzz with chainsaws unleashed by Clinton's signature on the Rescissions Bill. But here's the Sundance Kid, not even excusing Baucus as the lesser of two evils, rather hailing him as a true friend of nature. Redford should go back to the Blackfoot and take one last look.

THE GORE TEAM

W hy was the reaction to Babbitt's betrayal so subdued? Perhaps, like the Christian right during the era of Bush, the Beltway greens felt there was nowhere else to turn. It is also clear that many still placed their hopes in Vice President Al Gore. Gore's reputation among the Washington press corps as an environmentalist was largely based on his grandstanding at the Rio Earth summit in 1992 and on his book *Earth in the Balance*, which stresses environmental discipline for the Third World, while neglecting to mention the corporate plunder of North America's forests, rivers and mountains. (This is nothing new. Heading the rush to the Amazon to protest deforestation in the late 1980s were many US politicians who would be aghast at the thought of curbing timber companies operating in North America.) Gore is a tireless promoter of free-market environmentalism, and the probable ghostwriter of Clinton's "invisible hand has a green thumb" line. Since the mid-1980s Gore has argued with increasing stridency that the bracing forces of market capitalism are potent curatives for the ecological entropy now bearing down on the American environment. He is a passionate disciple of the gospel of efficiency, suffused with an inchoate technophilia.

Several of Gore's protégés landed top posts in the administration, most notably Carol Browner as EPA administrator. She had served as Gore's legislative director from 1989 through 1991, before leaving to become the head of Florida's Department of Environmental Regulation. During her tenure in Florida, Browner took two particularly high-profile stands. The first was a capitulation to sugar-growers and developers which allowed continued (though slightly filtered) dumping of pesticide-laced water into the Everglades. Second, Browner allowed the Walt Disney Company to destroy 800 acres of vital wetland habitat in central Florida, in exchange for a pledge from the eco-imagineers at Disney World to recreate several thousand acres of "wetlands", a feat which remains well beyond the capacities of modern science.

At EPA, Browner wasted little time in promoting ideas, such as wetland trading, that during the Bush administration had met with howls of derision from the green lobby. One of her very first actions was to put the imprimatur of the EPA on the Everglades deal she had brokered a year earlier in Florida. This was a precedent of sorts—the first time the federal government had officially sanctioned the pollution of a national park.

Following Gore, Browner initiated a campaign to reinvent the EPA by beginning to peel away "excessive environmental regulations". The theme here echoes back to the late 1970s and the writ-

Carol Browner, head of Clinton's EPA: When is a cancer risk not a cancer risk?
(EPA)

ings of Stephen Breyer, then an aide to Senator Ted Kennedy, who Clinton elevated in 1994 to a spot on the US Supreme Court. Breyer argued that federal regulations should be evaluated through two tests: risk assessment and cost/benefit analysis. The costs of pollution control would be weighed against the heavily-discounted benefits of human health and environmental quality—a certain recipe for more hazardous waste landfills, dioxin-belching incinerators and higher cancer rates.

Browner's first target was the so-called Delaney Clause in the Food and Drug Act, which placed a strict prohibition against any detectable level of carcinogens in processed food. Though long the bane of the American Farm Bureau and the Chemical Manufacturers'

Association, the Delaney Clause remained inviolate, even through the Reagan and Bush years. Within months of taking office Browner announced that she felt this standard was too severe and moved to gut it. "We just don't have unlimited financial resources to enforce all these measures and that can create a backlash", Browner complained. "So we need to be realistic. We need the strongest *possible* standards, but we need flexibility in how to achieve those standards."

ASIDE: THE NOT-SO-GREAT MCGINTY

One of the least popular of the Clinton administration's environmental staffers is 32-year-old Katie McGinty, whose nomination to head the Council on Environmental Quality has been blocked for more than a year by Senators Jesse Helms of North Carolina and Dirk Kempthorne of Idaho.

McGinty can blame herself for many of her troubles. In her previous post as an environmental adviser to the president, she tried unsuccessfully to withdraw the Council from congressional oversight and bring it under her own supervision in the White House. McGinty's incompetence as White House adviser was such that when Leon Panetta took over as Clinton's chief of staff in 1994 he promptly exiled her to run the agency she had tried to capture, from which position she was put face to face with Helms and Kempthorne.

Why did McGinty ever arrive at an eminence for which she was manifestly unqualified? Blame it on Rio. At the 1992 eco-summit, Senator Al Gore and McGinty, then his legislative aide, seem to have experienced that warming whose dire consequences for the planet was Gore's constant theme. By December of 1992, McGinty had become one of the first appointees to the Clinton White House, deputy assistant to the president, overseeing the Office of Environmental Policy.

McGinty's resumé shows her to be just the kind of technocrat Gore was summoning to remake government: a degree in chemistry, a stint for ARCO, a lobbyist for the American Chemical Society, where she first met Gore while working on the 1990 Clean Air Act. While McGinty won the affection of the vice president, she fumbled as White House adviser, at least from the environmental point of view. She helped orchestrate Clinton's infamous Portland forest summit in April 1993, and she helped round up the big green groups in support of NAFTA. Then Panetta evicted her.

★

L ike the pliant Browner, Vice President Gore has been in sync with the Clinton two-step. The best example of this is the case of the hazardous waste incinerator in Liverpool, Ohio. VP Gore had made the defeat of this incinerator the subject of the new administration's first policy statement on environmental matters. Three months later, again following the brisk intervention of McLarty, Browner's EPA issued the lethal plant its operating permit. Gore said nothing.

On other crucial matters, Clinton has used Gore to split environmentalists and thus advance pro-business policies, as in the fight over the North American Free Trade Agreement (NAFTA). The environmental defects of NAFTA were manifold and had helped to energize broad opposition to the agreement. When it looked as if the trade pact might go down, Gore pledged to Clinton that he could wrest an endorsement of NAFTA from the environmental organizations.

Gore turned to his long-time friend Jay Hair, who was the perfect person to marshal support for NAFTA. He was the self-proclaimed leader of the Gang of Ten, executives of the 10 largest environmental organizations, including the National Wildlife Federation, Natural Resources Defense Council, Sierra Club, Environmental Defense Fund, National Audubon Society, Izaak Walton League, World Wildlife Fund, League of Conservation Voters, Wilderness Society and Friends of the Earth. The Gang met six times a year in such pleasing circumstances as Kodiak, Alaska; Telluride, Colorado; Jackson, Wyoming; and the beaches of Belize.

Hair knew he couldn't sell the other eco-executives on the meager environmental provisions in NAFTA, so he outlined the political calculus at work. Hair said that the greens' endorsement of NAFTA would buy the administration's support for high priority environmental reforms, such as protection of ancient forests, reform of mining law, and strengthening of the Endangered Species Act. The more conservative and policy-oriented groups quickly aligned themselves behind Hair, including the Environmental Defense Fund,

Natural Resources Defense Council, World Wildlife Fund, Nature Conservancy, Conservation Foundation and the National Aububon Society.

When the Sierra Club and Friends of the Earth refused to endorse NAFTA and instead joined the opposition, Hair dashed off threatening letters to the executives of both organizations, accusing them of treachery.

In the end, the resistance of the Sierra Club and Friends of the Earth didn't matter. The groups assembled by Hair were more than enough for the purposes of the Clinton administration. Days after the trade deal squeaked through Congress, John Adams, head of NRDC, claimed credit, boasting about "breaking the back of the environmental opposition to NAFTA". A few months later the famous environmental "side agreement" to NAFTA was formally declared to be worthless.

ASIDE: THE ALASKA TROVE

Most of America's oil reserves, salmon, native settlements, grizzly bears, old-growth forests and public lands are packed into one state: Alaska. For more than a decade, the fate of Alaska's natural environment has been shaped by two men, Senator Frank Murkowski and Rep. Don Young. Murkowski and Young are an odd but savagely effective tandem. Murkowski, the millionaire, is a banker by trade, harmonized to the elite power circles of DC, a man who moves seamlessly from the Foreign Relations Committee to the Energy and Natural Resources Committee, which he now chairs.

Murkowski's financial records show that the senator owns $50,000 of stock in Louisiana-Pacific, the largest purchaser of timber from the national forests. Louisiana-Pacific owns the Ketchikan Pulp Company, which holds an exclusive 50-year contract for timber from southeast Alaska's Tongass National Forest. Over the past 10 years, Murkowski has intervened numerous times to keep timber flowing into the Ketchikan pulp mill despite evidence of severe environmental problems on the Tongass, the nation's largest national forest and the last intact temperate rainforest in North America. Murkowski's advocacy of Louisiana-Pacific was undiminished even after the company was convicted of criminal vio-

Frank Murkowski: A stock portfolio flush with rape and pillage.

Don Young: Trapped own hand; "It hurt like hell."

lations of the Clean Air Act and the Clean Water Act at the pulp mill.

Don Young, who has served in the House since 1973, is a different character entirely. He is a former trapper and riverboat captain, whose congressional office resembles a cheap Ketchikan taxidermy, its walls covered with the skins of Alaskan grizzlies, the lacquered corpses of king salmon, and the severed heads of Roosevelt elk and Sitka black-tailed deer.

Like Murkowski, Young's stock portfolio is flush with rape and pillage companies such as Homestake Mining, whose profits originate in the subsidies and regulatory exemptions doled out by the committees commandeered by the grizzled Alaskan.

In 1992 Young stood like Jeremiah on the floor of the House and excoriated the Congress for refusing to open the fragile plains of the Arctic National Wildlife Refuge to oil production, warning of dire shortages, gas lines, soaring prices and looming threats to national security. Then, three years later, Young calmly pleaded his case for lifting the ban on export of Alaskan crude oil: "There's an oil glut in America. Prices are too low. There's nowhere to market our product, except Japan."

★

The real power in environmental politics is held by those who control the money of the federal government. Here, the key player for the past decade has been Senator Mark Hatfield of Oregon, retiring at the end of 1996, who has dominated the Appropriations Committee of the Senate. Hatfield has long cultivated an image as a "senator of conscience", leading to his nickname, "St. Mark".

Hatfield received warm praise in the press for his "act of intellectual conscience" in breaking ranks with his party and casting the vote which killed the Balanced Budget Amendment in early 1995. This was no such thing, but merely one more instance in which Hatfield served the timber, mining, grazing and aluminum industries, which depend on billions of dollars a year in federal subsidies, corporate welfare payments. Hatfield wished to preserve his power as Appropriations chairman and not be hobbled by balanced-budget restrictions.

Much of Hatfield's liberal reputation derives from his early opposition to the war against Vietnam. In fact, fearing his anti-war stance might cost him the 1966 Senate election, Hatfield loudly advocated the saturation bombing of Haiphong and Hanoi to bring the war to a "rapid conclusion".

In the 1980s Hatfield received tens of thousands of dollars worth of cash, gifts and artwork from the president of the University of South Carolina. The university also offered a full scholarship to Hatfield's son, although he failed to meet the institution's admissions standards. In exchange, Hatfield steered millions in grants to the university. The Senate Ethics Committee delayed its investigation of the matter until after the 1990 senate election, where Hatfield narrowly defeated a maverick Democrat, Harry Lonsdale. In 1992, the ethics committee finally determined that Hatfield had violated the Ethics in Government Act and issued a mild rebuke.

This was not the first time Hatfield's ethical conduct had been questioned. In 1984 the FBI investigated Hatfield for possible criminal violations involving his dealings with the Greek financier Basil Tsaskos. Tsaskos paid Hatfield's wife Antoinette $55,000 to find him an apartment in the Watergate complex, which he never rented. In exchange, Hatfield agreed to use his influence to help Tsaskos build an oil pipeline from Somalia to Nigeria. Hatfield eventually fought off the lodging of bribery charges, but ended up donating the $55,000 "finder's fee" to charity.

Hatfield, a born-again Christian, has also benefited from more than half a million dollars in forgiven loans from wealthy members of his "prayer circle". Several of these loans originated from Del Dellenbach, a timber industry magnate from Medford, Oregon, who served in Congress in the early 1970s. Of course, those personal loans pale next to the millions of dollars that the timber, mining, agriculture and energy companies have shoveled into Hatfield's campaign war chest.

During the 1980s Hatfield teamed with former Idaho Senator James McClure to perfect the legislative art of the appropriations rider, laws quietly attached to spending bills which mandated that the Forest Service and Bureau of Land Management increase the amount of clearcutting on public lands, despite the impact on water quality or endangered species. The most notorious of these riders was affixed to the 1990 Interior Appropriations Bill. Known in environmental circles as the Rider from Hell, this provision overturned two federal court injunctions halting logging in ancient forests, mandated that the Forest Service sell twice its normal amount of timber to Northwest logging companies at highly subsidized rates and shielded all of those sales from any legal challenge. The half-million acres of clearcutting authorized by the Rider from Hell was a primary factor in the listing of the marbled murrelet and coastal salmon stocks as threatened species.

Hatfield's and McClure's partner in many of these maneuvers was Rep. Les AuCoin, a liberal Democrat who represented northwestern Oregon from 1974 until he vacated his seat for an unsuccessful challenge to Senator Bob Packwood in 1992. After his defeat, AuCoin vowed to reside forever in Oregon and swore he would never move back to Washington, DC, or work as a lobbyist. Three months later, AuCoin joined the DC law firm of Bogle and Gates as chairman of its Government Relations Group. His clients now include Weyerhaeuser, International Paper, the Global Forest Management

Mark Hatfield: God's appropriator; wrote Rider from Hell. (Shia photo/Impact Visuals)

Group, Northwest Forest Resource Council (a timber industry trade group) and Westinghouse.

Unlike Hatfield and AuCoin, McClure was unabashedly pro-industry. As the ranking member of the Natural Resources Committee, he single-handedly halted the designation of millions of acres of federal land in the West as wilderness. His enmity toward the Endangered Species Act was legendary. In 1989, he boasted, "We don't have spotted owls in Idaho, because we shoot them at the border."

McClure fought off numerous attempts to reform the 1872 Mining Law. Retired from the Senate in 1990, he wasted little time cashing in on his enormous influence. With two former staff members from the Natural Resources Committee, McClure established a DC law firm called McClure, Gerard and Neuenschwander to lighten further the burdens on mining corporations that do business on public lands. McClure's clients include the world's largest mining corporations: Barrick Resources, Battle Mountain Gold, Coeur d'Alene Mines, Cyprus Amax Minerals, Homestake, Newmont, Phelps Dodge, and Stillwater Mining Company (partially owned by Chevron), which operates a toxic gold mine north of Yellowstone Park.

McClure's firm represents other clients with a keen interest in the daily operations of the federal government, such as ASARCO, Cray Research, Lockheed, National Endangered Species Act Reform Coalition, Boise Cascade and the National Rifle Association.

MUNICH IN THE REDWOODS

The Wilderness Society was founded in 1930 by three early heroes of the environmental movement, Aldo Leopold, Benton MacKaye and Robert Marshall. MacKaye and Marshall were both socialists, who believed corporate-owned forest land should be seized by the federal government. Leopold was the father of modern forest ecology and author of *Sand County Almanac*, the classic book on "land ethics".

Today's Wilderness Society with its cautious political approach and $17 million a year budget bears little resemblance to the lean and radical organization started by Leopold and Marshall. The Society's board of directors is culled from the elite ranks of corpo-

James McClure: Idaho's dark heart. (Library of Congress)

rate America and the social register. In 1994, the board included John Bierworth (former CEO of Grumman International), David Bonderman (CEO of Continental Airlines), Caroline Getty, Christopher Elliman (Rockefeller heir) and Gilman Ordway (heir to the 3M fortune).

The Society's staff spends most of its time raising and reinvesting money. Indeed, the membership development, operations and financial staff of the Wilderness Society is three times the size of its conservation staff. Even so, in 1993 the Society shovelled out nearly $2 million in contracts to outside telemarketing companies to do additional fundraising.

An analysis of the Society's stock portfolio reveals an unsavory map of strange investments. For example, the country's self-proclaimed defender of America's last pristine lands owns thousands of shares of stock in Caterpillar, Cummins Engines, John Deere, Eaton and Ryder, corporations that build bulldozers, logging trucks, diesel engines and other heavy equipment used to invade roadless areas.

They also own investments in defense and energy companies, such as AMP, Inc., Baltimore Gas & Electric, Consolidated Edison, FPL Group, General Electric and Loral.

The Society occupies sumptuous quarters on 17th Street in DC. The halls, dressed in original prints by Ansel Adams, amplify the man-made connection between nature's grandeur and plutocrats' splendor. According to its annual report, starting in 1997 the Wilderness Society will pay $6 million a year for the DC office—more than one-third its annual budget.

Behind such Beltway greens as the Wilderness Society now stand the real power brokers of environmental politics: the shadowy syndicate of foundations known as the Environmental Grantmakers Association, which annually channels $400 million into the coffers of the nation's major green groups. Oil is the color of money here.

Pew entered the world of environmental funding cautiously. In 1994, Pew staffer Tom Wathen rejected a modest grant proposal by a broad swath of greens saying, "I like it, but my board's very conservative and they'd never approve it." The proposal was for a campaign to end the logging of native forests on public lands.

Yet the big foundations no longer function simply as dispensers of cash to green groups. At the Environmental Grantmakers Association's 1992 retreat on an island in Puget Sound the Association's president, Donald Ross, boasted that the foundations were quite capable of running their own environmental campaigns. "I think funders have a major role to play", Ross said. "And I know there are resentments in the [environmental] community towards funders doing that. And, too bad. We're players and they're players."

Sharing Ross's vision of a more interventionist role of foundations is Pete Meyers, the executive director of the W. Alton Jones Foundation. In 1991, Ross and Meyers decided to run a national campaign to protect the forests of the Pacific Northwest. They called their group Americans for the Ancient Forests and said their mission was to pass legislation in congress preserving the last of the old-growth trees.

To oversee their operation Ross and Meyers chose Bob Chlopak, who runs the DC lobbying firm of Chlopak, Leonard, Schechter and Associates. Chlopak's major clients include General Electric and the

Office of the President of Mexico. In the late 1980s, Chlopak served as the executive director of the Democratic Senatorial Campaign, where he developed close ties with many Democratic power brokers, including Al Gore and James Carville.

The Environmental Grantmakers Association foundations seeded Americans for the Ancient Forest with $2 million, some of which was diverted from hungrier green groups, such as the Native Forest Council and Project Lighthawk. When the money began to roll in Chlopak trilled to an Oregon environmentalist: "This contract has bought me my New Jersey beach house."

Chlopak was supposed to defend the forests in the strong language of dollars. Instead he counseled greens against pressing the new Clinton administration too hard. Finally he convinced them not to pursue passage of the very bill for which his organization had been created. Chlopak argued that the Clinton administration should be encouraged to develop its own plan for the management of the spotted owl and the Northwest's ancient forests, the plan which became Option Nine.

When Bruce Babbitt demanded that the environmentalists release their court injunction and permit logging to restart in spotted owl habitat, Chlopak, instead of lobbying the administration to back off, urged the environmentalists to agree to the deal. When the dazed greens acceded, Chlopak shut down the offices of Americans for the Ancient Forests. Mission accomplished.

Activists in the Pacific Northwest are only now beginning to appreciate the extent of Chlopak's betrayal. The truth began to emerge shortly after the new Republican Congress debated legislation purporting to slash $20 billion out of the 1995 budget, the so-called Rescissions Bill. When the bill finally emerged from the floor of the House, it was loaded like a MIRV warhead with anti-environmental amendments aimed at everything from institutionalizing current grazing practices to lowering drinking water standards to lifting a court injunction against logging on the Tongass National Forest. The most threatening of them all was the timber salvage rider cooked up by Don Young, Mark Hatfield and Senator Slade Gorton of Washington.

The rider promoted the traditional bogus claim of a "forest health crisis" in which millions of acres of old-growth forest were supposedly either burned over, decadent or diseased—a situation which, the senators argued, could only be cured by increased logging, chainsaw surgery. The salvage rider mandated that the Forest Service sell 5 billion board feet of timber (twice the amount sold in 1993), contained sufficiency language which exempted all of those sales from compliance with environmental laws, such as the Endangered Species Act, and shielded them from any possible court challenges brought by environmentalists.

Big timber backed the bill with messianic vigor, while the environmental lobby dubbed it "the logging without laws" rider, confident it would meet with a stern veto from Clinton. After all, the greens reasoned, the Clinton administration had promised to veto any "sufficiency language riders" affecting Northwest forests. This was a key part of the deal with Chlopak and Babbitt.

When the first version of the Rescissions Bill arrived at the White House, Clinton did veto it. Mainstream greens cheered the president in full-page ads in *The New York Times*. These accolades were over-loud and premature. In fact, concern for his own pet project, Americorps, which the bill would have gutted, sparked Clinton's veto.

Within days of the veto the White House helped draft a new version of the bill which contained both the Americorps funding and the anti-environmental riders. The new version sailed through the House, but could have been stopped in the Senate with an objection from a single senator.

Environmentalists had placed their hopes in Senator Patty Murray of Washington, who had intimated that she might filibuster against the bill. But when the time came Murray was nowhere to be found. It turns out Clinton had called her the night before the scheduled vote, demanding that she drop her challenge. The compliant senator quietly fled town for a leisurely weekend in Seattle.

After the final vote, Mark Hatfield strode to the podium, a smile on his face: "I would like to read this into the record. It is a letter denoting the Clinton administration's total support for this bill." In a final twist of the knife, the letter Hatfield brandished was signed by OMB director Alice Rivlin, a former adviser to the Wilderness Society.

A week later at the signing ceremony, Clinton rationalized his latest betrayal: "I support this salvage provision. I believe we need to do more salvage logging."

Nothing could better illustrate the shattered condition of the green lobby—when the most egregious assault yet on American environmental laws came before the Senate, not one senator could be roused to oppose it. Not one.

A quarter-century after the first Earth Day the corporate counter-attack launched in the late 1970s is nearly complete. As citizens virtuously warehouse their newspapers, seek redemption in glass and aluminum and recycle their direct mail pleas from mainstream environmental groups into properly labeled receptacles, they may be too busy acting locally to notice the national picture.

THE PRESIDENCY

President Bill: As Arkansas labor leader Bill Becker said bitterly, "This guy will pat you on the back and piss down your leg." (Alain McLaughlin/Impact Visuals)

CLINTON'S WORLD

The easiest guide to Bill Clinton's world comes in the form of a list of his campaign contributors through the 1980s, stretching from his successful bid for a second term as Arkansas governor in 1982, after the voters had kicked him out in 1980 following his first. Long before he hit the national spotlight (with a crashingly tedious keynote speech to the 1988 Democratic convention in Atlanta which earned him much ridicule), the big money had its eyes on the young governor.

Badly shaken by his 1980 upset and determined never to offend corporate power again, Clinton let the word go forth: the high and the mighty had a man they could trust in the governor's mansion in Little Rock. The high and the mighty responded in appropriate fashion. Money flowed south from Wall Street, from the big securities firms, banks and investment houses: Merrill Lynch, Goldman, Sachs & Co., Drexel Burnham, Citicorp, Morgan Stanley, Prudential Bache.

Look over these old lists today and the quid follows the pro quo like the buggy after a mule. Indeed the scandal that dogged Clinton through his term thus far—Whitewater—traces its origins to just such collusion. Of the 1,070 news stories written about the Whitewater scandal between 1992 and 1996, some 90 per cent have concerned themselves with the cover-up question: if or how the Clinton White House suppressed evidence in the wake of Vince Foster's suicide. Almost all the remaining stories deal with the efforts of Governor Bill and the First Lady of Arkansas to keep their friend James McDougal's Madison Guaranty Savings & Loan afloat.

All these reports overlook the actual origins of Whitewater, which began with a land deal. In 1978 state attorney general Bill Clinton was in the midst of his first campaign for the governorship when he and Hillary, along with Jim and Susan McDougal, bought 230 acres of riverfront land in the Ozark Mountains of northern Arkansas. Though title to the land was in the Clintons' name, the couple put down no money. McDougal did not yet have the S&L, and was a financial fixer and property dealer. He fronted the money for the down payment on the loan.

The land's previous owner-of-record was a partnership, 101 River Development, which bought it from a local business group. 101 had held the property for only three days, and went out of existence within a couple of weeks of the sale. The original seller of the land was International Paper, a $16 billion a year timber giant, Arkansas's largest landowner with 800,000 acres in the state and with 7 million acres of land across the US.

International Paper's powerful presence in Arkansas dates back to the 1950s with the arrival of Winthrop Rockefeller. The New York-based timber company had long been backed by Rockefeller interests, and when Winthrop went south, the company made a similar migration and set about building up its empire in the state.

The Whitewater sale came at a time when the timber giant was following the pronouncements of candidate Clinton with keen attention. The young attorney general was vowing that as governor he would restrict the use of clearcutting on land held by companies such as International Paper, Georgia-Pacific and Weyerhaeuser. These paper and timber companies had gone on a logging binge in the mid-Seventies, clearcutting thousand-acre chunks of forest at a time. Clinton promised to introduce legislation banning the practice as soon as he entered the governor's office.

101 River Development had given the Clintons and MacDougals a very good deal, selling the land for $500 an acre. Non-river front property in the area was selling at the time for nearly twice that amount.

The Whitewater sale went through in August of 1979. Clinton won the governorship in November of that year. Environmentalists eagerly awaited action from the new governor on clearcutting and other issues pertaining to the state's very serious problems with water and air pollution. But the promises of the campaign trail soon lost their fire. Indeed Clinton's commitment to them was pallid from the start. His two predecessors in the governor's mansion—successively, Dale Bumpers and David Pryor—had both tangled with the timber companies on the issue of clearcutting with far more vigor than was ever displayed by Governor Clinton.

The newly elected governor formed a task force on clearcutting stocked with conservationists. The task force swiftly took heat from loggers and executives from Weyerhaeuser and Georgia-Pacific. A startled Clinton kicked off the conservationists, put in industry hacks and recommended voluntary compliance with soft regulations.

In what proved to be a fatal blow, Clinton reneged on a pledge to poultry king Don Tyson of Tyson Foods and refused to raise the legal weight for trucks on Arkansas highways to 80,000 pounds. In 1980, Tyson and other moneyed interests shifted their support to Republican Frank White, who defeated Clinton.

When Arkansas voters turned out Clinton at the end of his two-year term, he left the governor's mansion and went to work at the Little Rock law firm of Wright, Lindsey, and Jennings. Hillary was at Rose law. Both firms represented the timber giants of Arkansas before state regulatory bodies such as the Pollution Control Board and the Department of Ecology.

Clinton recaptured the governor's office in 1982, the same year that McDougal bought Madison Guaranty Saving & Loan. Among those contributing to candidate Clinton's campaign treasury were International Paper, Georgia Pacific and Tyson Foods. Their investment was swiftly rewarded. Clinton redux was now equipped with a philosophical approach to regulation highly congenial to the resource industries and to the poultry factories.

Tyson in particular became a key ally of Clinton after the latter learned his lesson from the trucking dispute. Tyson planes ferried the First Family on its travels and Tyson funds poured into Clinton's campaign coffers.

In return, the poultry magnate received roughly $12 million worth of tax breaks during Clinton's years as governor. Nor was Clinton diligent in monitoring the environmental record of Tyson Foods or of the poultry industry in general. During Clinton's years as governor the White River turned into a cesspool. Animal wastes from the poultry and cattle industry polluted the river so badly that 400 miles of streams became unfit for swimming. In 1983, Clinton dallied for 17 months before taking action to control damage from a Tyson plant in Green Forest, Arkansas, which, after a sinkhole developed, poured a million gallons a day of chicken wastes into the water table.

The disastrous impact of Tyson's chicken farms on the Arkansas River is fairly well known. Less notorious but even more toxic are the pulp plants of International Paper, Georgia-Pacific and James River. International Paper's mill at Pine Bluff is one of the most toxic in the nation, venting nearly 2 million tons of chemicals a year into the air and water.

From 1982 forward, Clinton argued that compliance to environmental standards could best be achieved on a voluntary basis, rather than by the imposition of exigent (and politically perilous) rules and regulations. To this end Governor Clinton stacked his pollution control board with members friendly to industry. In 1985 he promoted and then signed into law a huge tax break for industrial corporations of his state, including the big timber companies. This easing of the corporate fiscal burden was offset by a regressive sales tax on the citizenry.

Clinton's big offering to the timber companies was the Manufacturers' Investment Sales and Use Tax Credit, known by critics as the "IP bailout law", after International Paper. Under this program state tax breaks were approved for more than $400 million in projects by International Paper and three other paper mills that then State Senator Ben Allen of Little Rock called "the worst corporate citizens in Arkansas"—all this in a state with one of the lowest per capita incomes in the nation and where 29 per cent of the children and half the state's black residents lived in poverty.

A few years later state officials tried to keep International Paper and two Georgia-Pacific mills off a toxic waterways list, despite evidence they were contaminating rivers with dioxin and rendering the eating of fish from them an unacceptable cancer risk. Meanwhile, International Paper, while taking repeated advantage of the manufacturers' sales tax credit, was ladling out money to candidate Clinton.

Clinton also supervised a land deal highly favorable to the timber giants. In later years, taunted with the fact that his state ranked 48th in environmental quality, Clinton would make much of the fact that as governor he had acquired thousands of acres for state-owned forests. Two types of deals were involved here. In one set of transactions state-owned lands with profitable timber on them were swapped to the big companies in return for parcels of their land which had been recently cut over. And, in other instances, the state simply acquired at inflated prices land which the timber companies had recently logged of its best trees.

Nourished by these benefices, the timber companies and Tyson urged Governor Clinton—now nearing the end of his third term—to consider challenging Dale Bumpers for the Senate seat he had held since the early Seventies. The companies had no love for Bumpers. He had led the charge to reform forest policies on federal lands, culminating in the passage of the National Forest Management Act. Bumpers was also a spirited critic of the clearcutting and pesticide practices of the big timber companies in Arkansas. But Clinton was already contemplating a run for the White House and so instead the timber companies, along with other corporate interests, funded the Democratic Leadership Council—Clinton's launching pad to the national scene and the presidency.

As president, Clinton has performed many kindly deeds for the timber giants, as noted in the preceding chapter. But for International Paper, in particular, Clinton wrought two spectacular favors as president. He refused to take any action to stem the flow of raw log exports from the Pacific Northwest, where International Paper holds about a half million acres. And the generous Habitat Conservation Plans tirelessly promoted by Interior Secretary and fellow DLC member Bruce Babbitt allowed International Paper and Georgia-Pacific to continue to cut trees in land occupied by endangered species such as the red-cockaded woodpecker.

The harmonious relationship between International Paper and Clinton that began in the late 1970s has many threads. It was International Paper that sold another piece of land to McDougal and the Clintons, and then kept the Clintons' names off a suit against the Whitewater partnership for non-payment. This was at the time that Clinton signed the IP bailout law.

Meanwhile, the nearby Castle Grande deal, for which Hillary Clinton spent the notorious 60 hours of legal billing on behalf of Madison S&L, began to fall apart and threaten Madison's financial health. McDougal and Clinton pressured timber executive Dean

HRC: Bad at math, parlayed $1,000 into $99,541 in futures trades. Perils of an untidy office; never know when or where subpoenaed papers might turn up. Thinks it a fine idea that welfare checks for mothers can be held ransom against unquestioned right of entry into private homes by state welfare snoops and therapy cops. Uncertain ideological moorings: from Goldwater girl to Wellesley anti-war stance to internship at radical Oakland law firm to elite liberal career path, board membership of waste incineration company and Children's Defense Fund. Waste not, want not. (Library of Congress)

Paul into taking out an $825,000 loan to bail out the Castle Grande project. Nearly $100,000 of that "loan" ended up in Whitewater accounts and some of that money may have also found its way into Clinton's campaign chest. And though Hillary's incredible record of success in commodities trading has been widely advertised as an exercise in cattle futures, in fact part of her successful conversion of $1,000 into nearly $100,000 came in trades on timber futures.

Hillary's famous trades yielded her $99,541 in the 10 months following the first $1,000 investment she made in August of 1978. The chances of such good fortune were calculated by three finance professors writing in the *Journal of Economics and Finance* at being four in a billion.

As Caroline Baum and Victor Niederhoffer pointed out in a devastating article in *The National Review*, Hillary's 10,000 per cent rate of return far outstrips the personal best of George Soros who, across 20 years, never achieved better than a 122 per cent rate. If the trades had gone bad, the Clintons would have been wiped out, owing more than $1 million. Bill's drive for the governorship would have been finished along with any other political ambitions. Hillary's investment adviser was James Blair, counsel to Tyson Foods. The broker of record at Refco in the Springdale, Arkansas, branch was Red Bone, who had previously worked for Tyson Foods. In 1979, he was handed a $250,000 fine by the Chicago Mercantile Exchange for violation of sundry procedures, the largest ever imposed for commodity trading violations.

When the Whitewater scandal finally exploded, Attorney General Janet Reno searched for a special prosecutor and finally came up with Robert Fiske, of the law firm of Davis, Polk and Wardwell. This was the New York law firm representing not only Clark Clifford and Roger Altman (whose First American bank had been introduced to the criminal enterprise know as BCCI by the Stephens financial empire in Arkansas), but also International Paper.

Tyson, Wal-Mart and the Stephens family are familiar pillars of the Arkansas power structure. Yet the timber companies are probably the most potent of the lot. Combined, International Paper, Weyerhaeuser, Georgia-Pacific and Potlatch control more than two and a half million acres of land in Arkansas and operate more than 30 timber mills.

CAPITAL'S MAN

Back at the start of the 1990s, Bill Becker, head of the AFL-CIO in Arkansas, wrote an internal memo on Clinton's record. It detailed a repeated sequence of betrayals by Clinton despite almost consistent support from labor in his Arkansas races over 16 years. Back in the dawn of his career, in 1974, Clinton sweet-talked the state AFL-CIO into endorsing him for the Democratic nomination in a congressional race, over a state senator with a pro-labor record. He got nowhere in that race but two years later, in his successful bid to be state attorney general, he gave labor the finger on their bottom line issue. The state AFL-CIO was circulating a petition to put a "rights of labor" initiative on the ballot that would have allowed union shops when members of a local union voted for it and management also agreed. Clinton announced, "I don't think it will pass, and I so far have very serious reservations about it", and claimed friends in the labor movement told him "it's the wrong time to bring it up".

Clinton lost labor's endorsement then, but he had it again for his first run for governor in 1978, repaying the favor by coming out against exemption of food and prescription medicine from the sales tax. In his first term he supported an increase in the gas tax, raised taxes on motor vehicles and supported a constitutional amendment to give tax breaks to utilities.

By 1986, Becker was telling *The Wall Street Journal* that "almost any [Clinton] activity, in so far as our folks are concerned, is reminiscent of what Reagan is doing to us".

Perhaps the most telling incident took place in 1990, when Morrilton Plastics faced a strike by employees belonging to the United Auto Workers. After Clinton's intervention, the Arkansas Industrial Development Commission (busy advertising the state's "right to work" allurements) gave the company a $300,000 loan guarantee to help the company build up inventory against the expected strike. Becker himself then delivered the famous judgment that the AFL-CIO would now prefer to forget: "This guy will pat you on the back and piss down your leg."

ASIDE: WILLARD'S WAY, MENA'S MYSTERIES

T he scandals that Clinton's advisers had long feared finally exploded amidst the New Hampshire primary, in February of 1992. The Clintons survived it, barely, while the major national papers and magazines, sympathetic to Clinton, wrote snootily about the "unverified reports of the supermarket tabloids" concerning Gennifer Flowers. In fact the tabloids, notably *The Star*, did a very thorough job of investigation, interviewing relevant witnesses such as the doorman in Flowers's building, making it clear that she was telling the truth about the long affair.

Flowers's charming book, *Passion and Betrayal*, published in 1995 and ignored by the reporters who had dubbed her a lying slut three years earlier, provided further detail right down to the names intimately exchanged for such portions of their anatomy as Willard and Precious.

The other scandal that swirled around Clinton's head in campaign season was his relationship with the West Arkansas air base known as Mena, used by the Reagan administration as a staging post in the undercover shuttle of supplies to the contras. The planes carried cocaine on their return swing. The cocaine smuggler Barry Seal, machine-gunned to death by Colombian hitmen in Baton Rouge in 1986, left papers establishing that he ran his gigantic

Gennifer Flowers: Precious to his Willard. (K. Condyles/Impact Visuals)

smuggling operation with the acquiescence of the Reagan administration.

Abundant efforts to get Governor Clinton to protest the flagrant arms/drug operation were futile. There was insistent speculation that drug money might have been washed through the state's financing system and associated network of bond brokers and banks. The best detailed reports of Mena appeared in *The Nation* in early 1992, as reported by Bryce Hoffman, JoAnn Wypijewski and Alexander Cockburn.

In January 1995, a long account of the Mena affairs, in part drawing on documents from Seal's papers, was being prepared by Sally Denton and Roger Morris for *The Washington Post*. Three days before scheduled publication on January 29, the article was held, then axed by the *Post*'s managing editor, Robert Kaiser. No explanation was ever given. Denton and Morris's story was finally published in *Penthouse* in June 1995.

One good guide to Clinton's past comes in the form of David Maraniss's biography, *First In His Class*. Among the book's disclosures:

• With sidekick Taylor Branch, mangled McGovern's presidential campaign in Texas. Snubbed Hispanics, blacks and labor while courting LBJ.

• Ideal Musician: Elvis, whose death Clinton mourned for a week.

• Ideal Woman: Dolly Parton, whose life-sized poster adorned the door of his private restroom in the governor's office in Little Rock.

• Clinton on Bob Dole, circa 1976: "The biggest prick in Congress."

• Hillary Clinton: the futures whiz needed tutoring in math and economics. "She had trouble with numbers", said an old school colleague, Geoffrey Shields.

• Bill on Hillary: "[She's] old-fashioned in every conceivable way. She's just a hard working, no nonsense, no frills, intelligent girl who has done well, who doesn't see any sense to extramarital sex." According to Betsey Wright, "Bill tried to run her off, but Hillary won't go."

• Places Clinton inhaled pot without smoking: Georgetown, New Haven, New York, Oxford, Fayetteville, Hope, Dallas, Little Rock, Los Angeles.

• Allowed his own brother to be set up in a coke sting.

• Clinton took up jogging as a way to run around on Hillary; slapped Betsey Wright in the face when she suggested state troopers escort him on his "outings". Later used troopers as his procurers.

• Clinton decked the diminutive Dick Morris on the back porch of the governor's mansion when Morris upbraided him for his abusive treatment of Wright.

• Dated Mary Steenbergen on the evening of the first execution in Arkansas after the Supreme Court legalized the death penalty.

• Refused to push for a civil rights law, leaving Arkansas as one of two states without such legislation.

★

G iven his record in Arkansas no one should have expected President Bill Clinton to live up to his campaign promises of attacking "special interests" and defending the "little guy". Any illusions about such a possibility disappeared even before the inauguration, when Clinton filled his administration with an assortment of corporate lawyers (Mickey Kantor of Manatt, Phelps and Phillips, US Trade Representative; and Bernard Nussbaum of Wachtell, Lipton, Rosen and Katz, White House counsel); financiers (Robert Rubin of Goldman, Sachs, National Economic Council); lobbyists (Howard Paster of Hill and Knowlton, chief congressional lobbyist; and Ron Brown of Patton, Boggs and Blow, Commerce Secretary); and corporate executives (Mack McClarty of ARKLA, the Arkansas-based natural gas company).

Eager to demonstrate to CEOs that business need not fear the Democrats, Clinton was just as accommodating to big business as his Republican predecessors. He pushed through the NAFTA agreement, extended an R&D tax break worth billions to big business, halved his proposed corporate tax increase and won the enthusiastic endorsement of the auto industry by breaking a campaign pledge to force the Big Three to increase fuel efficiency by 40 per cent.

By late 1994, the press was congratulating Clinton for his wise policies and wondering why CEOs weren't more appreciative of his efforts. "For all the arguments about whether Bill Clinton is a New Democrat or an old one, when it comes to pushing US business interests abroad, no recent President has demonstrated Clinton's willingness to roll up his sleeves and dive into the sometimes grubby details of international deal making," said *Time. The Washington Post* asked why CEOs weren't "singing 'Hail to the Chief'" since Clinton had been so diligent in "[serving] up pro-business policies". The newspaper quoted BP America Inc. chairman Charles Bowman as saying that Clinton's record was "doggone good".

Business Week was also pleased with Clinton's approach. "Guess who's coming to dinner—and lunch and breakfast—since Bill Clinton moved into 1600 Pennsylvania Avenue?" asked the magazine. "After years of hobnobbing with Republican presidents, blue-chip CEOs are discovering that they can do brisk business with a Democratic Chief Executive, too." *Business Week* said Clinton's "outreach campaign [to the corporate sector] transcends anything the Democrats attempted before", and quoted Democratic National Committee finance director Terence McAuliffe as saying that big donors were "screaming to give us checks".

One man surely pleased with the Democrats was Dwayne Andreas, top man at Archer-Daniels-Midland. Once known as "the kingpin of GOP fund raising"—his signature was on the check found with the Watergate burglars—Andreas changed trains in 1992 when it looked as if Clinton might capture the presidency. In the first 21 months following Clinton's coronation as the Democratic candidate, he gave the party some $270,000 in soft money contributions

In return for his public support of the president's 1993 budget plan, Andreas got ethanol (the "alternative" corn-based fuel of which ADM is the world's largest producer) exempted from Clinton's BTU tax proposal, an exemption that opened the door to so many other challenges that ultimately the entire proposal was scuttled. Clinton also maintained a Bush-era tax subsidy for ethanol which will cost the government an estimated $3.4 billion by the year 2000.

But Clinton's biggest gift, granted one week after Andreas co-chaired a fundraising dinner that netted the Democrats $2.5 million in June of 1994, was the EPA's ruling that by 1996 one-tenth of all gasoline sold in the United States must contain ethanol. ADM, producing 70 per cent of the country's ethanol, stands to gain some $100 million a year as a result of this environmentally dubious decision.

General Motors also made out well under the Clintonites. After chest-pounding pledges to recall the company's C/K pickup trucks, which have an unfortunate tendency to burst into flames after collisions, the Transportation Department in late 1994 abruptly changed course and merely required GM to pay $51 million over five years toward funding safety programs. That was a tiny price to pay for a defect which resulted in the deaths of over 600 people.

Possibly shedding light on Transportation Secretary Federico

Pena's decision is that deputy assistant attorney general John Rogovin, the man who brokered the deal between the government and the company, owns thousands of dollars worth of GM stock. Rogovin's last employer before joining the government was O'Melveny & Myers, a law firm that does sizeable work for GM and other auto makers.

Don Tyson, the Arkansas poultry magnate and head of Tyson Foods, seems to prosper no matter which party is in power but his success during the early Clinton years was so staggering that he and his firm were soon being investigated by a special prosecutor. The immediate focus: gifts of Super Bowl tickets, travel and a scholarship for the girlfriend of Clinton's first Agricultural Secretary, Mike Espy, who was charged with overseeing and enforcing rules on the poultry industry.

Tyson's expansion into the fishing industry—it is now the No. 2 company fishing for Pacific whiting—also became the subject of controversy. In 1993 and in 1994, Commerce Secretary Ron Brown took the highly unusual step of vetoing Commerce's own fisheries council in two decisions that collectively meant millions of dollars for the poultry company.

In the first case, which came a year after Tyson purchased the Arctic Alaska fishing company (and renamed it Tyson Seafood Group), Brown allotted 70 per cent of the whiting catch to Tyson and other companies with factory trawlers and only 30 per cent for small fishermen, who have increasingly been edged out of the business by the giant firms. Commerce's Pacific Fisheries Management Council had suggested that the trawlers get just 26 per cent.

In 1994, the Council ruled that factory trawlers, of which Tyson owns two, should pay 20 times more for permits than small boat owners, reflecting their far larger capacity. But Brown stepped in again, ruling that the ratio be cut to 12 to 1, thereby saving Tyson $800,000 with a stroke of the pen.

In a little noted case, Tyson also benefited from tens of millions of dollars authorized by the Federal Aviation Administration for the proposed Northwest Arkansas Regional Airport, a preposterous project whose prime function is to ferry Tyson chickens to Japan and to offer a hub for Wal-Mart's vast commercial operations. Backers of the airport—planned for the tiny town of Highfill, Arkansas, conveniently located near the headquarters of Tyson Foods and Wal-Mart—envision the construction of two 12,500-feet runways. Only O'Hare in Chicago currently has a longer runway—13,000 feet—than the two runways planned for the Tyson Poultryport at Highfill. The longest runway at JFK in New York is 11,351 feet; at Dulles in Washington, 11,501 feet; and at Los Angeles International, 12,091 feet.

Clinton's relationship with labor was not marked by the same generosity of spirit he showed the corporate sector. In addition to NAFTA, he pushed through the GATT agreement and made little effort to hike the minimum wage during his first two years in office, when the Democrats controlled Congress. Kevin Phillips rates Clinton as the most anti-labor president of the 20th century.

However, at least one labor leader and his union have been treated with extreme gentility by the Clinton team. In February of 1996, Attorney General Janet Reno announced that as a result of an agreement reached with the government, the Laborers' International Union of North America would hold elections that same year for its top two officers, for the first time since the mob took over the union in the 1920s. Laborers' president Arthur Coia hailed the deal, saying the union "must remove any lingering question of taint or corruption....We've made great strides in reforming this union, and we're grateful to the Justice Department for its cooperation."

This agreement was also greeted warmly in the press. In *The New York Times*, Dirk Johnson wrote that reforms at the Laborers' had taken place due to "scrutiny from Federal prosecutors", and said the deal would give the union "a chance to reform itself".

Studiously ignored was that the deal left Arthur Coia, a man said by the Justice Department itself to have mob ties, at the head of the Laborers'. Coia is one of President Clinton's closest friends in the labor movement, and his union is a major contributor to the Democratic Party.

The remarkable story of Coia and his White House ties was covered only by Dean Starkman and several colleagues at the *Providence Journal-Bulletin*. The rest of the press simply turned a blind eye to this rich and fragrant affair.

The Laborers', which has 700,000 members, mostly in construction and hospitals, has long been considered the most corrupt union in America, even worse than the pre-Ron Carey Teamsters. Back in

Arthur Coia: Head of the Laborers' union. The Justice Department said he had associated with and been controlled by the mob. Fought deft campaign, sent checks to Clinton, plus hand-crafted golf club. (Providence Journal-Bulletin Photo)

1986, a presidential commission laid bare the union's connections to the mob, saying that "organized crime had used its influence over the Laborers' to obtain workers' benefit funds" and to "provide no show jobs for [the mob]". The commission informed the Justice Department that a case was "waiting to be made".

The union is tightly controlled by its leaders. The only time that a dissident faction challenged the leadership, in 1981, its representatives were beaten on the convention floor. The union's secretary-treasurer at that time was Coia's father, who presided over the convention and railed against "outsiders" seeking to destroy the union as the dissidents were pummeled. Coia was re-elected along with the rest of the incumbent slate by a vote of 2,342 to 5.

On November 4, 1994, following a three-year investigation, the Justice Department served the Laborers' with a 212-page draft complaint. The document, signed by Paul Coffey, head of Justice's organized crime and racketeering section, and assistant attorney general JoAnn Harris, a Clinton appointee, accused the union of having "an aura of criminality and pervasive lawlessness".

The complaint charged that Coia, who rose through the union ranks in Providence, had "associated with and been controlled by organized crime figures". It accused him of pilfering union funds in an insurance scheme in the 1980s and of having helped a Mafia family in upstate New York divert funds from four union locals. The complaint also said Coia and other union officials had used "actual and threatened force, violence and fear" to seize funds from several locals in upstate New York. (In another link to the Mafia, though one not mentioned in the document, Coia once sought to mate his champion Rottweiler with a bitch owned by Raymond Patriarca of the New England mob.)

The draft complaint recommended that the government place the Laborers' in a trusteeship, as previously occurred with the Teamsters. It further recommended that Coia be permanently banned from the union.

By February of 1995, just three months later, the Justice Department had adopted a very different approach. Instead of a trusteeship, the government determined that the Laborers' should conduct its own internal clean-up. Coia was left in charge of the union and since Laborers' dissidents say they will not be able to launch an effective challenge in 1996, he will remain at the helm until at least the year 2001, the date of the next elections.

With the exception of the presidential and vice-presidential posts, the agreement decreed that the rest of the Laborers' 13-member general executive board be elected under the old rules whereby delegates at the union's convention select the leadership. Laborers' dissidents interviewed by the *Journal-Bulletin* were appalled by the deal. Chris White, an Alaska bus driver who was among those beaten at the 1981 convention, said the new rules allow only for "token democracy".

How was it that Coia and the Laborers' got off so easy? Perhaps in part due to a very clever strategy by Coia, who recast himself as a crusading reformer. In January of 1995, shortly after the Justice Department delivered its draft report, Coia suspended two Laborers' vice presidents, Samuel Caivano and John Serpico, who were suspected of having Mafia ties. The two men later sued Coia, claiming that he threw them overboard in order to save himself. Coia also approved a union code of ethics that makes associating with the mob grounds for dismissal.

In another clever move, Coia hired a former FBI agent, W. Douglas Gow, as the union's brand new inspector general, and charged him with rooting out corruption at the Laborers'. While Gow took some needed steps, the fact that he is paid by the union and reports directly to Coia and his board leaves doubts about his ability to investigate the top leadership. (Coia also hired some high-priced lawyers, including Brendan Sullivan, Oliver North's handler during the Iran/contra hearings.)

Within the union movement itself, Coia has also shifted gears. After briefly considering a challenge to AFL-CIO president Lane Kirkland, Coia threw his support behind John Sweeney, who won the Federation's presidency at its 1995 convention. Coia parrots Sweeney's lines and, in one indisputably positive move, created a vibrant organizing department which has launched vigorous campaigns in the US.

While all this has surely helped the Laborers' leader, it is Coia's ties to the White House that may have been decisive in the Justice Department's decision to forgo a trusteeship and leave Coia at the helm. Coia was one of the earliest labor backers of Clinton's health care plan and virtually alone among union leaders in supporting NAFTA. In addition, Coia:

• heads a union that loaned $100,000 to Clinton's inaugural committee and that is one of the Democratic Party's top 10 donors.

• co-chaired with Robert Strauss, Vernon Jordan, Dwayne Andreas and Ronald Perelman a 1994 Democratic National Committee black-tie dinner which raised $3.5 million.

• was part of the "host committee" of a 1995 fundraiser for the Democratic Congressional Campaign Committee which brought in additional millions for the president's party.

• joined with Garrison Keillor, Barbra Streisand, Sean Penn, Lloyd Cutler, Vidal Sassoon, Cyrus Vance, among others, in donating $1,000, the maximum allowed, to Clinton's legal defense fund for the Paula Jones and Whitewater affairs.

• pledged $100,000 of his union's money to the US Botanic Garden, one of Hillary Clinton's favorite charities.

Coia and the Clintons have also developed a personal friendship. The Laborers' leader commissioned Bob Hampton of Providence to design the president a golf club, replete with the presidential seal built into the base. (Clinton used the driver when he and former presidents Ford and Bush sent spectators scrambling for cover at the 1995 Bob Hope Classic). On the same day that the Justice Department delivered its 212-page draft complaint to the Laborers', Clinton wrote a personal note to Coia. Addressed "Dear Arthur", the note read: "I just heard you've become a grandfather—congratulations! Thanks for the gorgeous driver—it's a work of art."

In another token of his esteem, Clinton extended invitations to Coia to attend a number of prestigious affairs, including a reception for the emperor of Japan and the White House signing of the Israeli-Palestinian peace pact.

On February 13, 1995, exactly one week before Justice signed its deal with the Laborers', Hillary Clinton addressed a Laborers' conference in Florida at the request of Coia. Before heading to Florida, Mrs. Clinton was advised by the White House counsel that because Coia was "currently being investigated", the First Lady should avoid any "private meetings or conversations" with him.

Until 1998, the union is required to issue progress reports to the government every 90 days. If the Justice Department isn't satisfied, it could still take over the union.

Meanwhile, Coia continues to hold his job and his $220,000 yearly salary. He still drives a Ferrari, maintains two residences—one a family mansion overlooking Narragansett Bay in Rhode Island, the other a hotel suite in Washington—and enjoys access to the highest circles of the Democratic Party. No wonder Coia told the *Journal-Bulletin* in late 1995 that these "are the best of times".

THE CLINTONS' KID SCAMS

I n his January 1996 State of the Union Address to Congress Bill Clinton identified the national enemy: kids. He said he was going to ask the FBI to join the war on teen gangs. He urged parents to install V-chips in their TV sets to make sure the kids weren't watching dirt. He called for a national crusade against teen motherhood. While Bill begged the nation to throw rocks at pregnant girls, his wife Hillary sat with her daughter Chelsea at her side up in the gallery, fresh from launching her awful book *It Takes A Village*, in which she recommends that welfare mothers submit to mandatory house searches by social workers. So much for the right to privacy and the Fourth Amendment.

Right from the start, Bill and Hillary have grandstanded to the right about "responsibility" and the family, and tried to curry favor with Pecksniffs by beating up on mothers who receive welfare.

In February of 1994 President Bill traveled to the poor area of Anacostia in Washington, DC, where the kids, ready with questions about NAFTA and the Clean Water Act, were treated to homilies about "personal responsibility" and sex.

"We can't renew our country unless more of us, I mean all of us, are willing to join churches", he had told the joint session of Congress a few days earlier. Then he talked about family, work, community. This from a man who spent slabs of the 1980s with his nose between Gennifer Flowers's thighs and who can't even spend a Christmas vacation with his family without rushing to a conclave of power seekers in Hilton Head.

The whole notion of a (black) teenage sex epidemic, born of

teenage "irresponsibility", is utterly bogus. Less than one-eighth of all "teenage" births and one-fifth of all births to school-age girls match the myth of "children having children". In only about 20,000 births annually—less than 4 per cent of all births among teenage girls, or 1 per cent of the total births in the United States—are both partners minors under the age of 18.

In 60 per cent of all births to school-age girls, the male partners are over age 20. Men aged 23 and older are more likely to father a child with a school-age girl than boys under the age of 19. Similarly, more than 100,000 of the 150,000 annual cases of syphilis and gonorrhea among teenage girls appear attributable to post-teenage men.

If there was an "epidemic" in the growth of teenage parenthood, it was mostly in the late 1950s and the 1960s, coinciding with the falling age of puberty, rising post-war teenage populations and the "sexual revolution". Births among teenage girls peaked in 1958, declined through the mid-1980s and have since risen, for reasons of youth poverty. Among all age and race groups, the higher rates of poverty provoke higher rates of birth. Poverty, not age, is the problem.

As the sociologist Mike Males has pointed out, "The term 'teenage pregnancy', in most cases where it is labeled a social problem or assigned 'public costs', is simply a euphemism for the much larger category of 'low income pregnancy'."

And contrary to elite lore, a large majority of teenage parents appear to adapt well to parenthood. Most unmarried teen mothers are married within five years, most have jobs and few receive welfare. There are powerful arguments, best advanced by Arline Geronimus of the University of Michigan's School of Public Health, that for poor black teenagers, pregnancy can be an extremely rational choice given early death rates in the supportive kin structure, lead accumulation in the mother's blood that increases with age, and other factors. Among poor blacks, teenage mothers are likely to be healthier and to give birth to healthier babies than older women. Teenage childbearing creates more public costs than adult childbearing because teenagers are poorer in the same way that blacks are poorer.

A mythical teenage rutting boom fueled by a supposed absence of "family values" has produced an imaginary baby boom in which "irresponsible" teen mothers inseminated by feckless black youths (who all flee rocking the cradle) are lodged on lifetime welfare instead—in the fantasy of the liberal elites—of having Norplant under their skin as they train for those illusory good jobs at good wages.

An increasingly inegalitarian society pushes poor teenagers further and further to the margin and then blames them for lack of "responsibility". The Clintons latched onto this as a way of catering to the right.

The true facts were scarcely a secret to Clinton's advisers on these issues, such as Marian Wright Edelman of the Children's Defense Fund, Hillary Clinton and Donna Shalala. They must know that most pregnant teenagers come from abusive backgrounds and that the men who impregnate them, like the men who give them AIDS, are mostly over 20. But they kept quiet as Clinton picked on the social group least able to defend itself.

At least two-thirds of pregnant teenagers have childhood histories of violence and sexual abuse in their homes. This makes Clinton's threat in the State of the Union to cut off teenage mothers from welfare and force them to live with a parent or grandparent doubly cruel.

The Clintons set their moral agenda from polling data and hysterical news magazines. A 1993 report from the California Department of Justice found that 83 per cent of murdered children, half of murdered teenagers and 85 per cent of murdered adults are killed by adults over 20, not those "13-year-olds...with automatic weapons" the pudgy hypocrite in the White House loves to beat on.

When Jonathan Kozol visited a public school in Anacostia he asked the school principal what he found most frustrating about working with young people. "On Fridays in the cafeteria", the man answered, "I see small children putting chicken nuggets in their pockets. They're afraid of being hungry on the weekends." And there in 1994, this neo-liberal president fresh from cutting public spending lectured them about responsibility. It should have been the other way around. A few days later Clinton was leering to a labor convention in Louisiana, hinting about how he'd laid girls on the Astroturf in the back of his pickup in the 1970s.

Clinton dumped his Surgeon General Joycelyn Elders that same year because she thought kids should know that if they masturbate their hair won't fall out, nor warts grow on the palms of their hands.

Al Gore: Mindful of his father's role in helping push through Interstate Highway system in 1950s, Veep issued fervent promos for National Information Infrastructure, a sort of super-Internet, providing info services for society at low cost. Phone and computer companies mutinied at notion of low cost, government-constructed service; roared abuse: "The concept that Al Gore could build anything is absurd", cried one exec. Collapse of Veep on December 21, 1993: "Unlike the Interstate the NII will be built by the private sector." Democratic Party got over half a million in donations from phone and computer companies in short order. Twitted as "Ozone Man", has partaken in pell-mell Clinton administration retreat on big enviro issues like methyl bromide and PCBs, now being imported from Canada and Mexico under terms of NAFTA. Gore guru is *New Republic*'s Martin Peretz, who scrutinizes appointments; nixed hiring of speechwriter Richard Marius on ground latter too eloquent on the topic of Israeli troops and violence against Palestinians. Gore never disdainful of low road if map requires such itinerary; was first to raise Willie Horton issue in 1988 **primary fight.** (Shia photo/Impact Visuals)

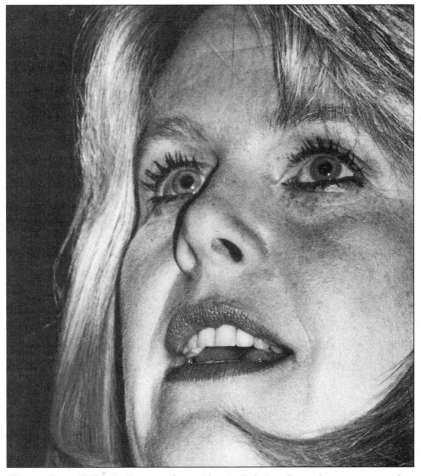

Tipper Gore: Zaftig belle, ray of sunshine in Babylon. Long hours spent reviewing filthy rock lyrics, concerned lest louche words sap nation's moral strength
and imperil youth. In December 1993 became big saleslady for Prozac, Eli Lilly's
anti-depressant. Held joint press conference with Fed mental health czar Fred
Goodwin to publicize Eli Lilly-sponsored study claiming "economic burden" of
mental depression to be $43.7 billion. Huffed in later letter to *Wall Street
Journal*, "You belittle decades of progress in psychopharmacology in your refer-
ence to the 'Prozac craze.'" Lilly execs ebullient at Second Lady Seal of
Approval. (Shia photo/Impact Visuals)

Sex education has always driven the right-wingers crazy. They
believe it's solidly entrenched in the school system and corrupting
youth toward the downward path. Actually, there's still not much
proper sex education available. Anne Hooper's *Pocket Sex Guide,* published in 1994, tells us that only 21 per cent of Americans today know

where the clitoris is. The rest of them probably think it's an island in the Aegean.

As Dr. Paul Pearsall put it in his book *Sexual Healing,* "The sexual liberals failed to get their 'erotic and selfish' version of sex into the schools, and the conservatives prevented any meaningful teaching about the role of values in sexuality in our lives. The real sex education that has had the most influence on our developing young adults is not offered by qualified teachers but by popular media, the sex syndicate's magazines, and the various sources of soft-core and hard-core pornography."

Direct relationships between "sex education" and measures of responsible sexuality are rarely studied. Back in the late 1970s Dr. Peter Scales did a survey for the Sex Information and Education Council of the US where he listed among his group's conclusions that:

• People don't become more predictably "liberal" or "permissive" after being in a sex education course, though they do become more tolerant of other people's behaviors, even if they would not engage in those behaviors themselves.

• Knowledge about sexuality is not associated with sex crimes, or with significant changes in the frequency or variety of a person's sexual behavior. In fact people who commit sex crimes are likely, in the words of the 1970 US Commission on Obscenity and Pornography, to have had "childhood experiences which encourage sexual repression and inhibition of sexual curiosity".

• In all areas of the world the highest fertility is associated with low levels of education, inadequate knowledge about conception and contraception, and an inferior status for women.

As Scales put it, "Our discomfort over sexuality has led to a sexual revolution based on the myth of the normal outlet—Isn't it abnormal for adults to masturbate? Isn't it abnormal to go too long without sex?—or a new myth of normality, Isn't it abnormal to want only one sexual relationship at a time? Sex education needs to communicate that there is no particular range of behavior people need to strive for in order to be 'normal'."

Here's the lunacy of public discussion today. The notion that we should return to a 19th-century orphanage system gets earnest attention. Elders's perfectly sensible remarks about masturbation—she was not urging classes in auto-eroticism, merely the demystification of the subject—get her fired as being a fringe liberal.

In the shambling jog of Clinton Time the departed Surgeon General rapidly became another sour memory of President Bill's political opportunism, like Lani Guinier. Elders was the perfect target from the point of view of Washington's white elites. After all, she was black and liberal. One pundit from *Newsweek* urged Clinton after the 1994 mid-term elections to "systematically attack [your] own base", and Clinton took this mad advice.

Black Democrats stayed home in unusually large numbers in 1994. With the firing of Elders, Clinton lost no time in reminding them that they did the right thing. Elders was sensible and humane. She said out loud what everyone knows, that the drug war was lost long ago and some new strategy—maybe decriminalization—was necessary. She said normal things which you hear in normal conversations as opposed to the frenzies of right-wing talk radio or sound-bite TV panels. She was for tolerance and education. Of course she had to go.

There's scant evidence that HRC actually likes children very much. Her book's title is *It Takes A Village—And Other Lessons Children Teach Us*, but not a single such lesson does Hillary ever cite. The Clintons' passion for talking about children as "investments" tells the whole story. Managed capitalism (liberalism's ideal) needs regulation, and just as the stock market requires the Securities and Exchange Commission, so too does the social investment (a child) require social workers, shrinks, guidance counselors and the whole vast army of the helping professions, to make sure the investment yields a respectable rate of return.

And if the yield looks to be poor? If the investment might fail? Enter the therapeutic cops, in whose ranks HRC eagerly enlisted when she got what she describes as her first real job, supervising children in a park. The "village"—HRC's cozy synonym for the state—moves in: "The village must act in the place of parents, it accepts those responsibilities in all our names through the authority we vest in the government."

A social worker suspects improper child maintenance? "States might also consider making public welfare or medical benefits contingent on agreement to allow home visits or to participate in other forms of parent education."

When Hillary looks at a child she sees a million chances for everything to go wrong, as though the little human were a computer without an adequate operating manual, into which the wrong software will most likely be installed. Her dream is doubtless a National Instruction Act for Parenting, encoded with the proper rules, as tested and certified by all the pedagogues, "guidance" counselors, nutritionists and psychologists HRC marshals to her side on every page.

The do-good progressives at the start of the century saw the family—particularly the immigrant family—as a conservative institution, obstructive to the progressive goals of society and the state. So they attacked it. Then their preferred economic system—consumer capitalism—began to rend the social fabric, and so today's do-gooders say that the family and the children, our "investment", must be saved by any means necessary. When the FBI was getting ready to incinerate the Branch Davidians they told Attorney General Janet Reno the group's children were being abused. Save them, she cried. Alas, to save them it was necessary to burn them alive.

THE MANY VICTIMS OF CHAIRMAN GREENSPAN

As Alan Greenspan's term as head of the Federal Reserve was heading to an end in March of 1996, there was much concern in the press that Bill Clinton would replace international banking's favorite son with a less reliable figure. "[Clinton can] ill afford to upset financial markets around the world by choosing someone without international stature and strong inflation-fighting credentials", *The Washington Post* fretted as anxiety mounted on Wall Street.

In fact, the bankers needn't have worried. Greenspan's chief competitor was Fed vice chairman Alan Blinder, a Democrat and friend of Treasury Secretary Robert Rubin. But Wall Street viewed him as a dangerous radical more concerned with stimulating economic growth than with the bondholder's No. 1 priority, fighting inflation. At a 1994 conference of Federal Reserve officials in Jackson Hole, Wyoming, Blinder stunned assembled dignitaries by having the effrontery to point out that "the central bank does have a role in reducing unemployment", and by suggesting that the Fed set targets for unemployment as well as inflation.

The reaction to Blinder's remarks was swift and violent. *Newsweek* columnist Robert Samuelson charged that Blinder's comments had made it painfully clear that he lacked "the moral or intellectual qualities needed to lead the Fed". In *National Review*, Lawrence Kudlow denounced Blinder for "contradicting the views of his boss, Alan Greenspan, and offending Bundesbank head Hans Tietmeyer, both of whom were present."

Blinder, of course, is hardly a menace to the upper classes. Walker Todd, a former Federal Reserve official, calculates the Greenspan-Blinder difference at about 0.5 per cent on inflation and 1 per cent on long-term bonds, troubling to the prudent investor but not cataclysmic.

Blinder eagerly sought to reassure Wall Street following the

Alan Greenspan with Andrea Mitchell and Katharine Graham: Found as a babe on mountainside by shepherds, taken to steamy salon of *Fountainhead* High Priestess Ayn Rand, whose nutty theories he eagerly espoused. Will work for food; wrote hot letter boosting Charles Keating's doomed S&L. (Vivian Ronay/Photoreporters)

Jackson Hole debacle. In a number of interviews, he promised that inflation was his top priority, that he was in entire agreement with Chairman Greenspan on economic matters, and that the growing size of the reserve army of the unemployed left him untroubled.

But the damage was already done. Blinder's chance to take charge of the Fed had been eliminated, and in early 1996 he stepped down from the Fed and returned to a teaching post at Princeton.

The high reputation of Greenspan among the opinion forming crowd is one of the great miracles of our age. On significant matters of economic policy he has a career of unmatched disaster.

• As Gerald Ford's economic adviser, Greenspan in 1974 counseled the president to tighten an economy already sliding into recession. Too late, flinging aside his "Whip Inflation Now" button, Ford discarded Greenspan's advice, but by that time his presidency was doomed by the "great recession".

• In 1983, Greenspan headed a bipartisan commission that advocated an enormous increase in regressive payroll taxes, thus prompting an entirely unnecessary (and deflationary) surplus in the Social Security fund.

• Two years before his elevation to the chairmanship of the Federal Reserve in 1987, Greenspan was running his own unsuccessful firm specializing in what he bravely called "statistical espionage" and what others less charitably described as rendering whatever opinion a given client paid for. One such customer was the thief Charles Keating, one of the S&L scandal's greatest scoundrels.

Keating paid Greenspan to write a letter to the Federal Home Loan Bank in San Francisco, urging that Keating's Lincoln Savings and Loan be exempted from the 10 per cent limitation on direct investments. Lincoln's new management, Greenspan promptly wrote on February 13, 1985, has "effectively restored the association to a vibrant and healthy state, with a strong net worth position". He praised Keating's "long and continuous track record of outstanding success". In 1989, Lincoln went under, at a cost to the taxpayers of $3 billion. Keating went to prison in 1991.

• More than anyone, Greenspan bore responsibility for the 1987 market crash, when stocks fell by more than 500 points. As recently appointed Fed chairman, Greenspan had raised the discount rate to exhibit to the world his credentials as a Volcker look-alike.

• As *The New York Times*'s Louis Uchitelle described in a 1995 review of newly released policy meetings from 1989, the Fed under Greenspan's direction was quick to slow down the economy that year—to the delight of the financial sector—but snail-like in boosting it. Thus, Greenspan's '89 money policies doomed Bush in 1992, even though Greenspan made belated efforts to re-elect him by lowering the federal funds rate from 6 per cent to 3 per cent over a six-month period. The economy did turn around, but the numbers weren't yet out by the time the voters went to the polls in November of 1992.

Greenspan tried to finish off Clinton with seven interest rate hikes during the first 18 months of his presidency, racking them up by more than three percentage points from early 1994.

The deadly nature of this medicine was well described by professors Timothy Canova and Lynn Turgeon in *Newsday*. Between mid-1994 and mid-1995, the interest rate on New York City's long-term municipal bonds (which finance the city's capital needs) rose by about 1.5 percentage points, adding around $67 million to the city's debt service at a time when fierce cuts were being imposed on summer education, training and work programs for thousands of children and teenagers. New York faced a budgetary shortfall of $2.5 billion in fiscal '95, while paying more than $2.4 billion just in interest on its capital debt.

At the other end of the country, the situation of Los Angeles in the wake of Orange County's financial collapse became even more desperate.

The central political point is that with the balanced budget mania now transfixing Congress and the White House, creative fiscal policy has gone out the window. The only game in town is monetary policy, currently dominated by Greenspan and the bond market. Six interest rate hikes after Clinton's election added $125 million to the federal deficit over the next years, thus wiping out more than one-fourth of the savings from Clinton's '93 deficit reduction package.

Canova and Turgeon identified the potential political dynamite in this situation:

"When the Federal Reserve regulates higher interest rates, it is mandating a higher price of money for most Americans—essentially mandating a redistribution of income from net borrowers (most of the middle and lower income population) to net creditors (including the wealthiest Americans). Higher interest rates constitute the largest and least recognized of the so-called 'unfunded mandates,' federal regulations which impose enormous costs on state and local governments, as well as the private sector. But unlike most Congressionally-imposed mandates, the Federal Reserve is shielded from public scrutiny and operates entirely behind closed doors."

Awaiting any political strategist of vision is a potent coalition ranging from manufacturers desiring lower interest rates, through to state, county and local governments who have seen their budgets lacerated by Fed policies, and on to the public workers and blue-collar populists, who have seen incomes and jobs destroyed and whose natural hatred of the Fed and the bankers reaches most vivid expression in the language of the militias.

A populist would call for greater congressional control over the Fed. But then, Clinton is no populist. His reappointment of Greenspan showed how irretrievably the Democrats are in the hands of the enemy.

ASIDE: BOB WOODWARD'S CLINTON—IT DIDN'T ADD UP

If you believe Bob Woodward of *The Washington Post*, it wasn't until January 7, 1993, just 13 days before his inauguration, that Bill Clinton found out who really calls the shots. In his 1994 book, *The Agenda*, Woodward described a January strategy meeting in Little Rock where the president-elect was advised that a credible deficit-reduction plan was required in order to placate the bond market. "Clinton's face turned red with anger and disbelief. 'You mean to tell me that the success of the program and my re-election hinges on the Federal Reserve and a bunch of fucking bond traders?' he responded in a half whisper."

This is a fair sample of Woodward's thesis, namely that Clinton was an idealistic candidate bursting with plans to rebuild the economy with a public investment strategy until Greenspan & Co. told him the facts of life.

From his very first economic plans outlined in early 1992 Bill Clinton was waving a white flag at Wall Street, striving to impart the message that he was a "New Democrat" and wouldn't rock the boat. His aides carefully floated the story that Paul Volcker, Wall Street's idol, might be Treasury Secretary. At the time an adoring press panted with enthusiasm for candidate Clinton's supposedly "detailed" economic proposals, but anyone who bothered to read the paltry manifestoes found only the vaguest pledges for public investment, said money to be balanced by cuts elsewhere in the budget.

The man allegedly thunderstruck at that January meeting had already appointed as his main economic advisers bond czar Robert Rubin and a junk-bond trader, Roger Altman, from the Blackstone Group. Woodward had Clinton getting red with anger all over again in April 1993, this time supposedly because it had somehow escaped the attention of this "hands-on" master of detail that in 1990 Congress had agreed on caps of domestic spending between 1991 and 1996. Hence his plans for public investment would mostly have to be scrapped.

If Clinton was so startled and distraught by the caps it's hard to explain something unmentioned by Woodward. Clinton extended the caps to the end of the century and furthermore made them more restrictive. Unless a new president insists on fundamental change there can't be any serious public investment strategy till the year 2000. Bill Clinton entered the White House accepting the proposition that if you worry the bond markets by talk of stimulus or expansion, then interest rates will shoot up. On Wall Street's orders he became a deficit buster and is now locked on a path of deficit reduction in a sluggish economy with no prospect of long-term improvement.

★

RON BROWN: MONEY TALKED

He died in the best of taste, at the head of a posse of big-time corporate pirates, intent on the capture of new Balkan markets. No one was more smoothly symbolic of fin de siècle corruption in Babylon than Commerce Secretary Ron Brown. His terminal trip, heading up a billion-dollar, state-subsidized package tour of construction and communications magnates from Bechtel, Boeing, Enron, Northwest Airlines et al., was typical.

From early in his tenure, press accounts glowed over the Commerce Department's Advocacy Center, a computer-lined "war room" where bureaucrats monitor bidding on dozens of global deals, and try to get an inside track for US firms by gathering intelligence (with help from the CIA) and coordinating financing from government sources. Brown led groups of executives on commercial trips to Brazil, Argentina, Chile, China, Hong Kong, South Africa, Russia, India and the Middle East. These hotly disputed journeys—some 300 CEOs applied for seats on the trip to Russia, of which only 28 were picked—provided a handy means for the Democrats to reward their campaign contributors. Melissa Moss, formerly with the Democratic Leadership Council and a fundraiser for the Democratic National Committee, picked the CEOs who got to fly along with Brown.

Twenty-five executives flew to China with Brown in September of 1994. This was three months after Clinton had bowed to business pressure and re-extended Most Favored Nation trade status to Peking, whose vast market makes CEOs quiver with excitement.

Lodwrick Cook of Atlantic Richfield was one of the CEOs who made the trip to Peking. His company gave $201,500 to the Democrats between 1992 and 1994. Cook is also close to Clinton, who in June 1994 presented the ARCO chieftain with a birthday cake during a lunch for executives at the White House. Another CEO touring with Brown was Edwin Lupberger of Entergy, who closed an $800 million deal to build a power plant during the China trip. Lupberger is a personal friend of Clinton, and his firm donated $60,000 to the Democrats during the election cycle preceding the trip.

Other executives accompanying Brown to China included:

• Bernard Schwartz of telecommunications giant Loral Corp., who negotiated deals which will net his company $1 billion over the next decade. Three months before the trip Schwartz donated $100,000 to the DNC.

• Raymond Smith of the Bell Atlantic Corporation, which has given nearly $200,000 to the Democrats since 1991. Smith is also a party "trustee", meaning he has helped raise $100,000 or more for the Democrats.

• Leslie McGraw of Fluor Corporation, which donated $108,450 to Democratic candidates during the last election cycle. McGraw's firm—like several of the companies that have been picked to go with Brown—is also a donor and board member of the Democratic Leadership Council.

All told, at least 12 of the 25 executives who traveled with Brown to China were major donors or fundraisers for the Democrats. Their

At least Ron Brown died on the A list, surrounded on that last Balkan trip by a phalanx of corporate might. He sold Boeing to Saudi Arabia; a Boeing took him down.
(Library of Congress)

companies gave almost $2 million to Democratic candidates during the 1993-94 election cycle.

The same pattern is found on Brown's other trips. Traveling with the Commerce Secretary to South Africa were Donald Anderson, an adviser to the president of Time Warner, which donated $508,333 to the Democrats from 1992 to 1994, and California-based Yucaipa Group's Ronald Burkle, a DNC "managing trustee", the honorary title for those who have helped the party raise $200,000 or more.

Brown's export promotions were highly profitable to his party. In 1994, Saudi Arabia was looking to increase the size of its commercial air fleet and examined proposals from American and European aircraft makers. After being furiously lobbied by President Clinton and Ron Brown, the Saudis placed a $3.6 billion order.

Almost immediately upon closing the Saudi deal, Boeing began making hefty contributions to the Democratic National Committee. Within six months the company had enriched party coffers to the tune of $65,000, four times more than it had donated during the previous three years.

It's not surprising that so many business leaders raved about Ron Brown. As James Treybig, CEO at Tandem Computers Inc.—who negotiated a $100 million joint venture agreement while in China with the Commerce Secretary—told *The Wall Street Journal*, "Whether you're a Democrat or a Republican, you really have to respect this guy for what he's done for Corporate America." He died among his friends.

RENO AT JUSTICE

After two stillborn nominations to the post of Attorney General, Bill Clinton successfully put forward Janet Reno, a prosecutor from Dade County, Florida. In 1984, in the midst of a fierce battle to be re-elected to that post, Reno exploited the Satanic abuse hysteria then beginning to sweep the nation. Trying to win a case against Frank and Ileana Fuster, who had run a day care service in a Miami suburb called Country Walk, Reno connived at treatment of Ileana that could be fairly described as brainwashing or, more crudely, torture.

The 17-year-old Honduran woman was placed in solitary, interrogated by psychologists using techniques of semi-hypnosis, conditioned response and other mind-bending techniques. The Reno-appointed couple who oversaw Fuster, from a business operation called Behavior Changers, would tell the terrified young woman in her isolation cell that she would grow old in prison unless she co-operated and testified against her husband. Then Reno would send investigators from her office to take Fuster out to fancy restaurants and ask her if she missed such pleasures.

Finally Fuster cracked and agreed to testify, making the coerced statements while sitting between the psychologist, who often hugged her, and Reno, who held her hand. (Reno, according to one source, would make visits to Fuster in her jail cell. The prosecutor denied this.)

Whenever Fuster said she was unable to recall something, the psychologist would retire for a private session with her. Fuster would then return and recall palpably preposterous episodes such as that her husband had put snakes inside her and the children's genitals. Real snakes. Reno got her convictions and her re-election.

Ten years later, Ileana Fuster, back in Honduras, recanted her confession in a 61-page deposition and described her year of isolation and intensive interrogation. Later still, a one-page retraction of the recantation was secured by the minister of a Florida church, who traveled to Honduras to obtain her signature of the document drafted and counter-signed by him.

In 1989, Reno used the same technique to try to extort a confession from a 14-year-old boy, Bobby Fijnje, accused of sadistically assaulting children at a church attended by some of the Fusters' accusers. Fijnje, a diabetic, was deprived of food and made to enter insulin shock, at which point he agreed with police that he had touched the pre-schoolers. As soon as he emerged from the interrogation he retracted this confession. Reno then had him placed in solitary for a year, thus isolated because she claimed his parents were probably Satanist pornographers which would explain his reluctance to confess. He was ultimately acquitted.

At her confirmation hearing, Reno's horrifying conduct in these cases was never raised.

Hardly was this relentless abuser of human rights installed in the Justice Department before she was seizing on claims by the FBI that David Koresh and the Branch Davidians in the beleaguered compound outside Waco were abusing children during the siege. The allegations weren't true but Reno sent in the FBI with tanks and CS chemicals in an attack that ended with the inferno and a death toll that included 17 children, whose charred bodies were found clinging to their mothers.

Thus Reno's Justice Department co-presided (with Treasury, which oversees the Bureau of Alcohol, Tobacco and Firearms) over the largest federal armed entry ever against an American home, as

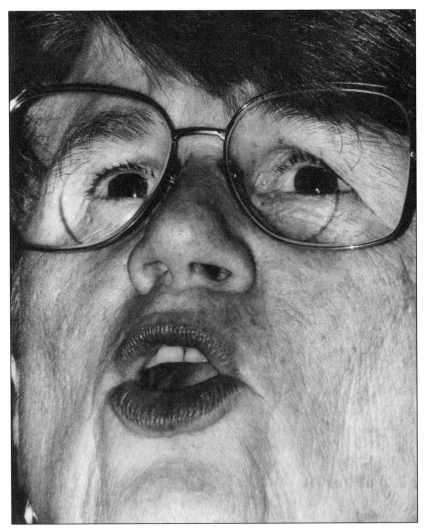

Janet Reno: Obsessed with "Satanic Abuse", supervised "Darkness at Noon" interrogation sessions with terrified 17-year-old Honduran, Ileana Fuster. Held 14-year-old Bobby Fijnje in solitary confinement for months after hysterical claims that he'd abused 17 tykes in church basement while their parents attended services upstairs. FBI told her Branch Davidian kids were being abused; Reno promptly gave green light for tanks to roll and CS gas to fly in final assault at Waco, leading to children's dreadful end. Signed off on Anti-Terrorism Act, a civil liberties' nightmare; endorsed maintenance of sentencing disparities for crack and powder cocaine which effectively mean a poor black user of crack gets a punishment 100 times more severe than a white high-flier busted for the same amount of powder. Plaque in office aptly represents the priorities of Justice in Clinton Time: "All furniture in this office was built by federal prison inmates".
(Shia photo/Impact Visuals)

well as the largest number of civilian deaths ever resulting from an operation by US "law" enforcement. As David Kopel of Denver's Independence Institute has written, "Not since the Wounded Knee massacre in 1890 had so many Americans been killed as a result of conflict with the Federal government. And the initial government response indicated almost equivalent lack of remorse."

The Waco catastrophe embodied almost everything wrong with federal law enforcement and justice, as administered from Babylon: out-of-control agencies, grotesque use of unnecessary force, denial of due process and elementary liberties, followed by cover-up and self-exculpation by the relevant officials, including Reno.

Her apologists—and there have been many—claim that Waco was an affair in which misjudgment and poor decisions were made under conditions of duress, where manipulation of Reno's emotions might make her errors forgivable.

But under conditions of calm and ordered reflection, Reno has exhibited equal contempt for due process and civil liberties. Her Justice Department has continued the attempts, begun under a previous Republican-appointed attorney general, to deport eight men and one woman of Palestinian origin, in the "LA 8" case. William Webster, then director of the FBI, told Congress in 1987, the year they were arrested, that the eight had "not been found to engage themselves in terrorist activities".

Reno has persisted with attempts to deport the eight (meeting with decisive rebuff in 1995 in the 9th Circuit Court) and has pushed the Comprehensive Anti-Terrorism Act, opposed by a wide range of groups across the political spectrum for its flouting of constitutional protections and guarantees.

Shamefully, Reno's Justice Department joined the White House in a particularly outrageous piece of politicking on the drug issue. The 100 to 1 disparity in sentencing of those convicted for crack cocaine possession (overwhelmingly poor and African-American) and for powder cocaine (more frequently rich and white) has been widely conceded. Yet in 1995 the White House said it would not ask Congress to end the disparities. A memo from Justice backed the president.

As one might expect from a former prosecutor, Reno has exhibited scant respect for the basic liberties, and indeed presided over their continued erosion.

ASIDE: THE SUPREMES

The current chief justice of the Supreme Court is William Rehnquist. As a clerk for Justice Robert Jackson in the 1950s, he urged that Julius and Ethel Rosenberg be promptly executed, writing that he was mystified at why "the highest court of the nation must behave like a bunch of old women every time they encounter the death penalty". He also opposed the Court's efforts to desegregate the South, saying it was "about time the Court faced the fact that the white people of the South don't like the colored people".

This same high sense of moral purpose has been evident during Rehnquist's years on the Supreme Court, as detailed by David Savage of the *Los Angeles Times*. He once opposed the Equal Rights Amendment because it would "turn holy wedlock into holy deadlock" and has been especially eager to remove all obstacles to the death penalty, including in cases involving teenagers and the mentally infirm. In 1992, the Court allowed the execution of Rickey Ray Rector, an Arkansas inmate charged with murder who asked that his jailers set aside the dessert from his last meal so he might eat it after he returned from the death chamber. Rector's death warrant was signed by then Governor Bill Clinton.

Under Rehnquist, the Court has embraced a radical view of the primacy of property and the marketplace. In 1994, it limited the right of communities to demand public goods—bike paths, parks, etc.—from real estate developers, declaring that such concessions amount to a "taking" of private property rights. In 1993, the Supremes ordered the State of South Carolina to compensate David Lucas for denying him permission to build on protected beach front property.

Rehnquist is fairly moderate when placed next to Clarence Thomas. The latter's sweeping intellect is seen in his post-confirmation cancellation of all newspaper subscriptions, with the exception of *Cowboy Weekly*, a publication for fans of the Dallas Cowboys.

The corrupt professional history of Thomas, though mostly ignored by the Senate during the confirmation hearings, is as shameful as his sexual escapades. Though sponsored throughout his career by ex-Senator John Danforth, Thomas failed to disqualify himself from a three-judge panel of the federal appeals court considering a case in which Ralston Purina faced heavy damages; Danforth's family had a major interest in the company. Thomas voted to reduce the penalty.

While Thomas is influential in the political culture, few justices in recent

Clarence Thomas with John Danforth of Missouri and South Carolina's Strom Thurmond: The least qualified Supreme with Senate's longest runner. (Rick Reinhard/Impact Visuals)

memory have been less influential on the Court itself. So flaccid and embarrassing are his judicial opinions that few justices sign on to his dissents, with the occasional exception of Antonin Scalia, the third member of the Court's trio of hard-line conservatives.

Bill Clinton's appointees have hardly been inspired, though all of liberal Babylon wailed that the Man from Hope must be supported against George Bush because the latter would nominate people who would destroy the integrity of the Court. Clinton's first nominee, Ruth Bader Ginsburg, is the wife of a millionaire real estate developer. She has done impressive work in the area of women's law, but is otherwise highly conservative. As an appeals court judge from the second district in Washington, DC, Ginsburg routinely voted the same pro-business line as her colleague Scalia in regard to bureaucratic and regulatory matters (as she has done on the high court).

About Stephen Breyer, Clinton's second nomination, one thing can safely be said: any man admired by both Senators Ted Kennedy and Orrin Hatch can't be all good. And in fact, Breyer's elevation to the highest bench illustrates concisely how, across the past 20 years, Kennedyesque liberalism and Hatchian conservatism have merged into a unified, pro-corporate posture.

Those with short memories often ascribe certain familiar features of the socio-economic landscape to the "Reagan revolution". Such features center around the erosion of government regulations unwelcome to business. But much of the intellectual groundwork and legislative demolition were engineered back in the late 1970s by Kennedy's people, of whom Breyer was one.

This was launch time for deregulation of airlines and trucking, and of erosion of environmental victories of the 1970s. Breyer and Alfred Kahn, another Kennedy man, predicted that in the bracing combat of the unregulated free market, the inefficient and unproductive would go to the wall, airline services would become more flexible and, above all, cheaper.

As any student of the real world could have told them, and many did, the true consequences would be greater business concentration, higher prices and reduction in the number of flights, seats and choices of destinations. Consumers paid the price and so did Kennedy's core constituency, organized labor.

Breyer, then Kennedy's chief legislative counsel, published in January 1979 an extremely influential article in the *Harvard Law Review* in which he argued an old business favorite: environmental hazards could best be dealt with by market mechanisms in which "rights" to pollute would be traded.

The country would be divided into zones, and a pollution index would be established for each zone, with companies allowed a certain amount of pollution within the overall permissible limit. But if Company A used only 25 per cent of its pollution "rights", it could trade the other 75 per cent to Company B in the same area that had reached its limit. On paper, Company B would not be exceeding regulations, though of course the people living next to Company B's plant would be dealing with higher levels of poison.

The Kennedy neo-liberals wanted to organize a market in Cancer Bonds. This offered relief to the Business Roundtable, which was screaming that in 1977 the operations of six regulatory agencies concerned with the environment caused $2.6 billion in incremental costs to 48 major companies, about 10 per cent of their total capital expenditures.

The regulatory theory promoted by Breyer was transmuted into law in the Clean Air Act of 1990. In May 1992, the Tennessee Valley Authority bought an estimated $2.5 million worth of credits from Wisconsin Power and Light, which didn't need them. These credits allowed the TVA to exceed its limit of sulfur dioxide and other toxic emissions. On the receiving end was Shelby County, Tennessee, which, as Benjamin Goldman shows in his useful book, *The Truth About Where You Live*, ranks 22nd among all counties for excess deaths from lung cancer. On the trading end, Sheboygan County, Wisconsin, ranks 28th from the bottom in the same category, an almost perfect reverse, mirroring the transfer of poisons from North to South.

In nominating safe corporatists like Ginsburg and Breyer, especially the latter, Clinton sent two messages: first, he indicated to CEOs that pro-business, anti-regulatory laws were on the way; to the Senate, Clinton indicated that the old boy's club system for nominations would again prevail, but the Senate would hold the balance of power.

★

THE MAN FROM GOLDMAN, SACHS

Another favorite of Corporate America is Treasury Secretary Robert Rubin. His selection in late 1994 to replace Lloyd Bentsen signified Bill Clinton's utter capitulation to Wall Street bond holders. The matching postures of Clinton's two secretaries is reflected in Rubin's management of Bentsen's financial portfolio in the late Eighties, when the former was co-chairman of Goldman, Sachs & Co and the latter was head of the Senate Finance Committee.

Rubin is a creature of Democratic lobbyist Robert Strauss, who in 1991 rented out the "F" Street Club and hosted a fete and gala to introduce Rubin—already a leading player on Wall Street but largely unknown in the capital—to Washington's elite. Attendees included Pamela Harriman, Katharine Graham and Senator Bill Bradley.

Rubin had first served as Clinton's chair of the newly-created National Economic Council, which marked Rubin's political debut. His entrance into the political arena was smoothed by the fact that Goldman, Sachs was the biggest single contributor to Clinton's presidential campaign, with partners and their spouses chipping in more than $100,000. The firm also organized a series of fundraising dinners which netted Clinton several million dollars, while Rubin and his wife donated $275,000 from their personal foundation to help pay for the 1992 Democratic convention in New York.

Rubin eagerly cultivates his image as a caring and compassionate type. In 1992, he announced that Goldman, Sachs would make huge cuts in its janitorial and dining room staffs, but that only men would be fired, saying this was part of the firm's "continuing effort to be more sensitive to women". Louis Proyect, who worked as a data base administrator at Goldman, Sachs until 1988, recalls a less understanding side to Rubin. According to Proyect, word came down in mid-1988 that the firm was concerned about the "excessive" salaries paid to computer professionals. Hence, older, more experienced and highly-paid employees would be phased out in favor of recent college graduates. Proyect got the message and soon found another job.

The axe soon fell. One Monday morning in early 1989 some 60 computer programmers and managers arrived at their desks and attempted to log on to the mainframe e-mail system, only to find that their ID's were not recognized. They were then ushered into the manager's office and told that their services would no longer be needed.

The ex-employees were allowed to clean out their desks before being escorted by security guards to the street, where Goldman, Sachs had dozens of livery cabs lined up to provide transportation home. "I ran into one of these fired managers a couple of years ago in the Business School cafeteria at Columbia University", Proyect reminisced in an interview. "He was in a flannel shirt and jeans, and told me that he was now sweeping floors. I think he was being sardonic, but I had the distinct impression that he had taken a great fall."

Many of the fired workers were Italian-Americans from Brooklyn who had joined Goldman, Sachs directly out of high school, and had been with the firm for 20 years or more. "These were guys who started at the bottom and rose strictly on merit", Proyect said. "Many of them had big houses in New Jersey and teenage kids, but they were just tossed out." Replacing the unlucky Italians was a fleet of Ivy League graduates.

The decision to implement this brutal policy of ethnic cleansing, which was overseen by Rubin, came at a time of fantastic prosperity for Goldman, Sachs. Despite the stock market crash, Goldman, Sachs made record profits in 1987 of more than $1 billion. The minimum firm bonus for the year was 24 per cent, with some partners and star performers receiving bonuses of up to 200 per cent.

At the NEC, Rubin demonstrated the same keen interest in the well-being of the working class. He was a chief promoter of NAFTA, pushed for an extension of China's Most Favored Nation status, worked to water down the administration's health care reform bill, and was one of the strongest voices arguing, successfully, that Clinton should drastically reduce proposed public investment spending in order to reduce the budget deficit. Rubin also urged Clinton to tone down his occasional populist rhetoric, saying he "felt it adversely affected the confidence of people who make economic decisions".

Shortly after Clinton selected him to head the NEC, Rubin sent a letter, written on Goldman, Sachs stationery, to hundreds of former business clients, saying he "looked forward to continuing to work with you in my new capacity". One recipient of the letter was natural gas giant Enron, listed on Rubin's 1993 financial disclosure statement as one of 44 firms with which he had "significant contact" while at Goldman, Sachs.

One would not have expected Enron to be a favorite with the Clinton administration. The firm had strong ties to the Republican Party, and company CEO, Kenneth Lay, was a close friend of George Bush. Enron advisers include former Secretary of State James Baker and former Secretary of Commerce Robert Mosbacher. On the company's board sits Wendy Gramm, wife of Texas's senior senator.

Perhaps it is mere coincidence, simply the normal workings of the bourgeoisie's executive committee, but Enron has done remarkably well during the Clinton years. Consider the following chronology of events:

February 1993: Enron and 10 other major power developers form the International Energy Development Council, which lobbies for greater government support for promoting US business abroad. Many of their proposals are implemented by the administration. These include a lifting of the ban on Export-Import Bank financing of projects in China and new rules which allow the bank to finance projects on the basis of projected cash flow and contractual arrangements, rather than on government guarantees.

March 1993: Ron Brown travels to Russia with executives from 28 major companies in tow. Enron, one of more than 300 firms that applied for a seat on the trip, is selected to join the Commerce Secretary. During the visit Enron negotiates a major deal to develop new European markets for Russian gas.

November 1993: Enron closes a $1 billion deal with Turkey to develop two 500 megawatt gas-fired power stations on the Sea of Marmara. Ex-Im will provide $285 million in financing; OPIC is covering project insurance.

May 1994: Enron, seeking a contract to construct several power plants in Indonesia, is assisted by State Department officials, who lobby Suharto's regime on the company's behalf.

August 1994: Enron finalizes $2.5 billion deal to build a power plant in India. Ex-Im will provide financing for the first phase of construction; OPIC backing is expected to reach $100 million.

August 1994: Enron arranges financing for its $320 million Mahanagdong Project in the Philippines, which includes two power plants on the island of Leyte. Ex-Im and OPIC will provide $240 million in loans.

September 1994: Energy Secretary Hazel O'Leary travels to Pakistan along with 50 corporate executives, including a representative from Enron. Fifteen deals are signed during the visit, with Enron among the winners.

November 1994: Enron is awarded contract to build a $130 million power plant in Hainan province, China. Ex-Im financing is to be negotiated.

It's one of the characteristics of the Clinton era that possible conflicts of interest that would have been occasions for commotion and rebuke a few years ago are now taken for granted. Rubin's career in government attests to the truth of this observation. A bond-house czar partakes in deals that net his former associates and Goldman, Sachs millions. Barely an eyebrow is raised amid the eulogies to his caring nature.

P erhaps nothing better signifies the hold corporate power exerts in Washington than the events leading up to and following the collapse of Mexico's economy in December of 1994. During the 1988 to 1994 reign of President Carlos Salinas de Gortari—"Harvard-educated", as the press here always likes to stress—the US government and media hailed Mexico's emergence as a model for Third World economic reform. (Overlooked was Salinas's and his family's pilfering of the state treasury, which blew up into a scandal after he left office.)

During the Salinas years, US industry reaped huge returns by exploiting cheap Mexican labor. American financiers also made big money south of the border with Mexico's rise as one of the world's hottest "emerging markets", the name big institutional investors give to Third World and Eastern European countries which deregulated their economies and allowed foreigners to buy domestic equities or debt, either directly or through mutual funds.

The powerful insiders running the show—most notably Goldman, Sachs & Co., Salomon Brothers, Merrill Lynch, Citibank, Chase Manhattan and J.P. Morgan—made a killing by trading and underwriting Mexican securities. Emerging market money also flowed into stock markets in Brazil, Argentina, Peru, Morocco, Tunisia, Ivory Coast, Ghana, Turkey, Malaysia, Indonesia, Poland and Russia.

The entire emerging markets phenomenon was driven by low US interest rates, which pushed investors abroad. However, most emerging market stocks fell badly after February of 1994, when the US Federal Reserve began raising domestic interest rates. Moreover, policies pleasing to institutional investors tend to annoy local populations. This was politely stated by *Emerging Markets Analyst*, a trade newsletter, which said in a May 1994 report that "market-oriented policies can initially foment the kind of political uncertainty which has recently rocked Mexico [the Zapatista rebellion, political assassinations] and Venezuela [coup attempts, popular protests]."

The Mexican economic "boom" of the Salinas years was highly dependent on foreign capital, especially in financing a current accounts deficit of more than $2 billion per month. That gave US institutional investors great leverage, all the more so because major banks—frightened by the temporary losses brought on by the 1980s debt crisis—have dramatically reduced direct lending to Mexico (and to the rest of the Third World). "In some ways, [investment houses and mutual funds] have taken over the financing role of big banks and quasi-governmental organizations such as the International Monetary Fund", writes *The Wall Street Journal*. "[But] fund managers have no long-term commitments. They want nearly instant returns on their investments, and are willing to use their clout to achieve those goals."

The bottom-line demands of the US financial community consist-

Treasury Secretary Robert Rubin's partial phone records (heavily censored by the Treasury Department) during the great Mexican peso crisis: Amid communications with politicians, press, financial heavies such as Felix Rohatyn and fixer/lobbyist Robert Strauss were three calls to corporate chieftains of Texas Instruments and Allied Signal, firms with big investments in Mexico. (Multinational Monitor)

ed most notably of an overvalued peso and high real interest rates, which protect bond yields and guarantee good returns for investors; cuts in government spending; support for privatizations; and loose rules on foreign investment. Such requirements are entirely incompatible with any type of social reform. As Francisco Drohojowski, managing director of New York's Capital Management Inc., was quoted as saying in late 1993, as the Mexican electoral race was heating up: "There are things that would disturb any investor when you talk about redefining income distribution."

American banks and brokers are not shy about flexing their muscle. After presidential candidate Luis Donaldo Colosio was assassinated in March of 1994, Fidelity's fund manager, Robert Citrone, quickly entered into contact with authorities at Mexico's Central Bank. He told them that he and other major players felt it was imperative that Mexico reassure investors by propping up the peso.

Days later, with the peso falling, Citrone forwarded a list of "suggestions" to Mexican officials, who were told that US fund managers were prepared to pump an additional $17 billion into Mexico if their advice was heeded. To emphasize the urgency of the situation, American investment firms cut back their purchases of short-term Mexican treasury certificates, ravaging stock prices and pushing up interest rates.

Mexican authorities soon took steps to bolster the peso. As Citrone told *The Wall Street Journal*, "If a country does the right things . . . they will get an additional push [from foreign capital]. If a country does something and the market doesn't like it, they pay immediately."

First proposed by George Bush and pushed through by Clinton, NAFTA finalized Mexico's effective insertion into the US economy. By guaranteeing "stability", the trade pact created fantastic opportunities for Corporate America.

All this explains the panic that ensued when Mexico's economy collapsed in December of 1994, and the Clinton administration's haste to patch together its $50 billion bail-out (about twice the amount of money the federal government spends annually for the Aid to Families with Dependent Children program). Though Mexico's people went down the drain despite the US "rescue"—Mexico's inflation for 1995 hit 50 per cent, 2 million people lost their jobs and loan defaults increased by 45 per cent—the press enthusiastically declared the bail-out a masterful foreign policy triumph for the Clinton administration.

But by enabling Mexico to make good on its commitment to bondholders, the bail-out was a publicly financed rescue of the big investment houses. Treasury Secretary Rubin even gained—via the "Framework Agreement for Mexican Economic Stabilization" signed

by the Treasury Department and the Mexican Ministry of Finance—
"the right to distribute, in such manner and in such order or priority
as it deems appropriate", Mexico's export revenues. Perhaps it's no
coincidence that of the $10.9 billion in international assistance
Mexico received during the first two months of 1995, nearly $9 bil-
lion was used to pay off holders of maturing government bonds and
bank certificates of deposit.

CLINTON TIME

B y the end of May 1993, the Clinton administration was over.
As an opposing, progressive challenge to business-as-usual it
had failed within five months, even by the standards of its
own timid promises. The recruitment of old Nixon/Reagan/Bush
hand David Gergen as the president's new public relations czar signaled the surrender.

As registers of liberal or conservative political potency, American
presidencies seldom coincide with the precise four-year terms that
march reassuringly down the quadrennial calendar. By the official
measure Jimmy Carter's administration stretched from 1977 through
to the end of 1980. But in fact by 1979, with Paul Volcker installed as
chairman of the Federal Reserve and arms spending pulsing up in
tune with the new Cold War, the Reagan years had already began.

The Clinton presidency actually got under way with the budget
compromise of 1990, when President Bush abandoned his party's
right wing and agreed to raise taxes. In terms of popularity and political strength Clinton peaked at the time of the Democratic Party convention in New York in July of 1992.

Decline was not long delayed. By the time of the official election
in November of 1994 the long sunset had already commenced. The
big vote for Ross Perot in 1992 had been one augury. Clinton's post-
election disclosure that there would be no tax cut for the middle
class was another. By the time of the inauguration the Clinton administration was already lurching. The president-elect and his advisers
had destroyed their room for maneuver in the formulation of economic policy. They fanned budget-cutting hysteria by accepting the
silly Republican claim that—surprise!—the prospective deficit was

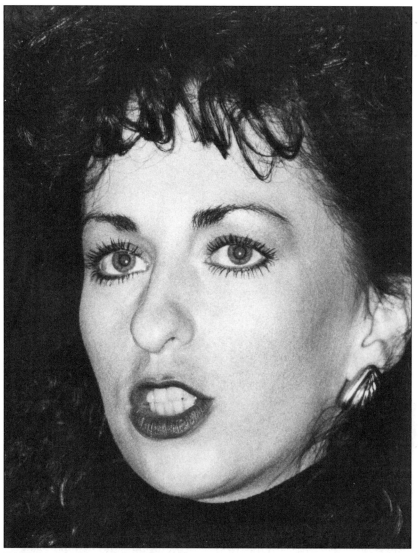

Paula Jones: Has charged Bill Clinton with sexual harassment when he was still Gov of Arkansas; says advances—abhorrent, she claims—were made by leering BC, with promises of career enhancement if Jones consented. Jones a profile in courage to the hate-Anita-Hill crowd, though Clintonites follow James Carville's lead and call her "trailer park trash". Undoubted authority on BC's m.o. in such matters, Gennifer Flowers, says she doubts Jones; regards latter's claim of Gov's cry "Kiss it, kiss it" out of character. Flowers's memories suggest BC's enthusiasm more for reverse procedure. Jones's lawsuit came with warning that she is ready to reveal certain "distinguishing features" of presidential member— already most discussed such appendage in White House history. Unlike Anita Hill, Jones deprecated by mainstream feminists. (Shia photo/Impact Visuals)

Funeral of deputy White House counsel Vince Foster: Discovered dead in Fort Marcy Park along the Potomac in July of 1993 with a gun in his hand and a bullet in his head. Though coroner ruled a suicide, Foster's death became vivid issue with the right. Dirigible of Drivel and Rev. Jerry Falwell proposed vast number of theories, including claim that Foster was murdered to prevent disclosure of affair with First Lady and former Rose Law colleague, HRC. Such claims have languished for lack of evidence. White House handling of the death fueled theories with saga of bungling and cover-up: belated discovery of suicide note, plus late-night migration of important files from Foster's office. Foster certainly under stress at time of demise: Clinton presidency imploding; Whitewater and Travelgate exploding. In latter instance, HRC sponsored firing of seven civil servants from White House travel office in order to install Arkansas cronies. HRC, heroine of mainstream feminists, set FBI and IRS on evicted team of seven, all subsequently cleared of wrongdoing. Foster case prompted right to overplay its hand, as in David Brock's squealing resumé of life in the Little Rock governor's mansion for *American Spectator.* (AP/Spencer Tirey)

going to be more severe than expected. And they were trapped by the turn-of-the-year talk about an economic recovery.

By the time he gave his presidential oath, Clinton's presidency, as anything other than a vehicle for economic orthodoxy and Wall Street wisdom, was heading toward the ditch. A few days later it was being hauled off for major repairs following the debacle of the issue of gays in the military. Clinton's inexperience and uncertainty had allowed Senator Sam Nunn and Chairman of the Joint Chiefs Colin Powell to seize the initiative. Before the week was out the Pentagon had its majority in Congress, and the Christian right was trumpeting renewal and victory.

Clinton's economic program outlined the terms of surrender and defeat. Wall Street orthodoxy was duly acknowledged with a deficit reduction program that will assure continued stagnation. The 'forgotten middle class' has been duly remembered with tax hikes. A modest stab at redistribution with raising of tax rates for the better off was accompanied with a renewal of the loophole and tax shelter industry. In short, by mid-1993 the wreck of the Clinton presidency was in the crusher, and the Republican administration had already begun.

At the end of 1994 the turnover was officially ratified by Republican capture of Congress, leaving Clinton the wondrous alibi of Newt Gingrich and permitting, once again, the usual calls to liberals to rally round colors that had long since been struck.

As Clinton settled in as the Republican president, his alter ego, Gingrich, sank to levels of public disesteem unmatched since Nixon's ratings when he fled the White House in 1974. Meanwhile, the people hunger for alternatives and fresh air.

AUTHORS' NOTE

Alexander Cockburn and Ken Silverstein edit *CounterPunch*, a fortnightly newsletter about power and evil in Washington. Cockburn contributes a regular column to *The Nation*, writes nationally syndicated columns, most recently published *The Golden Age Is in Us*. Silverstein covers politics for publications such as *Harper's* and *The Nation*, worked in Brazil for five years for AP, and is the author, with Emir Sader, of *Without Fear of Being Happy*, the story of Lula and Brazil's Workers' Party. *CounterPunch* ($40 for 22 issues a year, $25 for low income and seniors) can be reached at PO Box 18675, Washington, DC 20036, (202) 986-3665.

INDEX